2nd edition

Edexcel GCSE (9-1)

Physical Education

Tony Scott

PEARSON

Published by Pearson Education Limited, 80 Strand, London, WC2R 0RL.

www.pearsonschoolsandfecolleges.co.uk

Copies of official specifications for all Edexcel qualifications may be found on the website: www.edexcel.com

Text © Pearson Education.
Edited by Sarah Christopher
Typeset by Tek-Art, East Grinstead, West Sussex
Illustrations by Tek-Art, East Grinstead, West Sussex
Original illustrations © Pearson Education
Designed by Colin Tilley Loughrey
Cover photo: Getty Images: Koji Aoki
Indexed by Sophia Clapham, Index-Now

First published 2016

19 18 17 16
10 9 8 7 6 5 4 3 2 1

British Library Cataloguing in Publication Data
A catalogue record for this book is available from the British Library

ISBN 978 1 29212 988 4

Printed and bound in Great Britain at Bell & Bain, Glasgow

Acknowledgements
For image and text acknowledgements please see page viii.

A note from the publisher
In order to ensure that this resource offers high-quality support for the associated Pearson qualification, it has been through a review process by the awarding body. This process confirms that this resource fully covers the teaching and learning content of the specification or part of a specification at which it is aimed. It also confirms that it demonstrates an appropriate balance between the development of subject skills, knowledge and understanding, in addition to preparation for assessment.

Endorsement does not cover any guidance on assessment activities or processes (e.g. practice questions or advice on how to answer assessment questions), included in the resource nor does it prescribe any particular approach to the teaching or delivery of a related course.

While the publishers have made every attempt to ensure that advice on the qualification and its assessment is accurate, the official specification and associated assessment guidance materials are the only authoritative source of information and should always be referred to for definitive guidance.

Pearson examiners have not contributed to any sections in this resource relevant to examination papers for which they have responsibility.

Examiners will not use endorsed resources as a source of material for any assessment set by Pearson.

Endorsement of a resource does not mean that the resource is required to achieve this Pearson qualification, nor does it mean that it is the only suitable material available to support the qualification, and any resource lists produced by the awarding body shall include this and other appropriate resources.

Contents

Introduction iv

Component 1: Fitness and Body Systems 1
Topic 1: Applied anatomy and physiology 1
Topic 2: Movement analysis 50
Topic 3: Physical training 62

Preparing for your exam 118

Component 2: Health and Performance 124
Topic 1: Health, fitness and well-being 124
Topic 2: Sport psychology 153
Topic 3: Socio-cultural influences 164

Preparing for your exam 176

Component 3: Practical Performance 182

Component 4: Personal Exercise Programme (PEP) 196

Glossary 205

Index 210

About the author

I was born into a sporting family in Newport, South Wales and first started to play competitive sport (football) for my school (Lliswerry Primary) at the age of nine. I also represented my primary and secondary schools at football, baseball and cricket. My favourite subjects were PE and woodwork, but I left school at the age of 15 to become an apprentice carpenter. I attended college part-time and while I was there I became interested in teaching. However, I still really wanted to be a professional footballer and spent two years playing as a junior with my local professional club, Newport County.

Receiving my gold medal for the 1500m!

After college I moved to London and worked as a PE teacher in Barnet for 34 years. I coached football, basketball, track and field (athletics), cross country, trampoline, cricket, swimming and gymnastics. I also set up local school leagues for athletics and cross country – some of the teams I coached went on to National Schools finals competitions.

Alongside my teaching career, I played competitive football until I was 39. I ran in the first ever London Marathon in 1981 and again in 1984 and 1986, recording a best time of 2 hours 52 minutes (2 hours 40 from passing the start line!).

Soon after my last marathon I was diagnosed with serious liver disease and had a liver transplant in 1998. But that didn't stop me! Since 2004 I have represented the hospital where I had my transplant operation (Addenbrooke's in Cambridge) at the annual British Transplant Games. I have also represented Great Britain at the biannual World Transplant Games since 2003, winning gold medals in the 5000m and 1500m. In the 2015 World Transplant Games I won four gold medals: 5000m, 1500m, 800m and 400m – all in record times for World Transport Games for my age group.

In 2015, I was awarded an MBE for services to Physical Education and received my award from the Prince of Wales at Buckingham Palace.

I've had a wonderful career teaching PE and competing in my chosen sports all over the world. I wish all GCSE Physical Education students good luck! Enjoy the course and take what you learn with you for the rest of your life.

Receiving my MBE at Buckingham Palace

Tony Scott, MBE

Welcome to Edexcel GCSE (9-1) Physical Education

Learning through practice

This course is designed to help you develop your knowledge and understanding through practical involvement in a range of exciting sporting or physical activities. You will be able to develop and enjoy a healthy and active lifestyle by creating your own Personal Exercise Programme (PEP), which will also allow you to improve your own performance in your chosen sports.

There are many benefits to taking the Edexcel GCSE PE course.

- Firstly, it has a **real applied focus**. You will be encouraged to put the theory you are learning into context and apply what you have learned to your own practical performance. This makes it much more fun.
- It also reflects today's **global world** – the issues and topics you will learn about are up to date and will help you understand some of the key global influences in the world of sport today.
- You will gain a **well-rounded understanding of physical education**. Through an engaging introduction to the world of PE, sport and sport science you will genuinely appreciate how the human body allows us to perform amazing sporting feats, and how fitness and physical training contribute to a healthy lifestyle and improved performance.
- You will also have the opportunity to improve your **transferable skills**. These skills include analysing and interpreting data, communicating effectively and team working and will be valuable throughout your life. Having strong transferable skills can lead to a variety of employment opportunities in a range of different areas, for example, recreational management, leisure activities, coaching, the fitness industry, the armed forces or public services.
- If you do well in this course you will be in a good position to **progress to the next level of study** – whether this is A level PE or a vocational qualification, such as a BTEC National in Sport. The content of this GCSE is ideal grounding for other qualifications, and it has been designed using a similar approach, to make the experience of moving on a smooth one.

How you will be assessed

The GCSE course consists of four separate components:

- Component 1 Fitness and Body Systems
- Component 2 Health and Performance
- Component 3 Practical Performance
- Component 4 Personal Exercise Programme.

Components 1 and 2 are assessed by written exams, while Component 3 – Practical Performance – is internally assessed by your school. For more information about how you will be assessed, see the 'Preparing for your exam' sections. You will also find information about the assessment of your practical performance in Component 3.

Introduction

How to use this book

This book is organised in the same way as the Edexcel GCSE specification – there are four main sections, one for each component. Each component is divided into main topics; each topic section gives you all the information you need to know and guides you through the content of the course in a practical and engaging way, making it clear what you will cover and giving you useful activities and questions to help you practise what you have learned.

In this student book there are lots of different features. They are there to help you learn about the topics in your course in different ways, understand it from multiple perspectives and get the most from your learning.

- **Learning objectives** – these are listed at the beginning of each topic so you know exactly what you are going to learn and understand the related success criteria.

> ### Learning objectives
> By the end of this topic you will understand:
> - the different functions of the skeleton and its importance in physical activities
> - how bones and joints in the body are classified
> - the structure of the musculo-skeletal system
> - the different movement possibilities at joints within the body
> - the role of ligaments and tendons and their relevance to physical activity and sport
> - the classification and characteristics of muscle types
> - how the main muscles are used during physical activity
> - how the muscular system works with the skeleton to allow participation in physical activity and sport.

- **Getting started** – an activity or questions to check what you may already know and get you thinking about the topic before you start.

> ### Getting started
> People rely on their bones, joints and muscles to do sport.
> - How many bones, joints and muscles in the body can you name?
> - Why do sportspeople have such different bodies?
> - What injuries might happen to the bones, joints and muscles when taking part in sport?
> Select your favourite sporting activity. How do your bones, joints and muscles help you in this activity? Which ones are most important to your particular activity?

- **Key terms** – there are certain terms that you will need to know and be able to explain. These boxes explain what words that have been highlighted in **pink** mean. If the word is already defined in the text it is highlighted in **black**. All key terms can be found in the Glossary at the end of the book.

> ### Key terms
> **Tendons**: fibrous tissues that join bone to muscle.
>
> **Lever**: a rigid rod (bone) that turns round a pivot (joint).

- **Apply it** – the Apply it activities help you apply your knowledge and link it to a sporting context, as you will need to do in both the exam and your practical assessment.

- **Practice** – this feature is designed to build your practical skills and put your learning into practice immediately. Learning the theory of PE is not boring – it's what real sportspeople need to know in order to give their best performance.

> ### Practice
> Bone size determines your body size and, to an extent, your body shape or **somatotype.** In a group, measure around your wrists. How does the size of your wrist compare to your size and body shape? Is there a link with which sports you take part in?

> ### Apply it
> Give an example of one place in the body where the muscles are:
> - not in your control (involuntary)
> - where they are under your control (voluntary).

Exam-style question

1 Identify the waste product created by the muscles during anaerobic activity. (**1 mark**)

2 Explain the effects that this waste product can have on the body. (**2 marks**)

Exam tip

The prefix 'an-' means 'without', so 'anaerobic' means without oxygen. This question is asking about the type of activity in which muscles need more energy than can be supplied with oxygen.

Link it up

For more information on how bones and muscles work together as levers, see Topic 2, Section 2.1.

Use of data

Knowing how to create a graph will help you to interpret similar graphs when you come across them.

When you have a few training sessions in front of you, make a point of checking your heart rate before you start and again at the end. Take your recovery heart rate at one-minute intervals until your heart rate gets back to your resting heart rate.

At the end of a certain period – perhaps five days, or a week – use this information to create a graph showing your heart rate and recovery rate for each session. The more familiar you are with these graphs, the better.

- **Exam-style question** – these questions match the style of questions that you are likely to see in the written exams and will give you useful practice as you go through your course.

- **Exam tip** – hints and tips to aid your learning and help you in the exam.

- **Link it up** – these features show you how different parts of your course link together.

- **Use of data** – questions or activities designed to support your understanding of mathematical concepts, calculations or interpretation of data in a sports-related context.

- **Summary** – a handy revision checklist of key points you will need to remember about the topic.

Summary

Musculo-skeletal system
- Function
  - protecting organs
  - muscle attachment
  - joints for movement
  - blood cells and platelets

Cardio-respiratory system
- Structure
  - heart: atria, ventricles, valves
  - sequence of blood circulation
  - blood vessels: arteries, veins, capillaries

Preparing for your exams

At the end of Components 1 and 2 are exam preparation sections with tips and guidance for achieving success in your written exams. You will find example questions and answers, together with detailed notes and explanations about the quality of the answers shown. This will help you build your understanding of how to write better answers and achieve more marks.

Acknowledgements

The publisher would like to thank the following for their kind permission to reproduce their photographs:

(Key: b-bottom; c-centre; l-left; r-right; t-top)

Alamy Images: Action Plus Sports Images 37, 185t, George S de Blonsky 130, Cultura Creative (RF) 185b, Dash 90, Alan Edwards 57, Enigma 189, epa european pressphoto agency b.v. 162, Dan Galic 18, Rob Judges Rowing 182, Dennis MacDonald 79b, Richard Manning 187, Cesare Marchetti 50, PCN Photography 6, 69, PCN Photography 6, 69, Phanie 101, Grant Pritchard 54t, 54b, Nico Smit 104, View Pictures Ltd 159, Wavebreak Media ltd 79t, Jim West 81; Fotolia. com: Ammentorp 76, Ardijatree 129, Kris Butler 52tl, Dzmitry Fedarovich 52tr, Frinz 17cl, Indykb 52bl, Michael Ireland 166, Kasto 62, Kjekol 199, Lisovoy 17br, Pavel Losevsky 17bl, Monkey Business 72, 193, Mopic 3, Alexander Novikov 68, Royalty stock photo 29tr, WavebreakMediaMicro 188t; Getty Images: rolfo 188b, Clive Rose 13, Cultura 100, Franck Fife 73, John Foxx 78t, Fuse 1, Gallo Images 131, Paul Gilham 164, Halfpoint 196, Scott Halleran 146, Ken Hoskins - The FA 170, Image Source 192, Glyn Kirk 114, Mark Leech 154, Warren Little 120t, Alex Menendez 148, Dean Mouhtaropoulos 153, Mike Powell 124, David Price 134, Jung Yeon-Je 120b, Zero Creatives 67; Pearson Education Ltd: Pearson Education Australia Pty Ltd 53l, 53c, Tudor Photography 64; Tony Scott: ivt, ivb; Shutterstock.com: 74, Zai Aaragon 95, bikeriderlondon 194, Paolo Bona 198, Neale Cousland 17t, Stefano Ember 128, Eurobanks 78b, Fotokostic. 173, Mitch Gunn 160, Herbert Kratky 80, ifong 145, katatonia82 83, Sebastian Kaulitzki 29l, Mykola Komarovskyy 38, Maxisport 44, Monkey Business Images 195, 201, Mooinblack 126, Natursports 115, Pete Pahham 190, Photosebia 139, Pressmaster 53r, Rido 34, Royaltystockphoto.com 29tc, scyther5 136, Ljupco Smokovski 138, Laszlo Szirtesi 174

The publisher would also like to thank the following organisations for their kind permission to reproduce their materials:

p.69 Table 1.5: *Degrees of obesity in adults using BMI* has been reproduced with permission from the National Clinical Guideline Centre, (2014) Obesity: identification, assessment and management Clinical guideline 189. Published by the National Clinical Guidelines Centre at The Royal College of Physicians, 11 St Andrews Place, Regent's Park, London, NW11 4LE, **p.70** Figure 1.32: *Height/ weight chart*, has been reproduced with permission from NHS Choices, **p.142** Figure 2.1: *Percentage of people in different BMI ranges who have high blood pressure, by gender*, Figure 2.2: *People admitted to hospital in 2013 because of diabetes by age group* and **p.143**, Figure 2.3: *Numbers of people going to hospital because of diabetes from 2003/04, by gender*, have been reproduced with permission from The Health Survey for England, *2013.* Joint Health Surveys Unit (NatCen Social Research & UCL) 2016. The Health and Social Care Information Centre: Leeds. Copyright © 2016. All rights reserved. **p.168** Figure 2.6: *Perceived impact of school experience of sport on later participation* has been reproduced with permission from Sport England.

1 Fitness and Body Systems

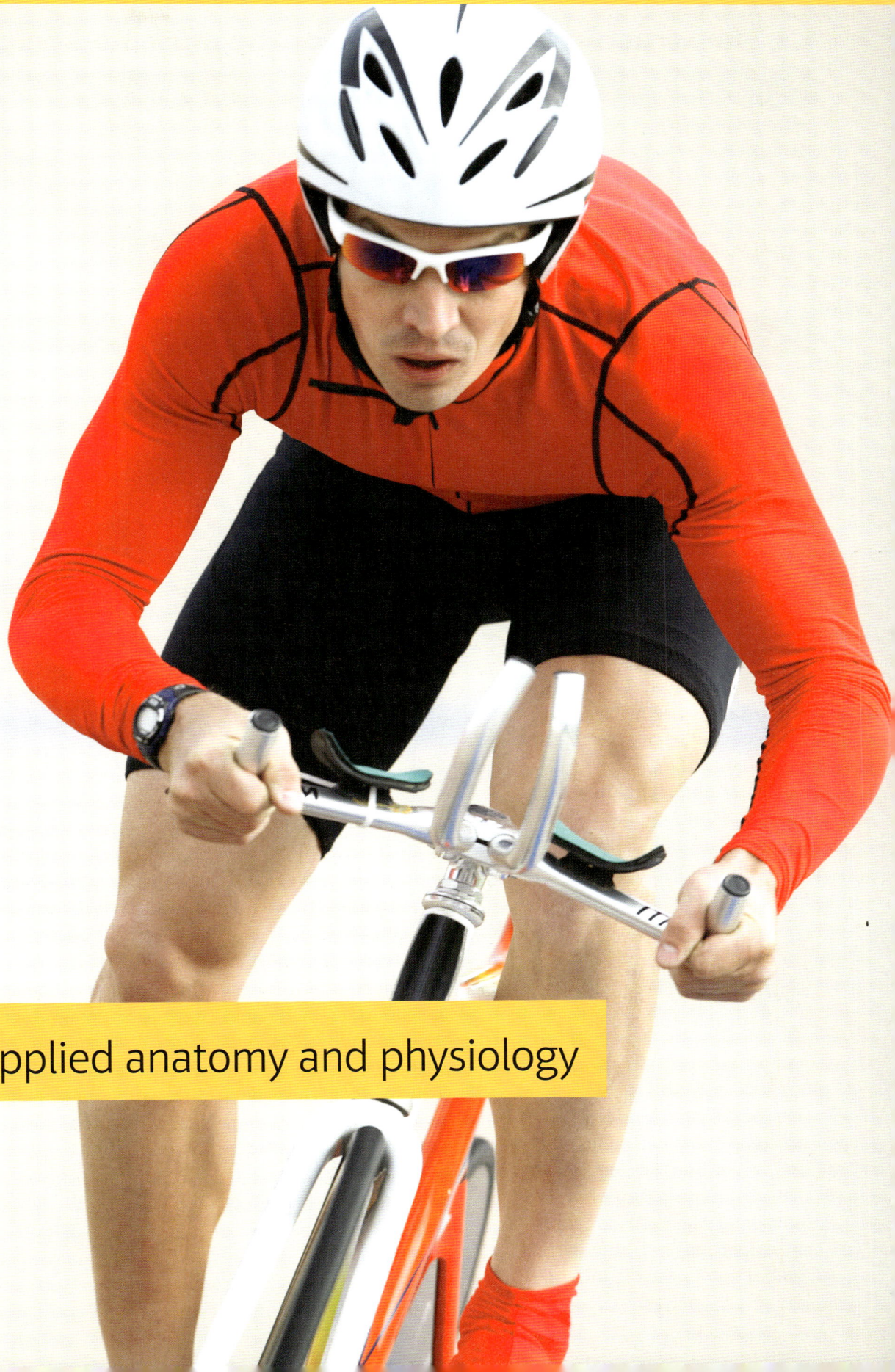

Topic 1 Applied anatomy and physiology

Fitness and Body Systems

1.1 The structure and functions of the musculo-skeletal system

Getting started

People rely on their bones, joints and muscles to do sport.
- How many bones, joints and muscles in the body can you name?
- Why do sportspeople have such different bodies?
- What injuries might happen to the bones, joints and muscles when taking part in sport?

Select your favourite sporting activity. How do your bones, joints and muscles help you in this activity? Which ones are most important to your particular activity?

Learning objectives

By the end of this topic you will understand:
- the different functions of the skeleton and its importance in physical activities
- how bones and joints in the body are classified
- the structure of the musculo-skeletal system
- the different movement possibilities at joints within the body
- the role of ligaments and tendons and their relevance to physical activity and sport
- the classification and characteristics of muscle types
- how the main muscles are used during physical activity
- how the muscular system works with the skeleton to allow participation in physical activity and sport.

Key terms

Muscular strength: the amount of force a muscle can exert against a resistance.

Muscular endurance: the ability to use voluntary muscles many times without getting tired.

Structure: how something complex is put together (called anatomy in animals and plants).

Anatomy: the bodily structure of humans and animals.

Physiology: how the whole body or a body part functions.

Link it up

Here we look at the body's structure – how it is put together. Later you will learn more about the body's **physiology** – how it functions – when you look at the circulatory and respiratory systems (see Section 1.2 later in this topic).

What is the musculo-skeletal system?

The skeleton includes all the bones in the body, from the cranium (skull) to the bones that make up the foot. Attached to the skeleton is a system of muscles, from large muscles like the gluteus maximus to the sheets of muscle that join bones together for example, the biceps and triceps. Working together, the joints, bones and skeletal muscles of the body comprise your musculo-skeletal system.

The main function of these components working together is to create movement, but they also work to provide stability, posture and protection.

Importance for sport

People need **muscular strength** and **muscular endurance** to be good at sport. The balance that someone needs between strength and endurance will depend on their sport. For example, the world's strongest man will need masses of muscular strength to lift the heaviest weight, but a long-distance runner will need muscular endurance to keep moving fast over 10,000 metres.

To understand muscular strength and endurance, you need to know about bones, joints and muscles, and the different roles they play. Bones, joints and muscles together form the **structure** of the body – the body's **anatomy**.

The functions of the skeleton for sport

The skeleton may seem like just a framework of bones on which our body is built, but it is much more than that. Bones protect your vital organs, give muscles somewhere to attach, create joints so you can move and store important minerals.

Protection of vital organs

Staying safe during sport is vital, and the skeleton plays a key role. The skull protects the brain, the spine protects the spinal cord, and the ribs protect the internal organs, including your heart. These bones act as cages around important body parts, though in some sports extra protection is needed, such as a helmet.

Muscle attachment

The muscles you use in sport need strong points to attach to. Bones provide that framework. The muscles are attached by **tendons**, and the bones act as anchors that muscles can pull on as they move.

Joints for movement

Look at a skeleton and you can see points where bones come together to form joints. Joints let the body make a variety of movements. Some are small, precise or 'fine' movements, like getting the right grip on a javelin. Others are larger or 'gross' movements, such as throwing the javelin. Joints work together with bones and muscles to form **levers**, so that a small force can generate a much bigger force elsewhere. For example, when you kick a football, this sort of lever turns the small movements in your leg muscle into the larger movement at the end of your leg.

Storing calcium and phosphorus

The bones act as a store for calcium and phosphorus, two minerals that are vital for developing and maintaining the strong and healthy bones you need for exercise. The best sources for both minerals are milk, cheese and yoghurt (choose the low-fat varieties). Phosphorus also helps to reduce muscle pain after a hard workout.

Red and white blood cell production

Some bones have hollow centres that hold bone marrow. Bone marrow makes most of the cells of the blood, including red blood cells, white blood cells and platelets.

Bone marrow responds to your activity and condition to keep you in good shape. When the oxygen content of the body's tissues drops or the number of red blood cells goes down, your bone marrow makes more red blood cells; if you have an infection, it makes more white blood cells; and if you have a cut, it makes more platelets to reduce the bleeding.

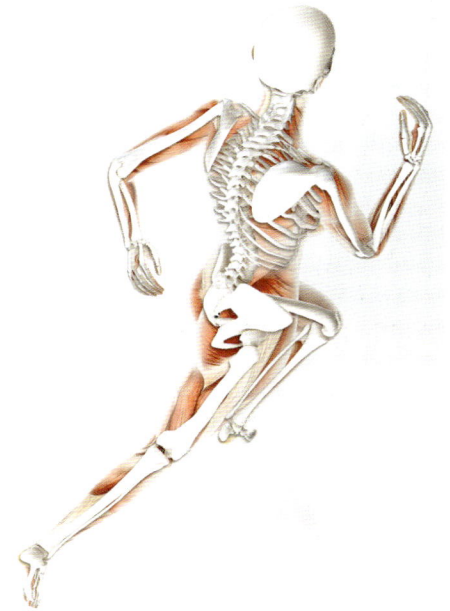

When it comes to sport, your skeleton is just as important as your muscles and organs

Link it up

For more information on how bones and muscles work together as levers, see Topic 2, Section 2.1.

Key terms

Tendons: fibrous tissues that join bone to muscle.

Lever: a rigid rod (bone) that turns round a pivot (joint).

Apply it

We only need most minerals in small amounts, but which foodstuffs provide them? Use the internet, books or magazines to find out. The BBC Bitesize website is a useful place to start.

Fitness and Body Systems

Practice

Bone size determines your body size and, to an extent, your body shape or **somatotype.** In a group, measure around your wrists. How does the size of your wrist compare to your size and body shape? Is there a link with which sports you take part in?

Facts about bones

- The bones of the skeleton are alive.
- Bones stop growing in length after about the age of 16-18, but still increase in density.
- Around the age of 35, bones begin to deteriorate (weaken).

Bone growth and development

All bones are formed from **cartilage**, except the clavicle (collarbone) and some parts of the cranium (skull). Bones begin to grow before children are born, and as growth takes place the cartilage, which forms their temporary skeleton is hardened into bone by calcium and other minerals. Bone growth begins in the centre of each bone, and in a long bone this is in the centre of the shaft. Growth takes place upwards, downwards and around the central marrow cavity, then secondary growth appears at both ends. Cartilage remains between the areas until bone growth is completed. These are known as growth plates. This process of development from cartilage to bone is known as **ossification**.

Classification of bones

Bones come in many shapes and sizes, but most can be put into groups that have something in common. For example, long bones tend to be used as levers, while flat bones are often for protection. Figure 1.1 shows the main types of bone.

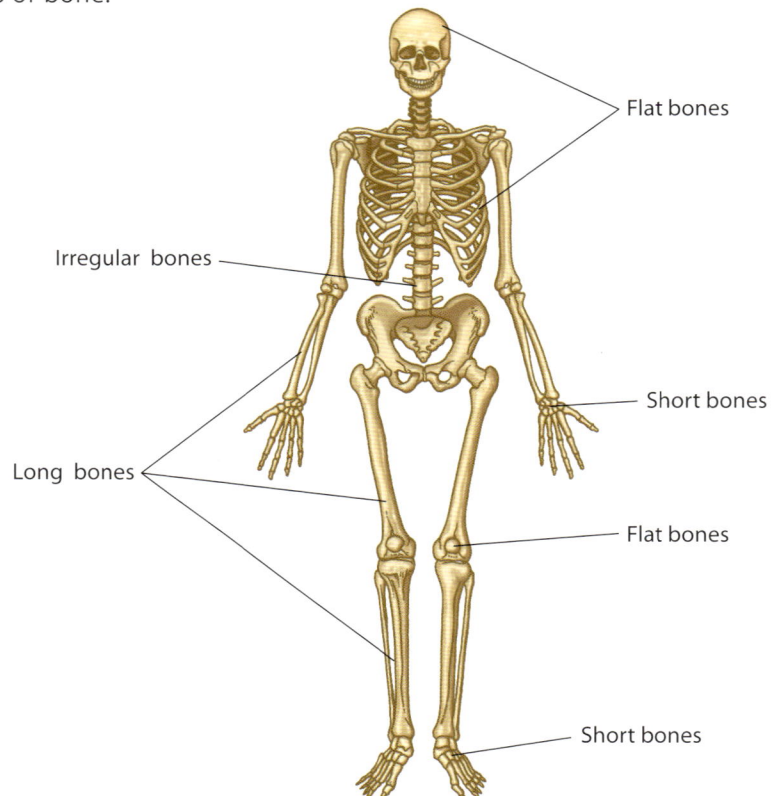

Figure 1.1 The main types of bone in the human body

Long bones

Long bones are bones that are longer than they are wide. They don't have to be big: small bones like finger bones (phalanges) count as long bones, because of their overall shape. A long bone has a shaft plus two ends.

All limb bones apart from the kneecap (patella) and the wrist and ankle bones are long bones.

In sport

These bones are vital to generate movement, strength and speed. They usually act as levers. When they are pulled by different muscles, they enable the body to move.

Short bones

Short bones are roughly the same size in length, width and thickness. The only short bones in the body are the carpals in the wrist and the tarsals in the foot. To remember which is which, think 'carpals and cuffs, tarsals and toes'.

In sport

Short bones are normally associated with weight-bearing, shock absorption and spreading loads. They play a key role in activities like jogging, playing tennis or dancing.

Flat bones

Flat bones, or plates, usually protect organs or offer a good surface for muscles to attach to. For example, the ribs protect the heart and lungs, while the broad shoulder blade (scapula) has three main muscle groups attached to it. Other flat bones are the kneecap (patella), skull (cranium), chest plate (sternum), collarbone (clavicle) and two of the hip bones, the ilium and ischium.

In sport

Flat bones protect your vital organs, especially in contact sports. They also provide attachment of muscles to help movement for every type of physical exercise.

Irregular bones

Irregular bones have odd shapes, and perform a range of functions. Some have a special shape so that they can protect something, like the vertebrae, which protect the spinal cord. Others have lots of attachment points for muscle, like the sacrum, a triangular bone in the lower back.

In sport

Irregular bones also offer protection when you are playing sport – for example, vertebrae in your back protect the spinal cord.
They tend to form specific functions – for example, the first and second vertebrae allow the head to nod and rotate, which is crucial in almost every sport.

Figure 1.2 shows some of the main terms associated with structure of bones.

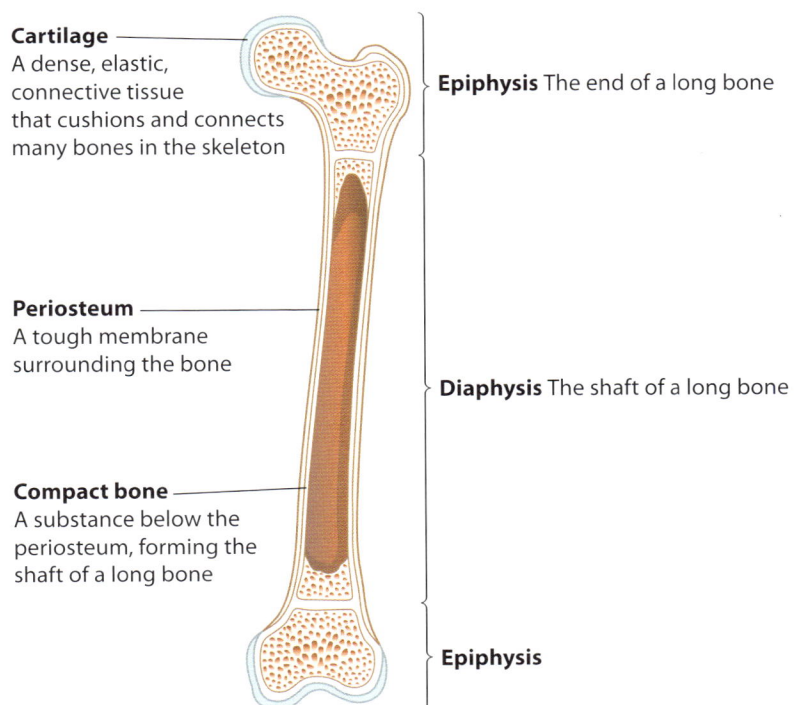

Cartilage
A dense, elastic, connective tissue that cushions and connects many bones in the skeleton

Epiphysis The end of a long bone

Periosteum
A tough membrane surrounding the bone

Diaphysis The shaft of a long bone

Compact bone
A substance below the periosteum, forming the shaft of a long bone

Epiphysis

Figure 1.2 Some of the main features of bone structure

Fitness and Body Systems

Apply it

Read this text about diver Tom Daley.

*In his dive from the 10 metre board, he uses energy climbing the steps to the diving platform as well as diving. This energy is transported in his blood in the form of **glycogen**, so blood production is vital. Movement takes place throughout the preparation (getting up the steps to the diving platform) and execution of the dive. For example, Tom Daley starts in a standing position but may have to take up a handstand position before diving. At this point he is supported upside down and balanced in the handstand position by his arms.*

He changes shape several times in a split second, going through a range of co-ordinated movements (somersaults and twists) at great speed using his agility and reaction time to complete the dive successfully. As he hits the water, his cranium protects his head, his ribs protect his heart, lungs and other vital organs.

Tom's event is a highly technical one and a fit body helped him to achieve success from a very young age. The way his body functions enables him to perform at this level.

- Think about which bones are key to Tom Daley's ability to dive.
- Name one bone of each of the four types that enables him to do his sport.

Key term

Glycogen: the stored form of carbohydrate primarily located in the muscles and liver and readily available as an energy fuel.

Exam tip

Choose a sport that you take part in. Think of your own experience of that sport and the sporting action and this will usually help you to get the answer right. Remember, with an 'explain' question you will be expected to do more than just state which part of the skeletal system is involved. You will need to say how it protects the body during the action.

Exam-style question

Think of a sport and an action in that sport (for example, diving; entering the water head first). Explain how the skeletal system protects the body during that action. You are not allowed to use diving as the sport. **(3 marks)**

The structure of the skeletal system

You will know many of the bones of your body by their common names, but it is important that you know the anatomical names too. For example, the bone you call your kneecap is technically called the patella.

Knowing these names is important. Doctors and other health professionals use them so that they can be precise about which bones they are talking about. For example, someone might say they have injured their finger bone – but the finger is made up of several bones, so which one do they mean? The scientific (Latin) name will identify exactly the right bone.

Apply it

If you take part in a lot of sport and physical exercise, you will probably already know some scientific names for bones. Cover up the next page and make a quick note of any of the Latin names you know for bones in your body.

Maxilla

Mandible

Clavicle

Humerus

Sternum

Rib

Pelvis

Radius

Ulna

Femur

Patella

Tarsals

Metatarsals

Phalanges

Cranium

Cervical vertebrae

Scapula

Thoracic vertebrae

Ilium

Sacrum

Lumbar vertebrae

Ischium

Carpals

Metacarpals

Phalanges

Tibia

Fibula

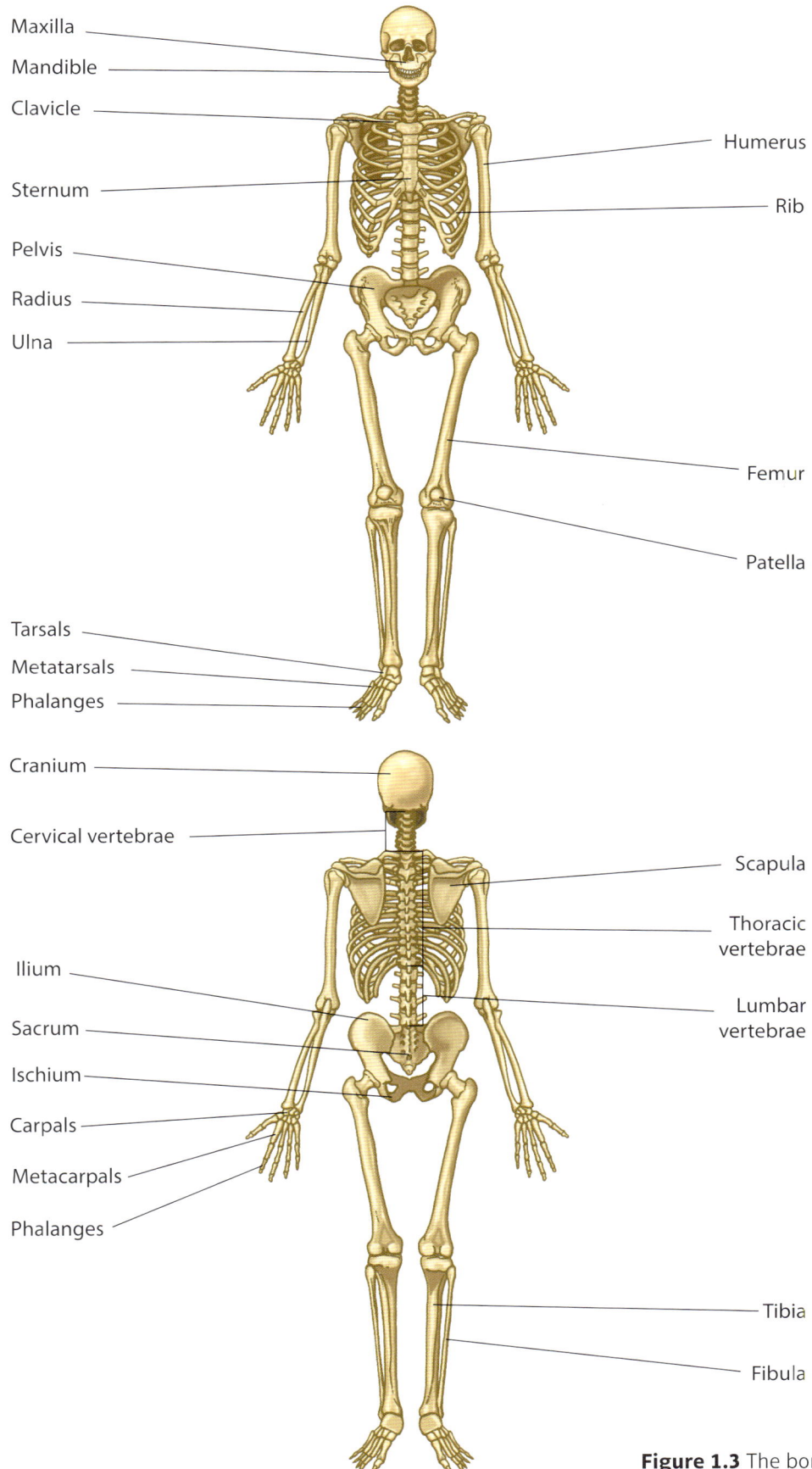

Figure 1.3 The bones of your skeleton

Fitness and Body Systems

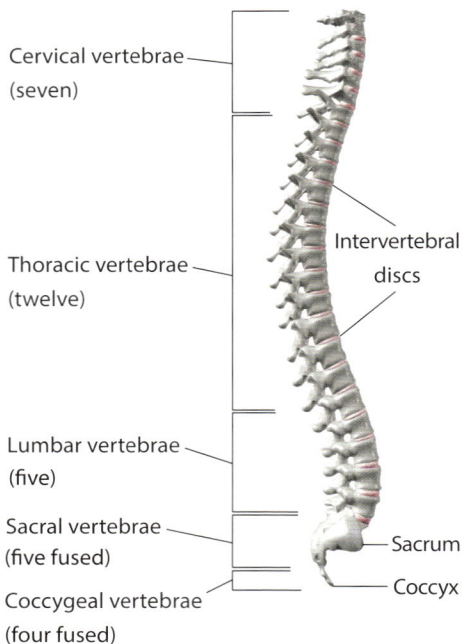

Cervical vertebrae (seven)

Thoracic vertebrae (twelve)

Intervertebral discs

Lumbar vertebrae (five)

Sacral vertebrae (five fused)

Sacrum

Coccygeal vertebrae (four fused)

Coccyx

Figure 1.4 The five groups of vertebrae that form the vertebral column

The vertebral column

The vertebral column consists of 33 bones, or vertebrae, which are divided into five groups. Starting from the top there are:

- seven in the cervical region which form the neck, and allow a variety of movement
- twelve in the chest or thoracic region, ten of which raise a pair of ribs when you breathe
- five in the lower back or lumbar region, where the discs between the vertebrae are relatively large to give you more mobility
- five in the sacrum, which in adults are fused together and work with the hip bones
- four in the coccyx.

Apply it

Working with a partner you feel comfortable with, take it in turns to feel down their spine. Can you identify which section of the spine you are in? See if you can learn the sections of the spine in the right order. Use Figure 1.4 to help you.

Exam-style question

1   Label the bones A to F shown in the diagram. **(6 marks)**

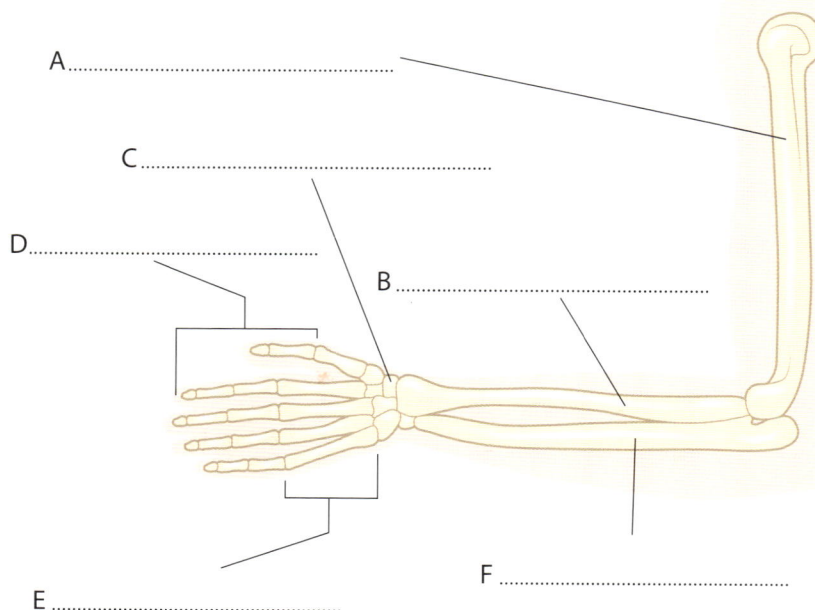

A..

C..

D..

B..

E..

F..

Figure 1.5

Exam tip

Make sure you label the correct bone! To help you remember which is which, practise labelling a diagram of a skeleton methodically from the top (cranium) down to the feet. Then memorise the names in the same order by reading over them again and again. You could even make up a rhyme or mnemonic that makes sense to you for different bones in different parts of the body.

Joints

What is a joint?

A joint is a place where two or more bones meet. Joints are important for movement and **rotation**. If our bodies were not jointed, we would not be able to deliberately move our bodies, and our movement and activities would be extremely restricted. All joints allow movement, although the extent and freedom of movement vary from joint to joint.

Our backs are flexible because the vertebral column is made up of a number of small bones. If our upper limbs were not jointed we could not eat as we do. If our lower limbs were not jointed we would not be able to stand, as our body is on too small a base to remain stable. A slight wind could knock us over if our muscles were not constantly moving and adjusting our balance by means of our joints.

Classification of joints

There are a number of different ways to classify joints. For sport and physical activity, the best way to group joints is according to how they function for movement. With this in mind, here are the four main types of joint:

- pivot
- hinge
- ball and socket
- condyloid.

Pivot joints

Pivot joints allow bones to rotate. In a pivot joint, one bone shaped like a cylinder rotates inside another bone or **ligament** that makes a ring round it. You have three pivot joints in your body: in your wrist, elbow and neck.

Key terms
Rotation: movement around a single axis or pivot point.
Ligament: strong, flexible connective tissue that connects bones to other bones.

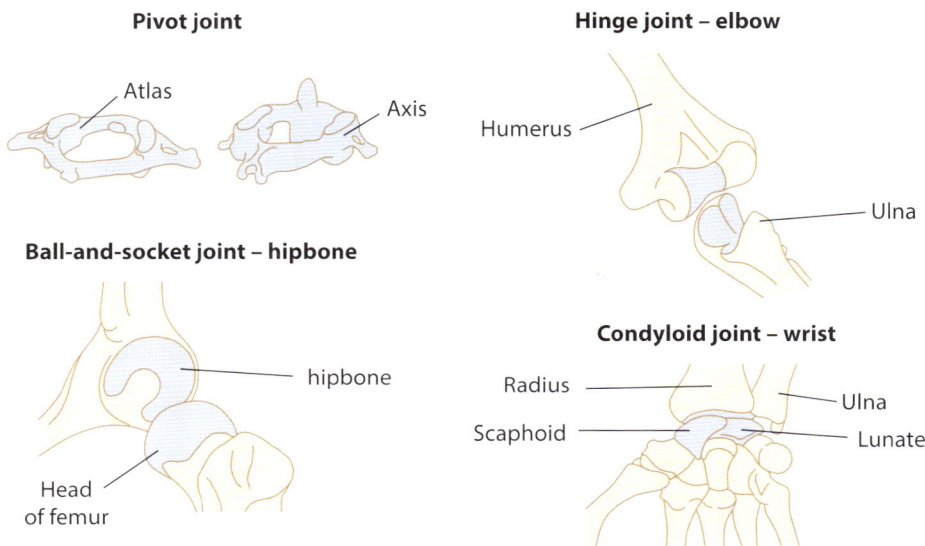

Pivot joint
Atlas
Axis

Hinge joint – elbow
Humerus
Ulna

Ball-and-socket joint – hipbone
hipbone
Head of femur

Condyloid joint – wrist
Radius
Ulna
Scaphoid
Lunate

Figure 1.6 How do you use different types of joint in your favourite sport?

Fitness and Body Systems

Each time you turn your head or rotate your wrist you are using a pivot joint – so you can imagine how important these joints are to sporting activity.

In the neck, the first two vertebrae – the atlas and the axis – form a pivot joint that connects the skull and the spine. This joint allows you to rotate your neck, so you can turn your head from side to side.

Hinge joints

A hinge joint is a joint that allows only backward and forward motion – just like the hinge on a door. There are three hinge joints: the knee, elbow and ankle.

Knee

In the knee joint, the tibia is hinged on the femur so that the leg can be bent (**flexion**) or straightened (**extension**). Examples of this movement include doing squats, or when a footballer bends the lower leg at the knee (flexion) then straightens it (extension) to kick the ball.

Elbow

The elbow has a hinge joint between the humerus and the ulna, which enables us to bend (flexion) or straighten (extension) the arm – for example, when doing bicep curls. The muscles that flex the joint are on the front (biceps) and the muscles that extend are on the back (triceps).

Ankle

The hinge joint in the ankle enables us to bend the foot up (**dorsi-flexion**) – for example, the leading leg when hurdling – and to point the toes down (**plantar-flexion**) – for example, pointing the toes when in the air during trampolining. When we turn the foot inwards (inversion), it is as a result of a gliding movement between the tarsal bones.

Ball and socket joints

In a ball and socket joint, the rounded head of a long bone (the ball) fits into a cup-shaped hole (the socket). Both the hip and the shoulder joints are ball and socket joints. With the hip, the long femur fits into the pelvis; with the shoulder, the long humerus fits into the scapula. In both the hip and the shoulder the bones are covered with cartilage and reinforced with ligaments, but the shoulder joint has more freedom than the hip and is capable of more variety and a bigger range of movement.

Condyloid joints

A condyloid joint is similar to a ball and socket joint, but the ball rests against the end of a bone, rather than inside a socket. This allows circular motion.

The wrist is a condyloid joint. You can bend it (flexion) and straighten it (extension), but you can also turn your hand inwards (**adduction**) and outwards (**abduction**). This allows for very complex movements, such as when a bowler spins a ball.

Key terms

Flexion: a bending movement that decreases the angle between body parts (the opposite of extension).

Extension: a straightening movement that increases the angle between body parts (the opposite of flexion).

Dorsi-flexion: bending or flexing the toes upwards, bringing them closer to the shin.

Plantar-flexion: extending or pointing the toes down, away from the shin.

Adduction: a movement that pulls towards the midline of the body (the opposite of abduction).

Abduction: a movement that pulls away from the midline of the body (the opposite of adduction).

(a) Flexion   **(b) Extension**   **(c) Abduction, adduction**

Abduction

Adduction

(d) Plantar-flexion and dorsi-flexion

Dorsi-flexion

Plantar-flexion

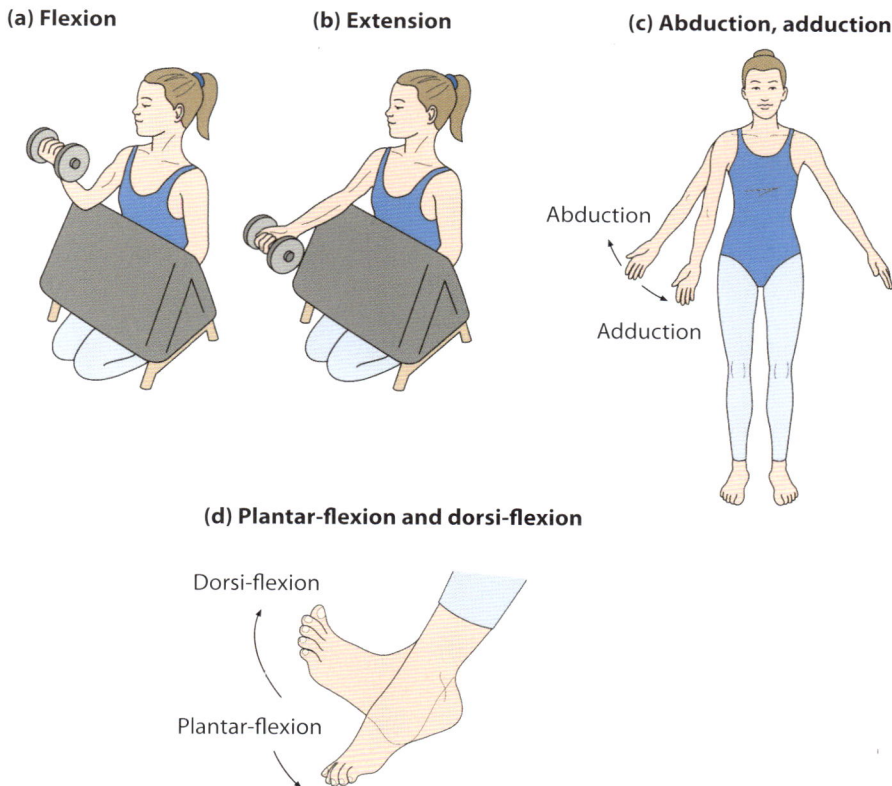

Figure 1.7 Types of movement at joints: flexion, extension, adduction, abduction, dorsi-flexion, plantar-flexion

Apply it

Draw a table with two columns, as shown below. Write an example for each joint type found in the body.

Joint type	Example
Pivot	
Hinge	
Ball and socket	
Condyloid	

Joints and movement

Joints allow movement. For example, the spine is made up of a number of small bones that allow the back to be flexible – a characteristic that lets high jumpers bend over a bar. Generally, the joints in the upper limbs allow mobility (for example, bringing food to your mouth) and joints in the lower limbs are for stability – you would easily fall over if your muscles were not constantly moving the joints to adjust your balance.

The shoulder joint and, to a lesser extent, the hip joint can perform flexion, extension, adduction, abduction and rotation. All of these movements can be performed quite easily in the shoulder as the head of the humerus can be rotated either forwards (as when bowling in cricket) or backwards (such as when swimming backstroke).

Jointed bones and flexible fingers make it possible to be able to play sport. For example, our fingers can be made into a fist (flexion), as when gripping a tennis ball, or straightened (extension), as when bowling underarm in cricket, or opened (abduction) and closed (adduction).

Table 1.1 shows you the different types of movement you need to know about, lists the joints that provide this sort of movement, and gives you some examples of where you can see this type of movement in sports practice.

Fitness and Body Systems

Type of movement	Joints that provide it	Examples in sport
Flexion – bending movement that decreases the angle between body parts	Shoulder, hip, elbow	Someone working out in the gym bends their arm up when doing a bicep curl
Extension – straightening movement that increases the angle between body parts	Shoulder, hip	A swimmer swings the arm backwards in preparation for a racing dive
Adduction – movement that pulls towards the midline of the body	Shoulder, hip	A golfer on the tee swings the club down towards the ball
Abduction – movement that pulls away from the midline of the body	Shoulder, hip	A gymnast moves their arms out sideways at the shoulder when performing 'the crucifix' on the rings
Rotation – movement around a single axis or pivot point	Shoulder, hip	A tennis player serves
Circumduction – moving in a circular or conical shape	Shoulder, hip	A cricketer bowls a ball
Dorsi-flexion – bending or flexing the toes up, closer to the shin	Ankle	A sprinter positions their feet in the starting blocks
Plantar-flexion – extending or pointing the toes down, away from the shin	Ankle	A floor gymnast points their toes

Table 1.1 Types of movement, related joints and examples from sport

Key term

Circumduction: moving a part of the body in a circular or conical shape, as with a ball-and-socket joint like the hip.

Apply it

Consider the shoulder joint and the hip joint.

Give an example from a sport of your choice for each type of movement possible in each joint: flexion, extension, adduction, abduction, rotation and circumduction.

Apply it

At any joint that has movement, ligaments, muscles and tendons hold the joint together – and there is the potential for injury. As part of your Personal Exercise Plan (PEP), identify and describe how you can:

- prevent injury occurring in the first place;
- deal with injuries if they occur.

Practice

Working with a partner, take it in turns to demonstrate a simple movement and ask your partner to explain the movement (for example, bending the arm shows flexion at a hinge joint).

With the same partner, take it in turns to name a type of joint, and ask them to demonstrate all types of movement possibilities at that joint (for example, hinge joint = elbow = flexion, extension and slight rotation).

Mime some sporting activities together, such as serving in tennis. Together, identify what joints are involved and discuss the types of movement taking place, for example: shoulder = ball and socket = rotation.

Ligaments and tendons

Ligaments and **tendons** are both types of strong fibrous tissue.

Ligaments are elastic fibres that join one bone to another, usually to hold things together and keep them stable. They keep your skeleton supported, while allowing movement at your joints.

An example of where ligaments are especially important in sport is the knee. When you walk or run, strong ligaments on either side of your knee keep it stable, while two ligaments crossing inside the knee hold the joint together.

Torn ligaments are one of the most serious injuries in footballers

Not much blood flows through ligaments (or tendons), which means they heal more slowly from strains or tears. Ligament injuries can be serious for sportsmen and women. Golfer Rory McIlroy ruptured his ankle ligament playing football for fun and missed the British Open at St Andrews in 2015.

Tendons are non-elastic fibres that attach muscle to bone, and help to move them. Tendons let you apply power and movement, and are designed to allow for pulley-like actions of muscles around a bone.

The tendons that you use more are stronger than the ones you don't use as much – so if you are a football player, the tendons supporting your ankle will be stronger than the tendons around your wrists.

However strong your muscles are, you can still injure a tendon when playing sport. This sort of injury can seem sudden, but it is usually the result of lots of tiny tears the tendon has picked up over time. It often takes a long time to recover from.

When you warm up, doing stretches helps prevent you injuring your ligaments and tendons by gradually stretching the joint (ligaments and tendons) further, before you actually perform.

Muscle types

Each of your muscles is made of many cells or muscle fibres. The muscles of the body each fall into one of three groups:

- voluntary muscles
- involuntary muscles
- cardiac (or heart) muscle.

This classification is very important. The muscles work either voluntarily, through different types of planned contraction, or involuntarily, contracting by themselves, as happens in the internal organs.

All muscles are made up of protein. When we eat fish or meat, which contains protein, we are actually eating the muscle of the animal.

Link it up

You will find more information on the role muscle plays in body composition in Topic 3, Section 3.2, including looking at Body Mass Index (BMI).

Voluntary muscles

Voluntary muscles are under your control: you can choose when to contract or relax them. All these muscles are attached to the skeleton by tendons, so they are also known as skeletal. When your muscle fibres contract, or pull against the skeleton, movement takes place.

These muscles are made up of cylindrical fibres, and are usually long and thin (but get shorter and thicker when they contract). On average, they make up 43 per cent of a man's weight, and 36 per cent of a woman's weight (women naturally have a higher proportion of fat).

Involuntary muscles

Involuntary muscles are not under your control. They contract and relax automatically, controlled by the involuntary nervous system, working all the time to keep you alive. Involuntary muscles are found in the organs in the digestive, circulatory and urinary systems. The muscles are made of spindle-shaped fibres.

> ### Key term
>
> **Vascular**: relating to blood vessels.

The involuntary muscles in blood vessels are especially important for sport and physical activity. **Vascular** smooth muscle makes up most of the wall of blood vessels. When it contracts or relaxes, it changes the volume and pressure of the vessel, helping to redistribute the blood to areas where it is needed most within the body – such as the active muscles you are using for your movement.

Cardiac muscle

Cardiac muscle is only found in the wall of the heart. It is a very specialised type of involuntary muscle – we cannot control when it contracts and relaxes. Cardiac muscle is made up of interlaced fibres. These fibres can spread electrochemical signals from the brain right through the heart, so that all the cells can contract together. This regulates your heart rate and pumps all the blood in your body through your heart in less than a minute. When you run, it is cardiac muscle that keeps your heart pumping in the right way.

> ### Apply it
>
> Give an example of one place in the body where the muscles are:
>
> - not in your control (involuntary)
> - under your control (voluntary).

Skeletal muscle   **Smooth muscle**   **Cardiac muscle**

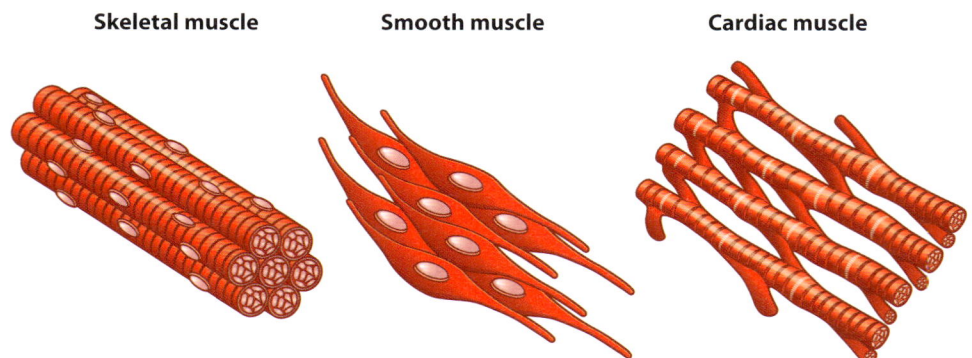

Figure 1.8 The structure of the three types of muscle tissue

The voluntary muscular system

The term 'muscular system' describes all the muscles in the body and the way they work together. Working with the skeletal system, the voluntary muscular system is the driving force behind movement, which happens as a result of muscles contracting and lengthening. Muscles also define body shape and help you to maintain your posture, whether you are sitting or standing.

The voluntary muscular system is crucial when you are exercising or playing sport. These are the muscles you can control. You can train them to be stronger and to work for longer without getting tired. They are the muscles you work on to improve flexibility and get a greater range of movement at the joints. They are also the muscles you work on through specific exercises – for example, sit-ups and step-ups – during a circuit training session.

Location and role of the main voluntary muscles

There are 12 specific muscles you need to know about. You need to know where to find them, what action they perform and how you might see them in action in sport or physical exercise.

Apply it

Devise a circuit training card to show what actions are taking place and when, and which muscles are responsible for each action in the following exercises:

- press-ups
- sit-ups
- step-ups.

Apply it

Using your own circuit training card, or a sample card from a circuit training session, identify which muscles you use for each exercise.

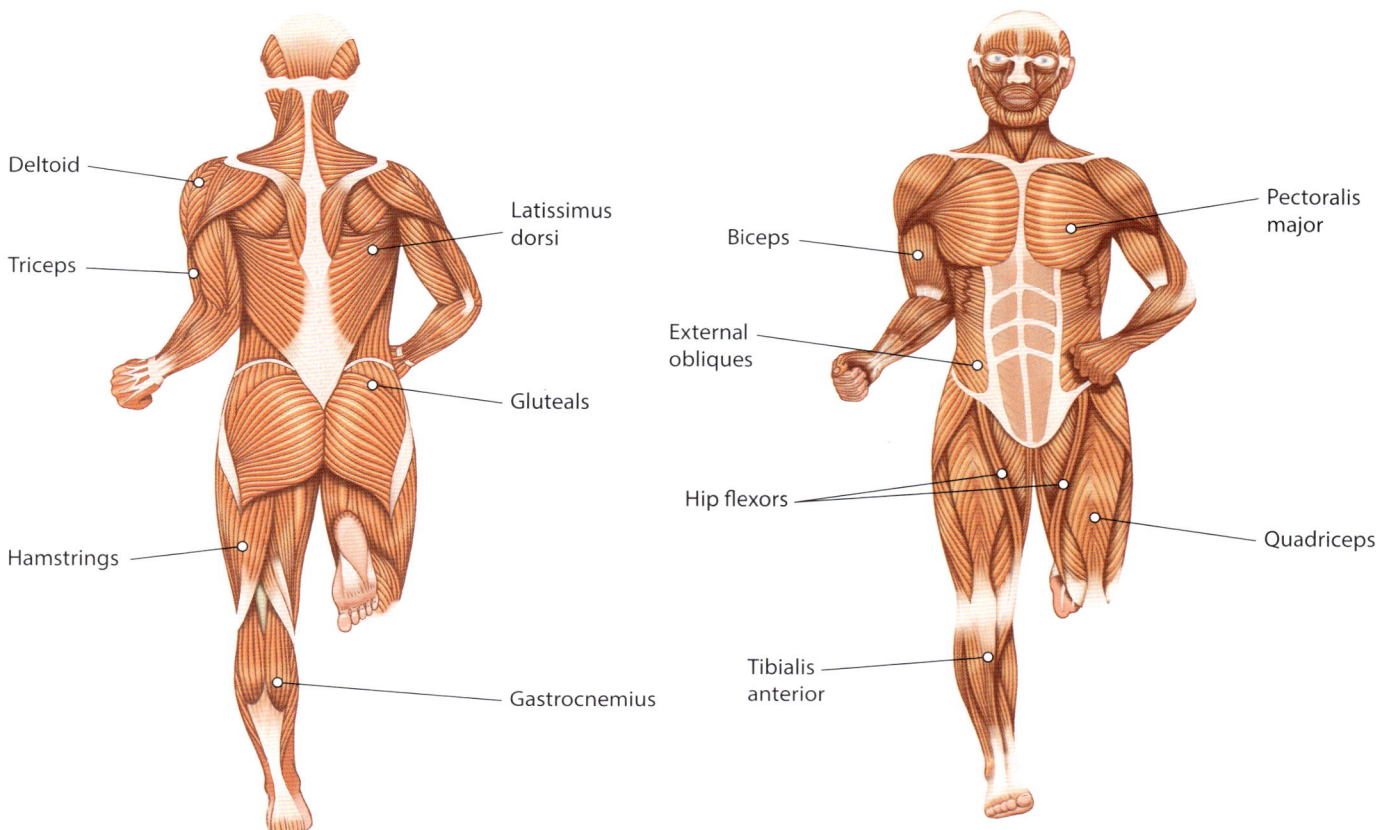

Deltoid

Triceps

Latissimus dorsi

Gluteals

Hamstrings

Gastrocnemius

Biceps

Pectoralis major

External obliques

Hip flexors

Quadriceps

Tibialis anterior

Figure 1.9 The main muscles in the body

Fitness and Body Systems

Table 1.2 tells you about each of these 12 muscles, starting from the top of the body and working downwards.

Muscle	Location	Function	Example in sport
Deltoid	Rounded, triangular muscle on the uppermost part of the arm and at the top of the shoulder	Move the arm in all directions at the shoulder	Serving in tennis
Pectoralis major	Covering the chest	Adduct the arm at the shoulder	Forehand drive in tennis
Latissimus dorsi	Broad sheet of muscle that extends from the lower region of the spine to the bone in the upper arm (humerus)	Adduct and extend the arm at the shoulder	Butterfly stroke in swimming
Biceps	Front of the upper arm	Flex the arm at the elbow	Pull-up, drawing a bow in archery
Triceps	Back of the upper arm	Extend the arm at the elbow	Press-up, throwing a javelin
External obliques	To the side of the abdomen, running from the lower half of the ribs down to the pelvis	Pull the chest downwards; flex and rotate the spinal column; one side contracting creates a side bend	Crunches in the gym
Gluteals	Form the buttocks. Gluteus maximus (the largest) lies just under the skin, and is attached to the femur (thigh bone)	Adduct and extend leg at the hips, pull the leg backwards	Pulling back leg before kicking a ball
Hip flexors	Sit deep in the front of the hip and connect the leg, pelvis and abdomen	Flex the hip, help move the leg and knee up towards the body	Lifting knees high in sprinting
Quadriceps	Four muscles found on the front of the upper leg	Extend the leg at the knee	Kicking a ball, jumping upwards
Hamstrings	Found on the back of the leg, stretching from the bottom part of the pelvis to the tibia (the shin bone)	Flex the leg at the knee	Bending knee before kicking a ball
Gastrocnemius	Starts at the back of the femur and comes together with the soleus muscle to form the Achilles tendon at the back of the ankle	Point the toes (plantar-flexes the ankle), help flex the knee	Running
Tibialis anterior	Runs down the shin	Pull the toes up towards the shin (dorsi-flexes the ankle)	Ski jumping

Table 1.2 Location and function of the main muscles in the body

Deltoid

The deltoid is a powerful muscle that takes away (abducts) the upper arm from the body. The deltoid is mainly responsible for lifting the arm above the head: for example, when serving in tennis.

You can improve deltoid strength through exercises such as bent-over rowing and military press.

Latissimus dorsi

Latissimus dorsi is a powerful muscle that brings the arms towards the body (adducts), rotates them and draws them back and inwards towards the body – as when someone swims butterfly stroke. The latissimus dorsi can be developed by performing lateral pull-downs on the weights machine, or pull-ups.

External obliques

The external obliques pull the chest downwards which compresses the abdominal cavity. These muscles also enable the spine to rotate. These muscles can be developed by side crunches or by performing the side plank.

Pectoralis major

The pectoral muscle is another powerful muscle that works to move the arm towards the body (adduct), draw the arm forwards and rotate it inwards. This muscle is important in the swimming strokes front crawl and butterfly. The bench press is a good exercise to improve the strength of the pectoral muscle.

Biceps and triceps

These muscles are described together because that is how they work – together. When the arm is straightened (extended), the triceps contracts while the biceps relaxes. The biceps and triceps are involved in throwing actions, such as throwing the javelin or a cricket ball.

You can use many exercises to strengthen the biceps, including barbell, dumbbell curls or preacher curls. For the triceps, you can use the triceps stretch (extension). Chin-ups, parallel bar dips, and press-ups improve the strength of both and are good tests of their fitness and strength.

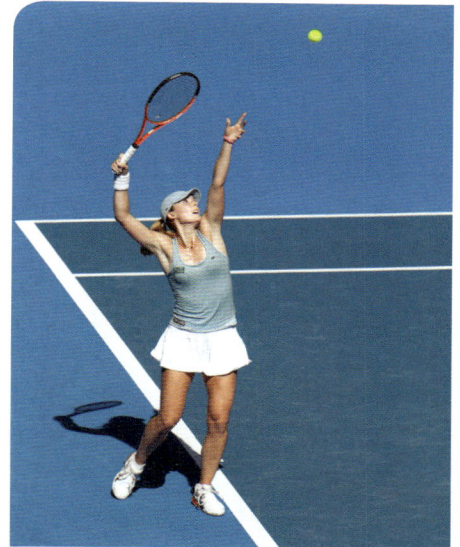

You would use your deltoid muscle when serving in tennis

The latissimus dorsi is one of the main drivers for your body as you swim

You use your pectoral muscles when doing the bench press

You use your biceps when performing the bicep (dumbbell) curl

17

Fitness and Body Systems

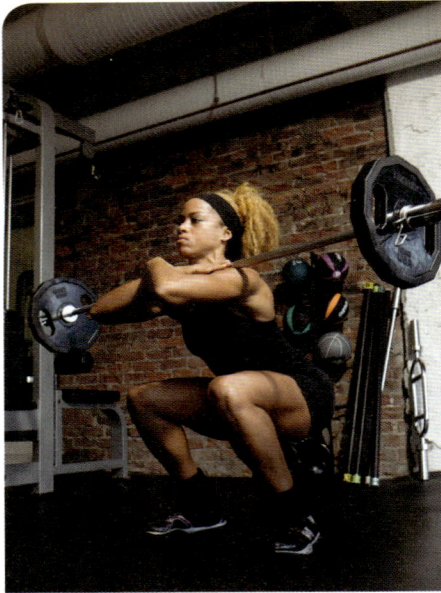

Squats can be useful for developing gluteal muscles and quadriceps

Gluteal muscles

The gluteal muscles pull the leg backwards (extension) – for example, before you kick a ball.

The gluteus maximus can cause poor posture if underdeveloped. Many weight-training exercises help to develop this muscle, including squats, leg presses and lunges.

Hip flexors

The hip flexors flex the hip to help you move your leg and knee up towards your body. Hip flexors control your stride length, so they are important for sprinting and hurdling, and they play a key role in being able to push forward in rugby. Hip flexors are often ignored in training programmes, but can be strengthened through exercises such as reverse lunges or straight leg raises.

Quadriceps

The four quadriceps straighten (extend) the leg at the knee joint. Their most common sporting use is when kicking a ball, which is why they are sometimes known as the kicking muscles. Many exercises are suitable for strengthening the quadriceps, including squats, seated leg press and leg extensions.

Practice

Take a netball or a basketball and pass it to a partner using one arm. Your partner should catch the ball and pass it back to you. With your other arm, feel the muscles in the upper arm.

- Which muscle is working when you straighten your arm to pass?
- Which muscle is working when you hold out your arm and bend it to receive the pass back from your partner?

Hamstrings

The hamstrings are so close to the surface that you can feel them behind the knee. Hamstrings bend (flex) the knee and its tendons. The hamstrings are so important in running that they are called the 'sprinter's muscle'. It is crucial to warm up your hamstrings properly before sprinting to avoid injury. Leg curls will help increase their strength, but use a lighter weight – hamstrings are not as strong as quadriceps.

Gastrocnemius and tibialis anterior

The gastrocnemius is one of two major muscles that make up the calf muscle. The gastrocnemius plantar-flexes the ankle. The tibialis anterior muscle runs down the shin, and dorsi-flexes the ankle.

The leg muscles are the strongest in the body, and are very important in most physical activities. In sports such as tennis, golf and especially throwing events in athletics, the initial movement comes from the legs and is finished in the upper body.

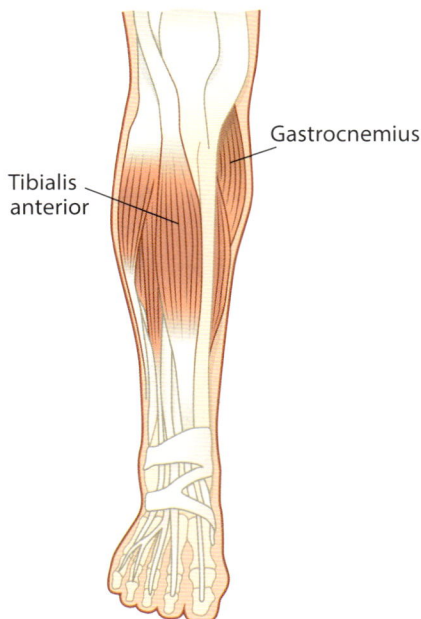

Tibialis anterior

Gastrocnemius

Figure 1.10 Gastrocnemius and tibialis anterior

Antagonistic pairs

When a muscle contracts and pulls on a bone, it can produce movement in one direction. However, muscles cannot push. So how can the bone move in the opposite direction? A second muscle is needed to pull the bone the other way.

To solve this problem, some muscles are arranged in twos, called an **antagonistic pair**. When one muscle contracts and pulls (agonist), the other relaxes (antagonist) to allow the joint to work. Examples include:

- the biceps and triceps muscles in the upper arm – these work together to bend (flex) and straighten (extend) the elbow joint. This is what happens during a press-up, biceps curl or triceps dip
- the quadriceps and hamstrings in the leg – when the quadriceps contract, the hamstrings relax and the leg straightens. This is what happens during a leg press or a squat
- the gastrocnemius and tibialis anterior in the leg – the first acts to plantar-flex the ankle, while the second acts to dorsi-flex it. This is what happens during hurdling, or when you do a reverse calf raise.

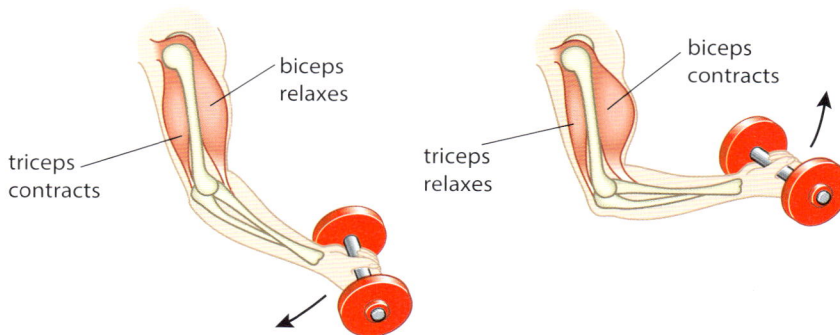

Figure 1.11 Two antagonistic pairs of muscles: the biceps and triceps

Key term

Antagonistic pair: muscles that work together to create movement.

Practice

The programme you plan and follow (PEP) will depend upon personal circumstances. For example, if you choose circuit training as one of your methods of training then you need to consider your age, current level of fitness, what you want to achieve, your activity and the time you have available to train. It is important to know which muscle groups you are going to work on so you know which exercises to use. For most people a core programme working on the upper body, abdominal muscles and lower body would be suitable.

Exam-style question

1 Give an example of an antagonistic pair of muscles. **(1 mark)**
2 For the pair you have chosen, explain how they function together to perform a specific action. **(3 marks)**

Apply it

Draw a table with eight columns. In the left-hand column, list each of the 12 muscles in Figure 1.9. Label the other columns with the words below. Add ticks to the columns to show the movements that can be created by each muscle. For example, biceps = flexion.

- flexion
- extension
- adduction
- abduction
- rotation
- plantar-flexion
- dorsi-flexion

Exam tip

You can learn and apply a lot of this knowledge while you are performing your Personal Exercise Programme. Make sure you write this sort of detail into your PEP so that you can revise it later and be able to apply it in exam questions.

Fitness and Body Systems

Key terms

Muscle fibres: make up voluntary (skeletal) muscle; divided into type I, type IIa and type IIx.

Type I: slow twitch muscle fibres; suited to low intensity work, e.g. marathon running, as they can be used for a long period without fatiguing.

Type IIa: fast twitch muscle fibres used in anaerobic work; can be improved through endurance training to increase their resistance to fatigue.

Type IIx: fast twitch muscle fibres used in anaerobic work and can generate much greater force than other fibre types, but fatigue quickly.

Myoglobin: a red pigment that transports oxygen to the muscles.

Apply it

Think of two sportspeople who participate in very different sports, for example, Usain Bolt and Mo Farah. Consider the sort of activities they do. Which would you associate fast twitch fibres with and which would you associate slow twitch fibres with?

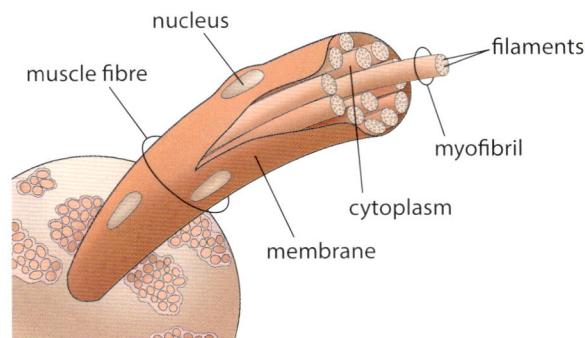

Fast and slow twitch muscle fibres

Voluntary muscle is made up of bundles of individual fibres. Each fibre contains many myofibrils, which are strands that can grab on to each other and pull to make the muscle contract.

Muscle fibres can be of two main types:

- slow twitch (**type I**)
- fast twitch (type II).

Fast twitch fibres can be broken down into two further types: **type IIa** and **type IIx**.

We all have both types of fibre in our muscles but in different quantities, probably determined by our genes – and this may affect what sports we are naturally good at.

Athletes with more slow twitch fibres tend to do better in endurance activities, such as long distance running or cycling. Slow twitch fibres (type I) are darker in colour because they contain a lot of **myoglobin**, and they have a good oxygen supply, which is necessary to supply energy to the working muscles. These muscles contract slowly, but they can work for long periods under great stress.

Athletes with more fast twitch fibres tend to do better in speed events, such as sprinting or jumping. Fast twitch fibres (types IIa and IIx) are lighter in colour because they don't use oxygen to make energy. They work much more quickly, but they also tire much more quickly.

Most of your muscles are made up of a mixture of both slow and fast twitch muscle fibres. However, muscles that help you keep your posture, like the soleus muscle in your lower leg and the muscles in your back, have mainly slow twitch muscle fibres, while your fast-moving eye muscles have mainly fast twitch muscle fibres.

Figure 1.12 Muscle fibres are made up of myofibrils

How the skeletal and muscular systems work together

The muscular system is composed of more than 600 muscles, including the involuntary muscles of the heart and the smooth muscles of the internal organs. The skeletal muscles connect to the bones and work with connective tissue at the joints to allow for movement. The muscles connect to the nervous system, which allows movement to start through nerve signals to and from the brain.

Working together, the joints, bones and skeletal muscles of the body make up your musculo-skeletal system. Together, their main function is to create movement, but they also work to keep you stable, protect you and give you good posture.

The bones, joints and muscles also work together as levers in the body. Depending on the location of the load in relation to the joint or **fulcrum**, when you lift an object your muscles and bones can create a mechanical advantage or a mechanical disadvantage. The closer the load is to the joint and the further away it is from the muscle, the easier it is to lift the object. On the other hand, the further the load is from the fulcrum and the closer the effort is to the fulcrum, the more difficult it is to move the object.

The point where the muscles and the bones connect – the point of **articulation** – is known as a joint.

Tendons are a form of connective tissue that connects muscle to bone. Skeletal muscles that produce movement are attached to two bones that **articulate** or meet. When movement occurs at a joint, only one of the articulating bones moves. The bone that doesn't move is called the point of origin for the skeletal muscle. The bone that moves is called the point of insertion for the muscle.

> ### Key terms
>
> **Fulcrum**: the point around which the lever rotates.
>
> **Articulation**: the state of having a joint; being a joint.
>
> **Articulate**: act as a joint.

> ### Exam-style question
>
> When performing press-ups in your circuit training session, which muscle contracts when you do a press-up? **(1 mark)**

> ### Exam tip
>
> Remember not to use abbreviations such as pecs for pectorals, abs for abdominal, glutes for gluteals or quads for quadriceps when you write answers in the exam. Try to use the correct terms when you are speaking too, as this will get you used to doing it correctly and help make sure you do not slip up in the exam.

Fitness and Body Systems

1.2 The structure and functions of the cardio-respiratory system

Getting started

A strong heart, healthy blood and good lungs are important for any athlete – but why?

- Which sorts of exercise makes your heart beat faster?
- Do you know any of the components that make up your blood?
- Which are the sports where having good lung capacity is key?

Look at the sports news on a national news website. Pick three athletes and explain why having a healthy heart and good lungs is particularly important in their particular sport.

Learning objectives

By the end of this topic you will understand:

- the main functions and structure of the cardiovascular system and its role in physical activity
- the structure of arteries, capillaries and veins
- how blood flows and is distributed
- the function and importance of red and white blood cells, platelets and plasma
- the composition of air, and how vital capacity and tidal volume impact on sporting activity
- the location and role of parts of the respiratory system
- the structure of the alveoli and the process of gas exchange
- how the cardiovascular and respiratory systems work together to let us take part in sport.

> **Key term**
>
> **Cardio-respiratory system:** the interaction of the heart and lungs to supply oxygen to muscles during exercise.
>
> **Cardiovascular:** to do with the heart, blood and blood vessels together.

What does the cardiovascular system do?

The **cardiovascular** system – sometimes called the circulatory system or circulation – is the system formed by your heart, blood vessels and blood. 'Cardio' means to do with the heart, and 'vascular' means to do with the blood vessels.

There are three important functions that the cardiovascular system performs.

1 It transports oxygen, carbon dioxide and nutrients

The heart pumps oxygen round the body, which releases energy stored as glucose in cells. If the muscles need to work for longer (e.g. for a long race) or harder (e.g. for a sprint) the heart works harder to increase oxygen levels. The circulatory system carries away waste products that cells produce, such as carbon dioxide, and gets nutrients, such as water and amino acids, to the places where they are needed.

2 It helps the blood clot

The blood contains platelets. If we cut ourselves, these platelets help to clot the blood, forming a scab that stops the bleeding and heals the wound. In some sports, such as rugby union, cuts are common, so this function of the cardiovascular system is crucial.

3 It controls the body's temperature

If your body gets too hot, the blood vessels close to your skin get bigger or dilate (**vasodilation**). Blood is diverted towards the surface of the skin to allow more heat to radiate out. If your body gets too cold, the blood vessels get smaller or constrict (**vasoconstriction**). Because the blood is diverted away from near the surface of the skin, less heat is lost and the body holds onto more heat.

Apply it

Investigate why temperature control is important in sport. Do some research to find out about the risks of getting too hot or too cold while doing physical activity. Make notes about the following:

- hypothermia
- hyperthermia
- dehydration
- core body temperature.

Explain the effects of, or changes to, one of the points you have researched to a partner.

The cardiovascular system and exercise

Cardiovascular fitness – the ability to exercise the entire body for long periods – is an important part of Health Related Exercise (HRE). It requires a strong heart and clear blood vessels to supply the muscles with plenty of oxygen via the blood.

Exercise makes your body work harder. As a result, your muscles require more oxygen, which means your body needs more oxygen and more nutrients, such as glycogen, to function properly. Oxygen and nutrients are carried to your muscles by the blood, so your heart has to work faster to pump blood around your body. This means that your heart rate (beats per minute) increases.

To bring about a change in your heart rate, your body releases **adrenaline**. Adrenaline is a hormone. It makes the heart beat faster and, among other things, causes glycogen to be released by the liver, and blood to be diverted away from the organs to the muscles, which need to work harder during exercise.

Stressful situations, such as taking part in an important competition, can also cause adrenaline to be released.

Apply it

List five sports that involve cardiovascular fitness: for example, in athletics running 1500 metres would involve cardiovascular activity but a long jump would not.

Key terms

Vasodilation: when veins swell up or dilate; widening of the internal diameter (lumen) of the blood vessel to allow increased blood flow.

Vasoconstriction: when veins shrink down; narrowing of the internal diameter (lumen) of the blood vessel to decrease blood flow.

Link it up

For more information on glycogen and glucose and their role in releasing energy, see Section 1.3 of this topic.

The heart

The heart is a muscular pump. It has four chambers: two **atria** that collect the blood as it comes into the heart, and two **ventricles** that pump the blood out of the heart. The atria make up the top half of the heart, with the ventricles below. **Valves** between the atria and the ventricles make sure that the blood cannot flow backwards.

Blood from the left ventricle has to go right round the body, so this ventricle is thicker. Blood from the right ventricle only has to reach the lungs, so this ventricle is thinner.

A central partition called the septum divides the heart into two halves, left and right. The right side of the heart pumps deoxygenated blood (blood not containing oxygen) to the lungs to pick up oxygen. The left side of the heart pumps the oxygenated blood from the lungs around the rest of the body.

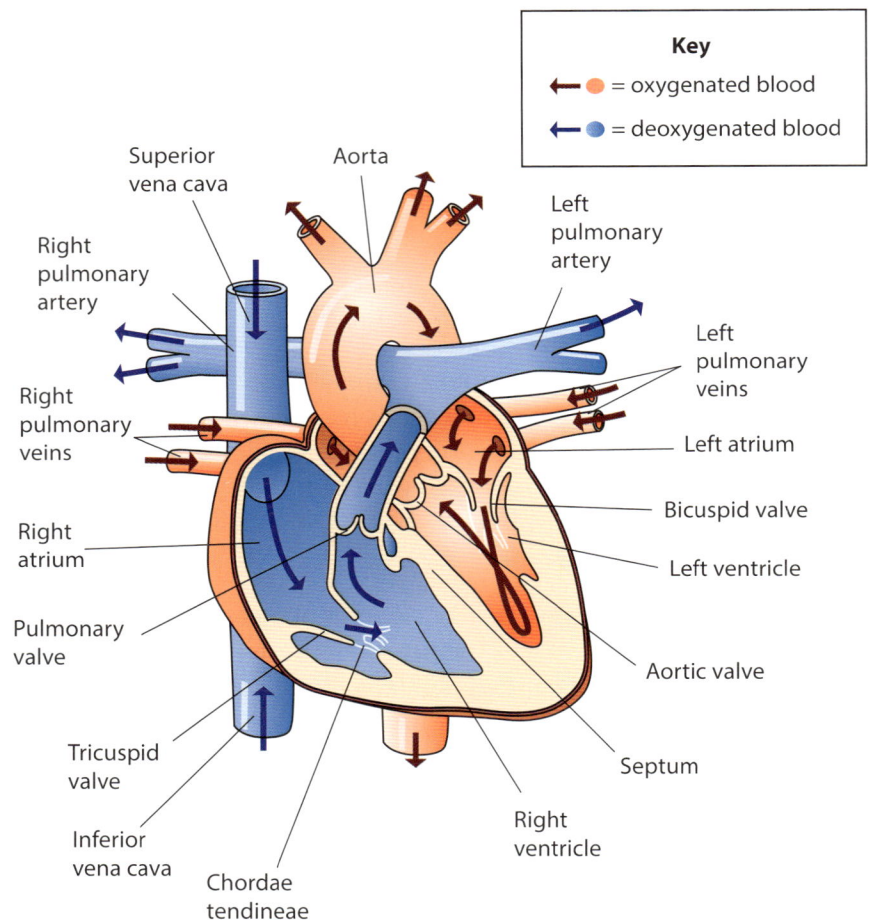

Figure 1.13 The structure of the heart

How deoxygenated blood gets oxygenated again

- The **vena cava** brings **venous** (deoxygenated) blood from the body into the right atrium, where it collects.

Key terms

Vena cava: large vein bringing deoxygenated blood into the heart.

Venous: to do with the veins.

- The venous blood passes from the right atrium to the right ventricle through a valve with three **cusps**, called the tricuspid valve.
- The blood then passes through the pulmonary (semilunar) valve into the **pulmonary** artery, and on into the lungs where it will pick up oxygen.
- Oxygenated blood from the lungs returns to the heart through the pulmonary **vein** and collects in the left atrium.
- It passes into the left ventricle through a valve with two cusps, the bicuspid valve.
- The oxygenated blood passes through the aortic (semilunar) valve and is ready to be sent round the body, through an **artery** called the aorta.

Key terms

Cusp: a triangular fold or flap of a heart valve.

Pulmonary: to do with the lungs.

Vein: tube that carries blood back to the heart.

Artery: a muscular tube that carries blood away from the heart.

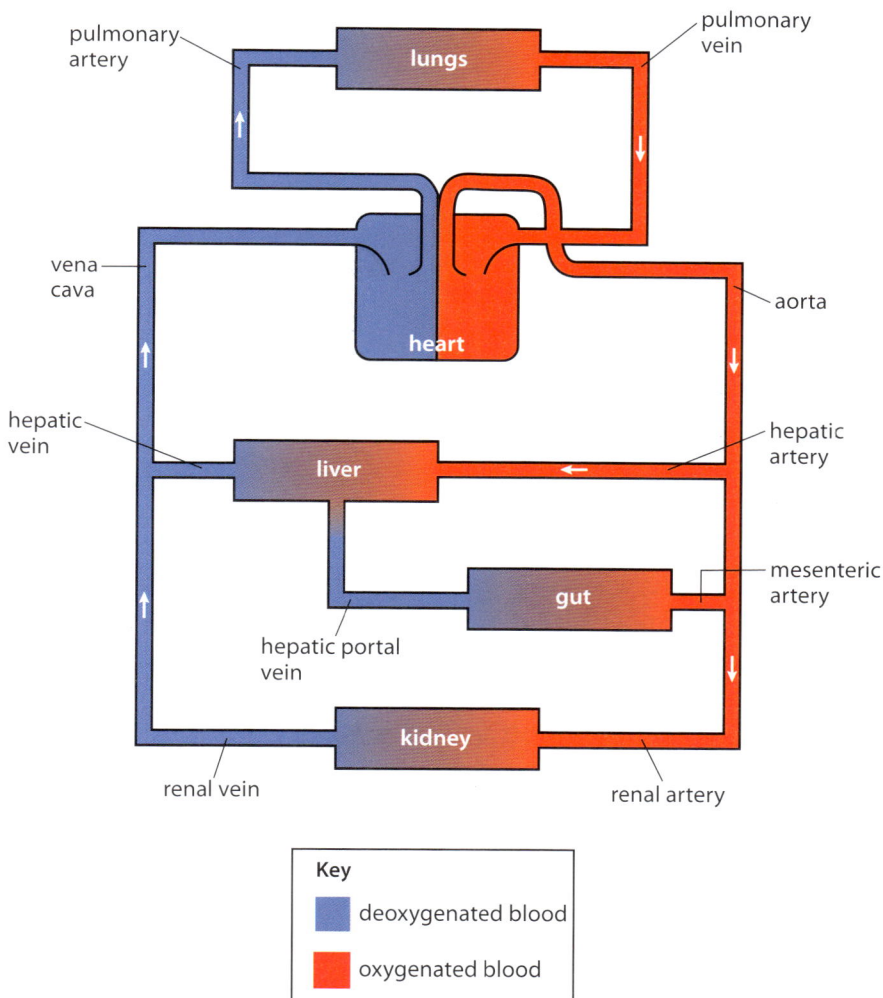

Figure 1.14 Blood vessels work to move blood around your entire body

Fitness and Body Systems

How the heart pumps the blood

You will be familiar with what a heartbeat is like, with its 'lub dub' rhythm. This rhythm is created by different phases in the heart's pumping cycle.

The first phase is when the heart contracts, called **systole**. Contractions happen in two waves (this is why we hear the lub-dub heartbeat). Firstly, blood is pumped from both atria into the ventricles; then both ventricles contract. This causes deoxygenated blood in the right ventricle to move towards the lungs via the pulmonary artery. At the same time, oxygenated blood in the left ventricle moves into the aorta, and on its way around the body.

The second phase is when the heart relaxes, called **diastole**. This is when the heart is refilling with blood. The ventricles are filling and relaxing, while the atria are just relaxing.

More oxygenated blood is required for respiration during exercise as more deoxygenated blood is generated when we are exercising and playing sport.

Blood pressure

Blood pressure is a measure of the force that your heart uses to pump the blood round your body. In sport, high blood pressure can indicate a higher risk of health problems in the future. Some experts say that blood pressure is the most important aspect of fitness that you should monitor, because it is such an important factor in participation and performance.

When you have your blood pressure read, the result has two numbers: for example, 135/95. The top number is your **systolic** blood pressure – the highest pressure, when your heart is pushing blood round your body. The bottom number is your **diastolic** blood pressure – the lowest pressure, when your heart is relaxing.

The structure of the blood vessels

There are three main types of blood vessel:

- **arteries** – which generally take blood away from the heart
- **veins** – which return blood to the heart
- **capillaries** – distribute blood within the organs

During exercise or physical activity the arteries, veins and capillaries work together to supply your muscles with the oxygen they need to work, by providing oxygenated blood and carrying away deoxygenated blood, taking it back to the heart so that it can be re-oxygenated. This process improves with cardiovascular fitness.

The structure of the arteries, veins and capillaries is different.

Arteries

An artery is a blood vessel taking blood away from the heart.

Arteries have thicker walls, are more elastic and carry blood which is at a higher pressure than veins. Arteries carry arterial or oxygenated blood away from the heart, and they pulsate as the heart beats.

The channel the blood flows through, called the lumen, can widen to allow more blood through the arteries. This happens when you exercise, so that more blood can reach your working muscles more quickly.

The pulmonary artery is different from other arteries, as it carries venous (deoxygenated) blood from the heart to the lungs. Even though it is carrying venous blood, it is still classed as an artery because it is carrying blood away from the heart.

Arteries are important in sport because they carry the oxygenated blood away from the heart, sending it on its way around your body to the muscles that need oxygen to respire/contract.

Veins

A vein is a vessel carrying blood to the heart.

Veins have much thinner walls, are less elastic and carry blood at a lower pressure than arteries. Veins rarely pulsate.

Veins contain many valves, which keep venous blood flowing to the heart, and make sure that it doesn't flow backwards. There is a tendency for this to happen because venous blood is at a much lower pressure than arterial blood.

The pulmonary veins are different from other veins, as they carry arterial (oxygenated) blood from the lungs back to the heart. Even though they carry arterial blood, they are still classed as veins because they are entering the heart.

Veins are important in sport because they bring the deoxygenated blood back to the heart for it to be re-oxygenated, ready for use in the process of releasing energy.

Capillaries

Capillaries are microscopic vessels – just one cell thick – that link arteries with veins. The blood pressure in capillaries is very low.

At one end, capillaries carry arterial blood, which transfers oxygen and nutrients to the muscles. At the other end, they carry venous blood into the veins, picking up waste products and taking them round the body to be disposed of. For example, veins carry carbon dioxide back to the alveoli, to be released into the lungs and breathed out.

Capillaries are where gas exchange takes place. Oxygen goes through the capillary wall and into the tissues, while carbon dioxide passes from the tissues into the blood.

Exam tip

Arteries carry blood away from the heart. You can remember this as A for arteries = A for away.

Apply it

Make two lists headed 'arteries' and 'veins'. List the differences and similarities between the two. For example, arteries carry blood at higher pressure than veins. Compare your answers with a partner.

Fitness and Body Systems

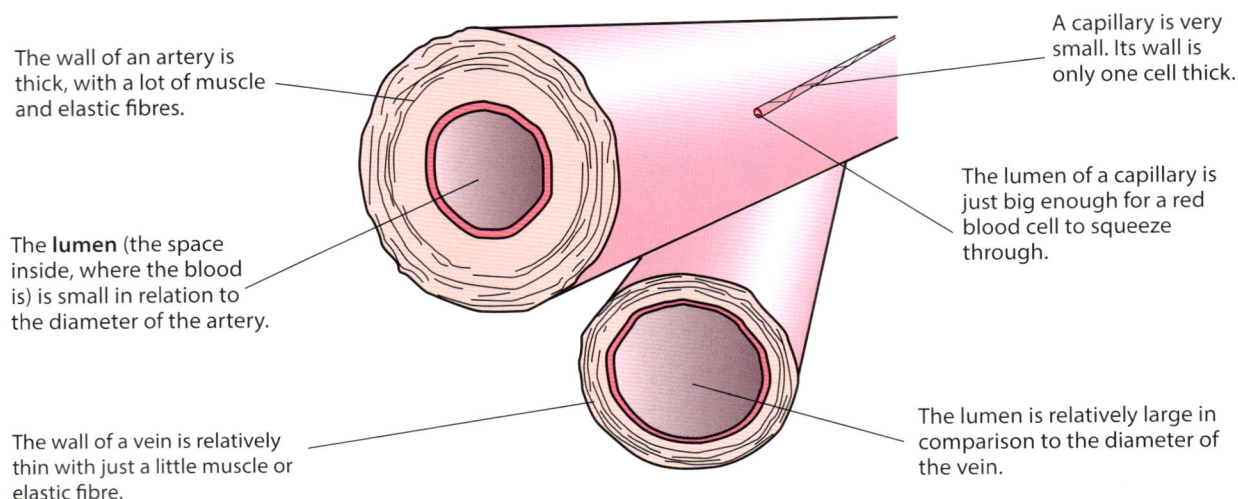

The wall of an artery is thick, with a lot of muscle and elastic fibres.

The **lumen** (the space inside, where the blood is) is small in relation to the diameter of the artery.

The wall of a vein is relatively thin with just a little muscle or elastic fibre.

A capillary is very small. Its wall is only one cell thick.

The lumen of a capillary is just big enough for a red blood cell to squeeze through.

The lumen is relatively large in comparison to the diameter of the vein.

Figure 1.15 Cross-sections through an artery, a vein and a capillary show the difference in size and structure of the vessels

Capillaries are important in sport because they are the points where oxygenated blood is delivered to the muscles, and where deoxygenated blood is taken away from the muscles.

Exam-style question

Explain the importance of the capillaries in the cardiovascular system.
(3 marks)

Exam tip

Remember that capillaries come in between arteries and veins, and that they carry both types of blood – oxygenated and deoxygenated.

Key term

Vascular shunting: process that increases blood flow to active areas during exercise by diverting blood away from inactive areas; achieved by vasodilation and vasoconstriction.

Apply it

Smoking can create many serious health problems for people because of its impact on the arteries. Research the reasons why it is so harmful, and write notes to help you explain your findings to a partner.

Blood distribution

When you exercise, the distribution of blood in your body changes. Your muscles need a lot more blood for movement, so your body works to get more blood to your muscles. This process is called **vascular shunting**.

When you start to exercise or play a physical game, your heart starts to beat faster and your blood vessels get narrower (constrict). Blood is sent to the working muscles to help them work harder and more efficiently, so your blood pressure rises. Your reflexes get faster and your muscles may tense up, allowing the blood to reach your muscles and the waste products to be taken away more efficiently.

As your muscles work harder, the oxygen levels drop, causing a build-up of lactic acid and carbon dioxide. This makes your blood vessels widen (dilate), to make it easier to get the oxygen to the muscles, and causes the blood pressure to drop. Exercise can make your temperature rise, and this makes the blood vessels in the skin dilate so that the blood can flow more easily to get rid of the heat.

Regular exercise helps this process work better and more efficiently. When you warm up, you are setting this process into action before your event or game. When you cool down, you are gradually returning your body to its pre-exercise levels.

Red blood cells, platelets and plasma

It is easy to think of blood as a simple red liquid. However, when you look at it through a microscope, blood looks quite different – millions of cells floating in a yellowish liquid.

In fact, blood is made up of four distinct components: red blood cells, white blood cells, platelets and plasma. Each component plays an important role in physical activity and sport.

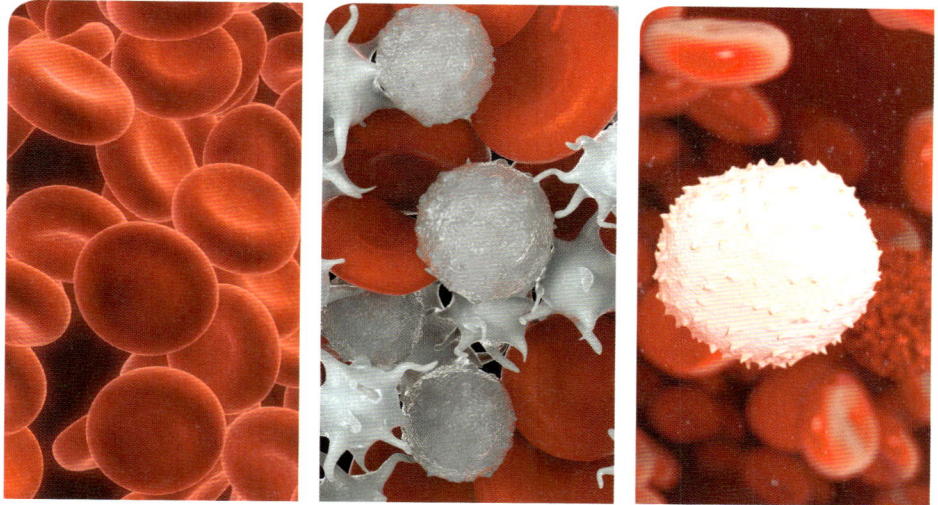

From left to right, a red blood cell, a platelet and a white blood cell

Red blood cells

Most of the cells in your blood are discs called red blood cells or **erythrocytes**. The pigment that gives the cells their colour is **haemoglobin**, and this is the part of blood that attracts oxygen, picking it up in the lungs and delivering it to the tissues.

When it comes to health and fitness, red blood cells play a key role. Having the right concentration of red blood cells (cell or blood count) can make the difference between health and illness, or between success and failure.

High cell count

One cubic millimetre of healthy blood contains an average of five million red blood cells – but this may vary considerably. People born at high altitude (for example, in the Kenyan highlands) have a higher cell count because there is less oxygen in the air, so their blood has to be super-efficient at picking up oxygen. Athletes from these countries often do exceptionally well in long-distance races, such as 5000m, 10000m and the marathon. Other athletes may go to train in these countries to improve their red cell count and therefore performance in distance races.

Low cell count

A low red blood cell count – known as **anaemia** – causes you to be breathless and lacking in energy. This condition has many causes. For example, if you lose a lot of blood you can become anaemic. A lack of iron can cause anaemia too, because the body needs iron to create red blood cells. Taking iron supplements or eating iron-rich foods, such as liver or spinach, can help.

White blood cells

The blood also contains transparent cells called white blood cells or **leukocytes**. These have an important function as the defence system of the body, because they destroy **pathogens**, which can cause illness. Some white blood cells completely engulf bacteria or viruses and digest them, while others destroy the pathogens with chemicals called **antibodies**.

Key terms

Erythrocyte: red blood cell.

Haemoglobin: a red protein in the blood that transports oxygen.

Anaemia: a condition where there is a lack of red cells or haemoglobin in the blood.

Leukocyte: white blood cell.

Pathogen: an agent that causes disease, such as a virus.

Antibody: chemical that destroys a pathogen.

Fitness and Body Systems

Apply it

Research the term a 'rainbow of foods'. Explain to a partner why a varied and balanced diet is important. What other ways can you improve your **immune system**? Do some research and discuss your findings with a partner or small group.

Blood platelets

Blood platelets are formed in the red bone marrow. They are concerned with the production of a substance called **thrombokinase**, which is essential for the clotting of blood. A decreased number of platelets in the blood can be an extremely serious condition, for example when undergoing an operation.

In fact, blood is the first line of defence for the repair of an open wound. This is brought about by a series of chemical reactions. When a blood vessel is cut, platelets rush to the site of the injury and swell into odd irregular shapes. They become sticky and block the cut, acting as a plug. If the platelets cannot cope with a large cut, a signal is sent out for the blood to start clotting by releasing a hormone called **serotonin**. Serotonin causes the blood vessels to contract and this reduces the flow of blood. As well as stopping the bleeding, clotting also helps to build new tissue. When giving first aid we can assist the repair process by pushing together the edges of the wound and compressing firmly with a sterile pad.

Plasma

Blood **plasma** is a pale, straw-coloured liquid made up of 90 per cent water. It contains a range of substances including sodium chloride (common salt), calcium, sugar (glucose), antibodies, urea and other waste products. Plasma also contains substances called plasma proteins, which are important for maintaining circulation between the cells and the tissues.

Plasma is important in sport because, without circulation between the cells and the tissues, oxygen transportation cannot happen – and that means muscles cannot get the energy they need to work. Also, carbon dioxide mostly dissolves in plasma when it is being removed into the blood.

Exam tip

Remember that 'explain' questions are asking you to give reasons why something happens. So to answer the first part of this question, don't just say what the problems are; explain why they happen. In the second part of the question, all you need to do is state a type of athletic event.

Exam-style question

1 Explain what problems may face athletes not used to competing or training at high altitude. **(3 marks)**

2 What type of athletic event might cause this problem? **(1 mark)**

The respiratory system

Every tissue within the body needs oxygen to function. The respiratory system is the system of organs and vessels that gets oxygenated blood to the body tissues and removes waste gases. It has two main jobs:

- to get oxygen into the body
- to remove carbon dioxide from the body.

In any sort of sport or physical activity, the respiratory and cardiovascular systems must work closely together to keep the body supplied with the oxygen it needs, and to keep it functioning efficiently.

Inhaled and exhaled air

The air you breathe in is 20 per cent oxygen and 0.4 per cent carbon dioxide. The air you breathe out is 16 per cent oxygen and 4 per cent carbon dioxide. How does this happen?

When you are resting, you breathe about 21 times per minute, taking in around half a litre of air with each breath. When you exercise, you breathe more often and take in more air with each breath – because you need more oxygen to give your muscles energy. When you take part in vigorous exercise, you breathe even more deeply or pant.

Being able to breathe more deeply can improve your performance in certain sports. Taking regular exercise enables you to take in more air with each breath, and thus improve the supply of oxygen to your muscles.

Vital capacity and tidal volume

Vital capacity and tidal volume are two measures that feature in sports training and evaluation. Sports coaches and physiotherapists can use them to estimate the efficiency of a sportsperson's respiratory system.

- **Vital capacity** is the greatest amount of air that can be made to pass into and out of the lungs by the most forceful **inspiration** and **expiration**. Normally this is about four to five litres.
- **Tidal volume** is the amount of air inspired and expired with each normal breath at rest or during exercise.

When you exercise, your tidal volume increases because the amount of oxygen you need goes up. Your lungs have to work harder to meet your body's demand for oxygen, so that your cells can produce the extra energy they need. During exercise, your body produces more carbon dioxide too. Increasing tidal volume is one way for your lungs to exhale this extra carbon dioxide more rapidly.

Interestingly, studies show that exercise makes little difference to your vital capacity. The maximum amount of air you can take in and breathe stays around the same. What changes is your ability to take oxygen in and get it to where it is needed.

Practice

Devise a way to measure your breathing rate and then measure your breathing rate when resting. Then perform a short, fast exercise and record your breathing rate again. Compare the two scores with a partner. How have the rates changed?

Key terms

Inspiration: breathing in.
Expiration: breathing out.

Fitness and Body Systems

Main components of the respiratory system

The lungs are the main organ involved in **respiration**, but other organs and parts of the body are involved.

When breathing in (inhaling), the intercostal muscles (the muscles between the ribs) contract and lift the chest upwards and outwards while the **diaphragm** tightens and lowers. The diaphragm changes from a dome shape to a flatter shape when we breathe in, and relaxes when we breathe out, moving upwards back to a dome shape. These actions open the lungs and create a vacuum inside so that air (with oxygen) can rush in through the nose and mouth, where it is warmed, moistened and filtered.

The air passes through the **trachea** into one of two branches called the **bronchi**, through which air passes into either lung. Smaller branches called **bronchioles** extend out from the bronchi and at the very ends of these they form millions of tiny sacs called **alveoli**. In the alveoli, oxygen passes into the blood so it can be transported around the body.

Structure of alveoli

The alveoli are surrounded by capillaries (very narrow tubes) that carry blood. **Haemoglobin** inside red blood cells binds to oxygen, which diffuses into the blood so it can be transported around the body to be deposited in the living cells.

A series of chemical reactions (called cellular respiration) then takes place, which combines glucose (from the food you eat) with the oxygen to release energy, along with carbon dioxide and water. The energy released is used to help us move, grow and to keep warm.

While oxygen is taken in, carbon dioxide is given out, or exchanged, into the alveoli and is then breathed out.

This whole process is known as **gaseous exchange**. To make this process as efficient as possible, the alveoli have a very large surface area. If all the alveoli in one person's body were flattened out, they would cover over 55 square metres – about half the floor space of the average family house in the UK! It is the alveoli that give your lungs their spongy texture.

The linings of the alveoli are very thin and only work well when they are moist and clean. A healthy person has an efficient mechanism for ensuring this. When you breathe air in through your nose it is:

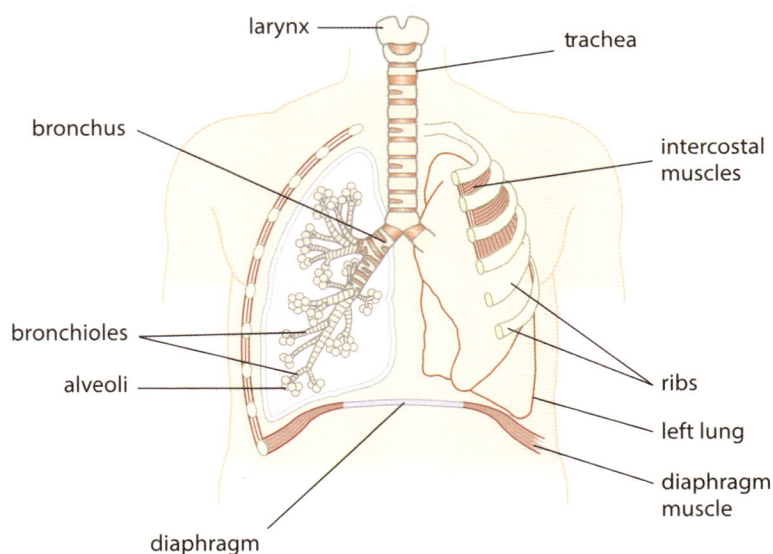

Figure 1.16 Can you describe the functions of each part of the respiratory system?

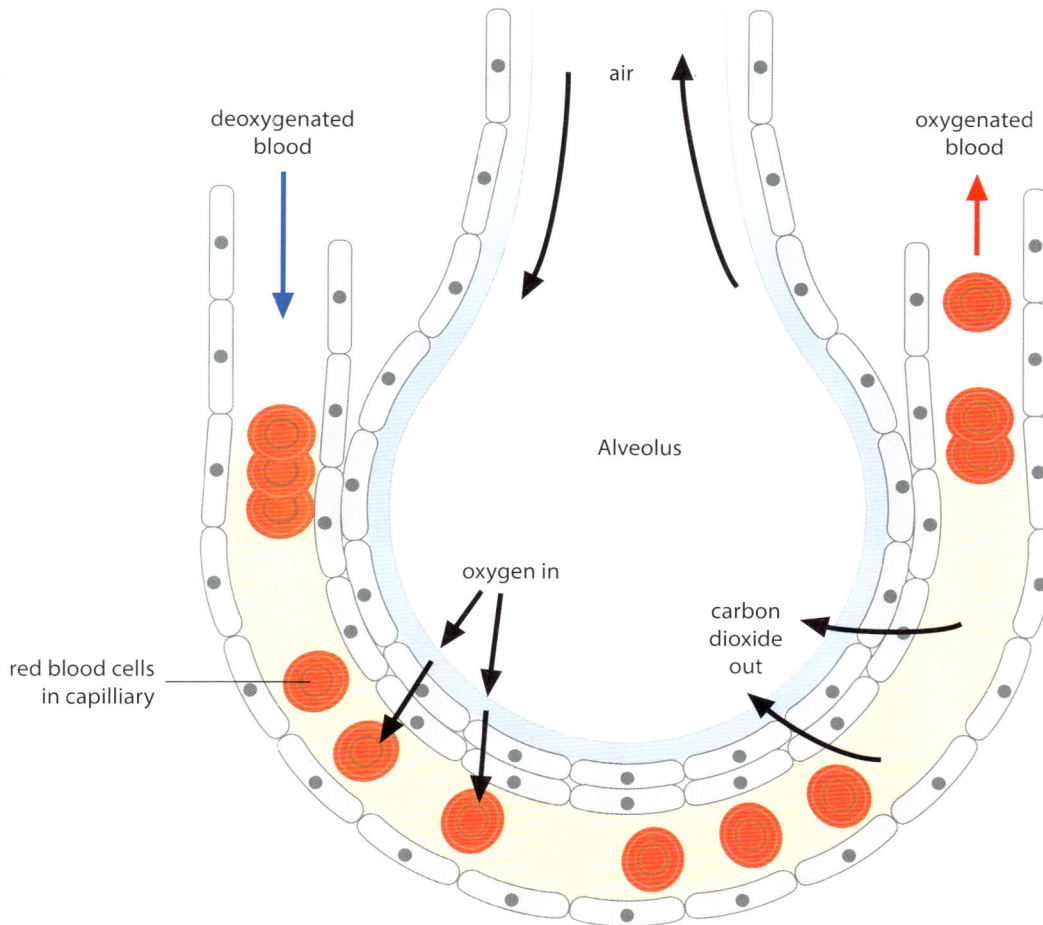

Figure 1.17 Gas exchange in an alveolus

- filtered by the hairs at the entrance to your nose and by your mucus, which is sticky
- warmed by blood vessels passing close to the linings of your nose
- moistened by water vapour.

How the cardiovascular and respiratory systems work together

It is very important to remember that an efficient respiratory system aids the cardiovascular system by providing a constant supply of oxygen for the muscles and by removing carbon dioxide. This is why efficient cardiovascular and respiratory systems (cardio-respiratory systems) are so important to everyone, not just elite sports stars, and are vital to both health and performance in sport and physical activity.

During exercise, the body needs to take in a sufficient supply of oxygen and eliminate the carbon dioxide produced by the muscles while they are working. Oxygen is breathed in and carbon dioxide breathed out in a process known as gaseous exchange.

Fitness and Body Systems

After intense exercise, athletes often gasp for air

An efficient respiratory system allows more oxygen to reach the blood and consequently the muscles. This is important because the harder and longer (intensity and time) the physical activity, the more oxygen is needed to keep the muscles working and the more carbon dioxide is produced.

Oxygen debt

The amount of oxygen needed at the end of a physical activity to break down any lactic acid is known as **oxygen debt**.

Oxygen used during **anaerobic exercise** often results in oxygen debt. This is the amount of oxygen needed to oxidise lactic acid to carbon dioxide and water. Oxygen debt is repaid through deep, gasping breaths at the end of the activity. These enable as much oxygen as possible to be taken into the respiratory system, while eliminating as much as possible of the waste produced, mainly in the form of carbon dioxide.

This may occur, for example, at the end of a race such as the 400m, which the best runners complete in around 45 seconds and are very out of breath at the end.

Exam tip

Generally these are questions where you either know or do not know the answer. You cannot work them out. You have to learn the correct terms. It will help you if you test yourself on all the key terms in this topic and make sure you understand them.

Exam-style question

Give the term for each action described in the following statements.

1 The amount of air breathed in or out of the lungs in one breath. **(1 mark)**

2 The maximum amount of air that can be forcibly exhaled after breathing in as much as possible. **(1 mark)**

3 The amount of oxygen consumed during recovery, greater than that which would usually have been consumed in the same time at rest. **(1 mark)**

Your body at rest and at work

Your body needs less oxygen when you are at rest because your muscles are not working so hard. An average person breathes about 21 times a minute during rest. You take in more air with each breath during exercise, as you need more oxygen to give your muscles energy. Vigorous exercise may result in you breathing more deeply or panting, but your breathing should still sound smooth, without any wheezing or bubbling sounds as might occur during a cold or flu.

The impact of exercise

Breathing is greatly affected by exercise. However quickly the heart beats, it cannot carry enough oxygen if not enough is reaching the lungs. The efficiency of breathing depends on how much oxygen can be removed from the air. The most important structures in oxygen uptake are the alveoli, and these can be damaged, for example, by smoking.

After a sustained period of regular exercise, the improved efficiency of the lungs will allow better delivery of oxygen to the working muscles, which means that the body will be able to cope better during exercise. Carbon dioxide will be removed more efficiently, which means that the body will be able to cope with a greater increase in the production of carbon dioxide during exercise.

More alveoli become available for gaseous exchange after regular exercise too, which means that more oxygen can be absorbed by the capillaries and more carbon dioxide taken from them. As a result, **VO_2 max** (aerobic capacity) is increased.

Regular exercise also increases the number of blood vessels. The increase in capillaries around the alveoli means more oxygen can get into the blood and to the muscles.

> **Key term**
>
> **VO_2 max**: the volume of oxygen an athlete can consume while exercising at maximum capacity.

Fitness and Body Systems

1.3 Anaerobic and aerobic exercise

Learning objectives

By the end of this section you will know about:

- how the body uses glucose and oxygen to release energy
- how fats and carbohydrates give energy for different sorts of activity.

Key terms

Glucose: a major source of energy for most cells in the body.

Aerobic respiration: the process of releasing energy from glucose, using oxygen.

Anaerobic respiration: the process of releasing energy from glucose, without oxygen.

Aerobic exercise: working at a moderate intensity allowing the body time to utilise oxygen for energy production and to work for a continuous period, e.g. long-distance events.

Link it up

For more information on respiration see Section 1.2 in this topic.

Exam tip

Know which training methods work aerobically and which work anaerobically, and take notice of this when you use them in your PEP.

Energy

Muscles need energy to work. That energy comes from food, which is mainly converted to glucose in the body. The muscles and liver store **glucose** as glycogen. This can then be converted back to glucose for use during exercise. To work most efficiently muscles also need plenty of oxygen.

Production of energy with oxygen is called **aerobic respiration**; production of energy without oxygen is called **anaerobic respiration**.

Aerobic respiration

The usual process for releasing energy for your muscles is called **aerobic** respiration. 'Aerobic' means with oxygen, and for this sort of respiration, your body's usual intake of oxygen is enough to give your muscles what they need.

The equation for aerobic respiration is:

$$\text{glucose} + \text{oxygen} \rightarrow \text{energy} + CO_2 + \text{water}$$

Glucose and oxygen are brought to the muscles in the blood, where respiration takes place and energy is released. The waste products – carbon dioxide and water – are absorbed by the blood and taken away.

Any exercise that increases your heart rate to a certain level – between 65 and 85 per cent of its maximum – is **aerobic exercise**. Examples are sports like running, swimming and cycling.

Exam-style question

Identify two training methods that can be used to improve aerobic fitness. **(2 marks)**

Anaerobic respiration

However, when your muscles have to work really hard, a different process kicks in. Your muscles need more energy, but your body cannot deliver enough oxygen to them, so anaerobic respiration begins. Anaerobic respiration is a different way to get energy, without oxygen. Glucose is still used, but now there is a waste product called lactic acid.

glucose ➜ energy + lactic acid

Anaerobic activities are usually short but intense: you work your muscles, but then have a break. Examples of anaerobic sports include sprinting, lifting weights and playing football.

Lactic acid

Lactic acid is toxic. After a while, it makes your muscles ache. Eventually it causes cramp, and the muscles stop working. You have to rest while the blood supplies oxygen to your muscles so that they can recover.

During more gentle exercise – up to 75 per cent of your maximum work rate – lactic acid builds up slowly. However, when you exercise at a higher work rate, it builds up in the muscles much faster.

Cramp oftens strikes at the end of a long, hard game of football

Key terms

Lactic acid: a colourless acid produced in muscle tissues during strenuous exercise when the body is exercising anaerobically at high intensity.

Cramp: painful, involuntary contraction of a muscle, usually caused by fatigue.

Link it up

For more information on cramp, see Section 1.4 later in this topic.

Fitness and Body Systems

Think about the different sports and physical activities you do.

- Which of these are aerobic and which are anaerobic?
- Which activities involve both types of respiration?

Write a list of your findings and discuss these with a partner.

Exam tip

The prefix 'an-' means 'without', so 'anaerobic' means without oxygen. This question is asking about the type of activity in which muscles need more energy than can be supplied with oxygen.

Key terms

Fats: a rich source of energy, but many modern diets provide more than our bodies need.

Carbohydrates: the body's main source of energy.

Build-up of lactic acid can happen because of poor training, or can simply be because of the level of effort you are putting in. For example, someone who is running a marathon or playing a football match that has gone into extra time may find they suffer from cramp because of the lactic acid in their muscles.

Exam-style question

1 Identify the waste product created by the muscles during anaerobic activity. **(1 mark)**

2 Explain the effects that this waste product can have on the body. **(2 marks)**

Energy sources

Energy comes from a range of different foods, including fats and carbohydrates. Carbohydrate is the main energy source for high-intensity exercise, while fat can provide energy for low-intensity exercise for long periods. For moderate-intensity exercise, energy will come from equal amounts of carbohydrate and fat.

Fats

Fats usually provide most of the body's energy needs. When you eat fat, it is broken down into fatty acids, which are absorbed into your blood and delivered to your cells. Any fatty acids that are not needed straight away can be stored in fat cells. Storing fat is easy for our bodies to do.

Fats are found in butter, margarine and cooking oils, as well as in foods such as bacon, cheese, fish and nuts. Your daily intake of fats should be no more than 30 per cent of your total diet.

Carbohydrates

Your body's cells use this source of energy more easily than fat. **Carbohydrates** can only be stored in small amounts – enough to last a day or two – so your body tends to use them first for energy.

When you eat carbohydrates, they are broken down into glucose or glycogen, which can be absorbed through the walls of your small intestine and into the blood. Glucose will pass into the blood, be transported to the liver (hepatic portal vein) and then circulated around the body.

Once your cells have used as much glucose as they need, some of the

However talented you are, and however hard you train, you still need a balanced, sensible diet to do your best

excess is stored in the liver, ready to be distributed if your blood glucose levels get too low. The rest can be turned into fat for longer-term storage.

There are two types of carbohydrates, complex and simple.

- **Complex carbohydrates** (for example, starch) are found in natural foods such as bananas, brown rice, wholemeal bread, wholemeal pasta, nuts and potatoes. Foods of this type help to provide energy for exercise and should form about half of your daily intake.
- **Simple carbohydrates** (such as glucose, fructose and sucrose) are found in their natural form in fruit and vegetables, and in their refined form in biscuits, cakes, chocolate and confectionery.

The energy you need to work and to exercise should come from complex carbohydrates because they provide a slower and longer lasting release of energy than simple carbohydrates, and can contribute to good long-term health.

Free sugars

Free sugars are any sugars added to food or drinks, or found naturally in honey, syrups and unsweetened fruit juices. The Government recommends that free sugars shouldn't make up more than 5 per cent of the energy you get from food and drink each day. That's a maximum of 30g of added sugar a day for adults, which is roughly seven sugar cubes.

> **Key term**
>
> **Free sugars**: extra sugar added to food and drink.

Think about how you will include energy sources and nutrition in your PEP. Consider which sports and activities you will be focusing on, what demands these will make of you, how you will train – and how all of this could link to your diet. Make a few notes, then bear them in mind as you read on through this section.

Fats, carbohydrates and physical activity

The fuel sources you need for physical activity depend on the type of activity you are doing.

- For short, high-intensity exercise – anaerobic exercise – the energy you need will come from carbohydrates.
- For longer exercise (up to two hours) of moderate intensity – a mix of aerobic and anaerobic exercise – the energy you use will come from equal amounts of carbohydrate and fat.
- For exercise of a longer duration and lower intensity – aerobic exercise – the amount of energy derived from your fat stores will increase.

Training and competing

You should have a light meal, high in carbohydrate, at least two hours before training or competing. If you have large amounts of food to digest, this will divert blood away from the muscles you need for performance.

Fitness and Body Systems

1.4 The short- and long-term effects of exercise

Getting started

Think about how exercise changes your body – in the short-term and the long-term.

- What things do you notice changing when you sprint?
- What sort of exercise makes your muscles ache the most – and when?
- Why does it take longer to recover from some sports than from others?

Learning objectives

By the end of this section you will know about:

- the short-term effects of physical activity and sport on:
  - the muscles
  - the heart
  - the respiratory system
- how the respiratory and cardiovascular systems work together so people can take part in physical activity – and recover from it
- how to interpret graphs showing heart rate, stroke volume and cardiac output values at rest and during exercise.

Link it up

For more information on the long-term effects of exercise on the body, see Topic 3, Section 3.4.

Effects on the muscles

There are a number of different ways in which your muscles can be affected by physical activity.

Muscle fatigue

When you exercise, your muscles can feel weak, painful and tired. This is **muscle fatigue**.

Muscle fatigue usually occurs as a result of anaerobic respiration. Your cells need oxygen to provide energy for your muscles. When there is plenty of oxygen available, they get energy through aerobic respiration. However, when there is not enough oxygen available, your cells respire anaerobically, and lactic acid is produced.

When lactic acid gathers – a process called **lactate accumulation** – this causes your muscles to feel painful and tired. You'll notice that muscle fatigue often comes when you have been doing the sort of exercise that makes you out of breath – so when you have to respire anaerobically.

Link it up

For more information about lactic acid and anaerobic respiration see Section 1.3 of this topic.

Key terms

Muscle fatigue: when muscles get tired.

Lactate accumulation: when lactic acid gathers in the muscles/blood due to increased work intensity, e.g. moving from aerobic to anaerobic exercise.

Cramp

As you saw in Section 1.3, sportspeople may get cramp – for example, when they have played a long, hard match. A footballer might get cramp in their calf muscle, or a tennis player may get cramp in their arm.

Cramp is a severe sort of muscle fatigue, which causes the muscle to contract in a particularly painful way. It usually hits a sportsperson when it is hot and they are tired, or when they are dehydrated because they have not taken on enough water. Good fitness levels, a proper warm up and drinking plenty of water are the obvious ways to avoid it.

Effects on the heart

Your heart plays a crucial role in your performance in sport. Exercise has many effects on it, some of which are easy to spot.

Heart rate

When you exercise, particularly when you do high-intensity exercise, your heart beats faster. Your **heart rate** is the number of times your heart beats per minute. When someone takes your pulse, they are feeling the effects of the heart beating which can be used to measure the heart rate. The pulse is caused by the impact of the blood on the arteries as the heart contracts.

Practice

Take your pulse to measure your heart rate before and after a short burst of exercise.

To take your pulse, look for the spot between the bone and the tendon on the thumb side of your wrist. You will feel a dip there. Gently place two fingers of your other hand there and feel for the pulse. Count the beats for 30 seconds, then double the result to get the number of beats per minute (**BPM**).

- What is your heart rate before exercising (resting heart rate)?
- How much does it go up by when you exercise?

How heart rate varies

A trained athlete's heart rate is likely to be lower than that of someone who is not as fit, so the heart rate can be used to indicate a person's fitness level. For example, someone like Bradley Wiggins could have a resting heart rate as low as 40 bpm, while an untrained person's resting heart rate could be nearer to 90 bpm.

Average heart rate is usually given as 72 bpm. However, heart rate can vary considerably from person to person and even within the same individual, so it is difficult to say what is normal. Resting heart rate can also be affected by factors including age, gender, size and diet.

Heart recovery rate is the time it takes for the heart to return to its resting heart rate after stopping exercise or physical activity. This is also a good indicator of fitness. The faster the person's heart rate returns to their normal heart rate, the fitter the individual.

Apply it

What should you do if you get cramp? Research ways to help prevent and stop cramp. Explain your findings to a partner.

Key terms

Heart rate: the number of times the heart beats per minute.
BPM: beats per minute.

Apply it

What other factors can affect heart rate? Write down your initial thoughts then research these factors and check your answers.

Fitness and Body Systems

Maximum heart rate

Your maximum heart rate (MHR) is the highest number of beats your heart makes when you exercise. Sportspeople use MHR to measure their fitness and to monitor their training programmes.

One formula used to calculate what your MHR should be is:

220 – age = maximum heart rate

This is the same for men and for women. So, for example, someone aged 20 would aim for a maximum heart rate of 200. However, this formula doesn't reflect differences in heart rate according to age. According to a study published in *Medicine & Science in Sports & Exercise*, a more accurate formula is:

206.9 – (0.67 × age) = maximum heart rate

Apply it

Work out your maximum heart rate using these formulae.

Use of data

Look at the formula: 220 – your age = your maximum heart rate.

You obviously know your age, but it can be easy to slip up on the easiest of sums in an exam situation.

Work out your maximum heart rate now. For example, if you are 16, 220 – your age = 204; if you are 15, 220 – your age = 205. Write your answer down, and remember it – but always write this simple part of the sum down in the exam, because you need to show your working.

When it comes to questions about training thresholds later, you will need to be able to work out 80 per cent and 60 per cent of your maximum heart rate. Why not do that now, check the answers with a friend and make a mental note?

Key term

Stroke volume: the amount of blood pumped by the heart during each beat.

Stroke volume

Stroke volume is the amount of blood pumped by the heart during each beat. At rest, stroke volume may be 75 ml per beat, but when exercising it could go up to 130 ml. How much stroke volume increases depends on the type of physical activity you are doing and your training level.

When someone trains regularly, their heart becomes more efficient. Their stroke volume increases – both at rest and when they are exercising – and their heart rate decreases. Training increases the heart muscle in size, thickness and strength, the chambers increase in volume and the heart itself gets bigger – all of which help the person perform better.

People with higher cardiovascular fitness levels have lower resting heart rates, so the heart has more time to fill with blood. This extra time for filling means that more blood gets pumped out with each beat – so they have a higher stroke volume. People with lower cardiovascular fitness levels have higher resting heart rates, so their heart has less time to fill up with blood, so their stroke volume is lower.

Cardiac output

Cardiac output is the amount of blood pumped by the heart in one minute.

The two factors that determine your cardiac output are your heart rate (the number of times your heart beats each minute) and your stroke volume (the amount of blood pumped out with each heartbeat). The formula used is:

Cardiac output = stroke volume × heart rate

When you exercise, your cardiac output rises as the intensity of your activity increases, reflecting your body's response as it works to meet your increasing physiological needs. Generally, the higher your cardiac output, the better your performance can be – and the healthier your heart is.

Your body holds roughly five to six litres of blood in total, and all this blood can pass through the heart in one minute – even when you are resting. Active people can have a cardiac output of up to 21 litres per minute and elite athletes may even go as high as 35 litres per minute.

Effects on your breathing

As you will have seen in Section 1.2, when you exercise you need to bring in more oxygen and get rid of more carbon dioxide. As you exercise, the depth and rate of your breathing increase, so that you can bring in and get rid of more air with each breath you take.

When you exercise hard, you use up more oxygen than you take in. This shortfall creates an oxygen debt. When you stop exercising, as you recover you keep breathing deeply, so that you can 'repay' this oxygen debt.

This may mean different things to different sportspeople. For example, sprinters will pay back their oxygen debt when they have finished their race. However, marathon runners will not build up such a big oxygen debt because they are not working at such intensity; they will cope with their needs by concentrating on breathing out carbon dioxide to make room for more oxygen in their lungs.

In other sports, participants may be able to take a break: for example, in tennis when the players sit down and rest for a few minutes between service games. In football, players may get a break if play stops for a foul, after a goal has been scored or during half-time.

Most of these activities are aerobic. In an anaerobic activity – the 400 metres, for example – athletes go into oxygen debt and still have a long distance still to go. However, they can prepare themselves to be able to cope with this, by doing specific training. For example, a 400-metre runner may use interval training, where they have short rests between high-intensity exercises, such as running fast.

Link it up

For more information on oxygen debt see Section 1.2 of this topic.

Link it up

For more information on the long-term effects of exercise on the body systems see Topic 3, Section 3.4.

Fitness and Body Systems

Link it up

For information on how the respiratory and cardiovascular systems work together to allow participation in – and recovery from – physical activity and sport, see Section 1.2 of this topic.

Different types of training enable sportspeople to cope with their specific sport

Interpreting graphs

Graphs are important tools in training and sport. They enable you to:

- look at a particular aspect of what is happening as an athlete exercises
- be able to make a quick visual comparison, between athletes or between sports
- look in more detail at where changes or issues occur, by analysing what is found on the graph.

You will need to produce graphs for your Personal Exercise Programme, and you will also need to be able to interpret them during the exam.

Heart rate graphs

Earlier in this section, you learned about heart rate – the number of times your heart beats per minute. You may remember that you can use resting heart rate (before exercise) and heart rate recovery time (after exercise) as indicators of someone's fitness.

Figure 1.18 shows the heart rate patterns for two athletes: one unfit and the other fit. Have a look and you will see some key differences between the two.

- The fit person has a **lower resting heart rate** to start with than the unfit person.
- The fit person's **heart rate rises more slowly** than the unfit person's – so the slope on their line is more gentle when they both start exercising.
- The fit person has a **lower maximum heart rate** than the unfit person – the highest point their line reaches on the graph.

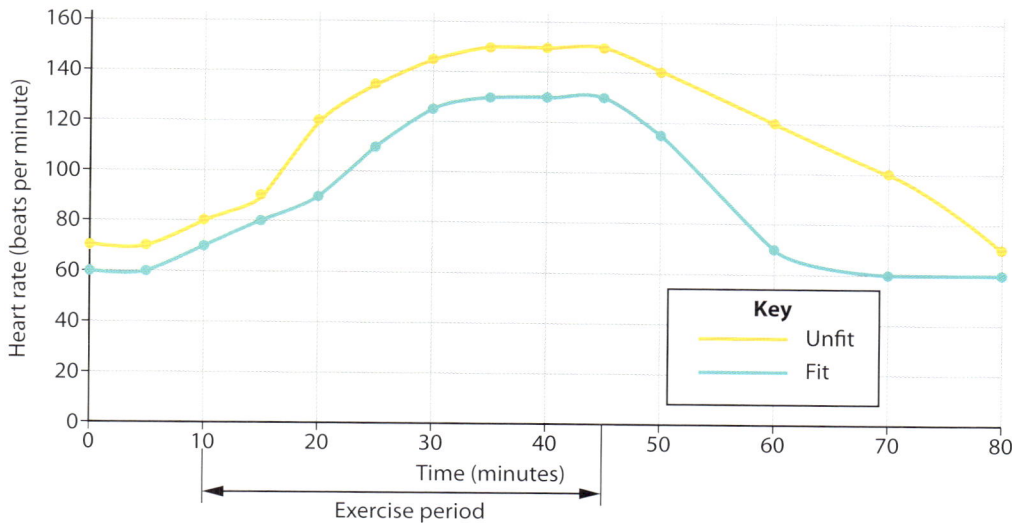

Figure 1.18 Heart rate patterns before, during and after exercise for two different athletes

- When they finish doing exercise, the fit person's **heart rate drops faster** than the unfit person's.
- As they recover from their exercise, the fit person's heart **gets back to resting heart rate faster** than the unfit person's does – so their **heart rate recovery time is shorter**.

Stroke volume graphs

Earlier in this section, you learned about stroke volume – the amount of blood pumped by the heart at each beat.

Figure 1.19 shows someone's stroke volume as they do some exercise, from a resting start, through the exercise period and while they recover.

Look at the graph below and you will notice that:

- stroke volume is relatively low when you are at rest, then increases as you exercise
- stroke volume rises during exercise but eventually reaches a plateau – a steady level
- as you recover from exercise, stroke volume gradually decreases, back to resting level.

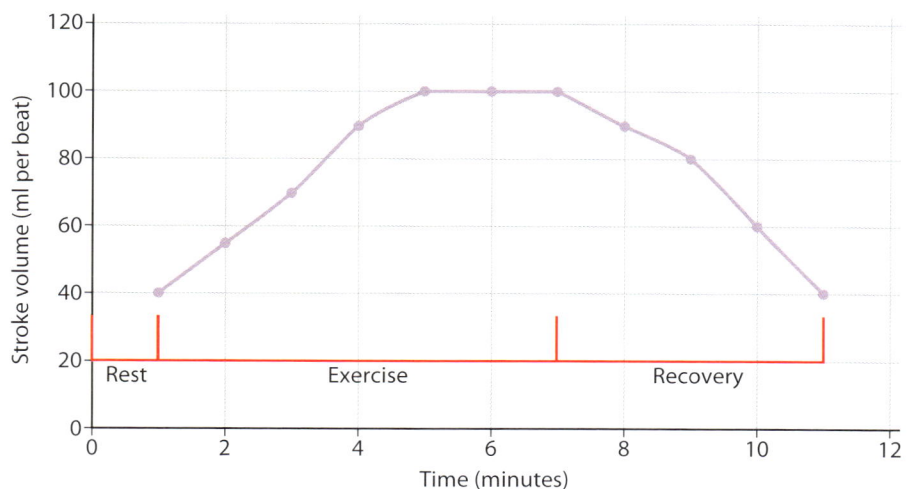

Figure 1.19 Stroke volume over time as someone goes from rest to exercise to recovery

The plateau happens because there is a limit to the amount of blood your body can pump during physical activity. Once you hit that point, your stroke volume may stay at the same level until you stop, or may tail off if you become exhausted and start to exercise more gently.

As you learned earlier in this section, stroke volume varies according to the type of activity and the person's level of fitness – and this will be reflected in the graph.

Type of activity

The bar chart below shows the different average stroke volumes for an athlete moving at different speeds: walking, jogging and running.

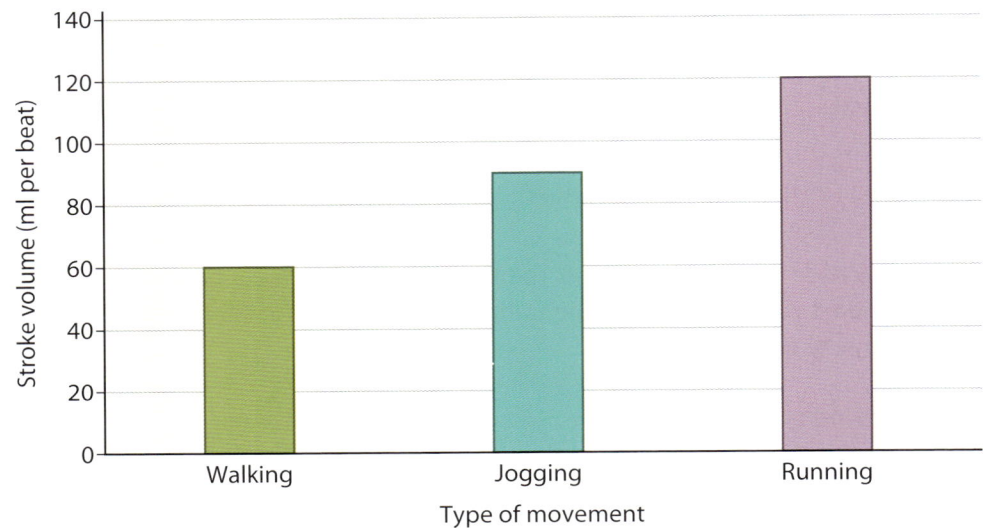

Figure 1.20 Average stroke volume for an athlete moving at different speeds

---

Exam-style question

Using Figure 1.20 explain why stroke volume varies for the athlete when they move at different speeds. **(3 marks)**

Exam tip

With graphs, read the information on the axes carefully, and make sure you use the right terms and units in your answer.

Level of fitness

A graph will also reflect the level of fitness of the person whose stroke volume is being measured.

For example, if an average person is doing a gentle activity like jogging, their stroke volume could increase from about 50 ml at rest to 120 ml at maximum intensity. However, for a trained Olympic athlete, their heart will pump more efficiently. This would mean that their stroke volume at rest would already be higher, and their maximum stroke volume during exercise would be higher too – so their stroke volume might increase from 80 ml at rest to 200 ml at maximum intensity.

Exam-style question

Look at the graph below, showing the stroke volumes during exercise for two different athletes. One of the athletes (A) is very fit; the other athlete (B) does not do much exercise.

1 Which line belongs to which athlete?
2 Explain your answer. **(4 marks)**

Exam tip

Make sure you don't lose easy marks simply by getting A and B the wrong way round.

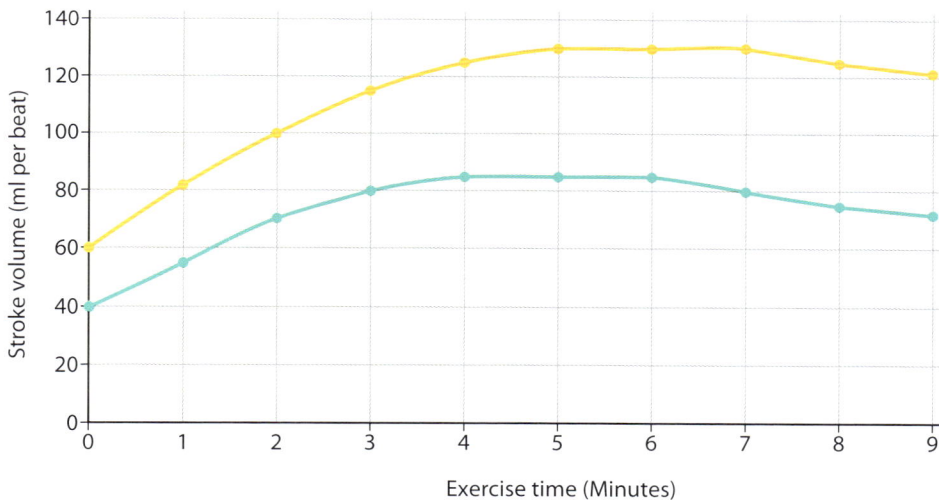

Figure 1.21 Stroke volume graphs for two different athletes

Cardiac output graphs

Earlier in this section, you learned about cardiac output – the amount of blood pumped by the heart at each beat.

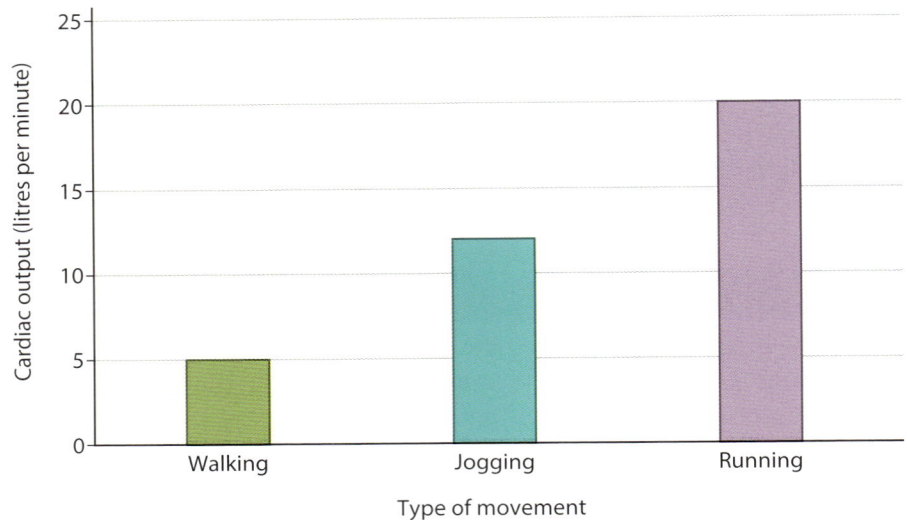

Figure 1.22 Cardiac output for an athlete moving at different speeds

Exam tip

Graphs give you data that you can keep referring to. Check, then check again to make sure you have the right answer!

Exam-style question

Using Figure 1.22, explain the changes in cardiac output when moving at different speeds: walking, jogging and running. **(3 marks)**.

Use of data

Knowing how to create a graph will help you to interpret similar graphs when you come across them.

When you have a few training sessions in front of you, make a point of checking your heart rate before you start and again at the end. Take your recovery heart rate at one-minute intervals until your heart rate gets back to your resting heart rate.

Take this information at the start of your first week of your PEP and again at the end of each week until the end of your PEP. Evaluate the graphs at the end of your PEP.

Exam-style question

1. Define the term heart rate. **(1 mark)**
2. What will happen to a person's heart rate at the start of a training session? **(1 mark)**
3. What effect will this have on their cardiac output? **(1 mark)**
4. Explain why it is important for the heart rate to alter in this way. **(2 marks)**

Exam tip

Remember that heart rate is the number of times the heart beats **per minute**, not just the number of times the heart beats.

Summary

Key points to remember:

Musculo-skeletal system
- Function
  - protecting organs
  - muscle attachment
  - joints for movement
  - blood cells and platelets
- Bone types
  - long (levers)
  - short (weight bearing)
  - flat (protection, muscle attachment)
  - irregular
- Joints
  - pivot
  - hinge
  - ball and socket
  - condyloid
- Movement at joints
  - flexion/extension
  - adduction/abduction
  - rotation, circumduction
  - plantar-/dorsi-flexion
- Muscles
  - voluntary – you can control it
  - involuntary – you can't control it
  - cardiac muscle – special muscle only in the heart
  - antagonistic pairs work together for movement
  - slow and fast twitch muscle fibres

Cardio-respiratory system
- Function
  - transports oxygen and carbon dioxide
  - clots blood
  - regulates body temperature

- Structure
  - heart: atria, ventricles, valves
  - sequence of blood circulation
  - blood vessels: arteries, veins, capillaries
- Blood
  - red blood cells to carry oxygen
  - white blood cells to fight illness
  - platelets for clotting
- Respiratory system
  - tidal volume and vital capacity
  - lungs: trachea, bronchi, bronchioles, alveoli

Aerobic and anaerobic exercise
- Aerobic
  - uses oxygen
  - usual work rate, moderate intensity
  - glucose + oxygen ➔ energy + CO_2 + water
- Anaerobic
  - does not use oxygen
  - high work rate, high intensity
  - glucose ➔ energy + lactic acid
- Energy sources
  - fat for aerobic activity
  - predominantly carbohydrate for anaerobic activity
- Short- and long-term effects
  - muscles – fatigue, cramp
  - heart – heart rate, stroke volume, cardiac output
  - breathing – oxygen debt

Topic 2 Movement analysis

2.1 Lever systems

Getting started

Think about the actions your body makes in a gym workout.

- In what ways do you think your body acts like a machine?
- Which moves do you make when you lift things?

Without reading on further, draw a picture of a lever. What have you drawn?

Learning objectives

By the end of this section you will know about:

- first, second and third class levers and how they are used in physical activity and sport
- how lever systems affect the range of movement and their impact on sporting performance.

Levers and your body

What do you think of when you hear the word 'lever'? Perhaps you think of a crowbar or a see-saw, or some part of a machine. In fact, parts of your body work as a lever too – and this mechanism is very important when it comes to sport and exercise.

In your body, the term 'lever' refers to a system of muscles and bones working together to help you – for example, to enable you to move or carry weight. When you exercise, your muscles pull on your bones, and the bones create movement, acting as levers.

How a lever works

A lever is a rigid structure, such as a bar or bone, that rotates around an **axis**. Each lever has three components:

- a **fulcrum** (or pivot) – the point around which the lever rotates
- a **load** – the force that is applied by the lever system
- an **effort** – the force that is applied by the user of the lever system.

In your body, when you want to move something:

- the fulcrum is your joint
- the load is the thing you want to move, which could be a dumbbell or barbell, or just your arm or leg
- the effort is supplied by your muscles.

Different classes of lever

Levers are classified according to the placement of the fulcrum, load and effort. This affects how the lever operates.

There are three different classes of lever: first class, second class and third class. Most exercises use third class levers, which are the most common in our body, but some use first and second class levers.

Link it up

For more information on the musculo-skeletal system, see Topic 1, Section 1.1.

Apply it

Describe the action of a lever to a partner.

Key term

Axis: an imaginary straight line around which a body or object rotates.

Fulcrum: the point around which the lever rotates.

Load: the force that is applied by the lever system.

Effort: the force that is applied by the user of the lever system.

Fitness and Body Systems

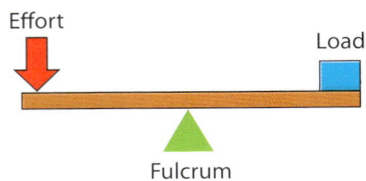

Figure 1.23 Diagram showing a first class lever

First class levers

In a first class lever, the fulcrum sits in the middle, between the load and the effort.

A good example of a first class lever is the oar on a boat. To move the boat through the water, the rower applies effort by pulling on one end of the oar, and this applies force on the water (the load).

In your body

There are not many first class levers in the body, so few exercises use them. The main examples are exercises where the elbow or the knee straightens, such as the elbow in triceps extensions and triceps dips.

In these examples, the elbow joint is the fulcrum, because it lies between the load (weight held in the hand) and the effort applied by the triceps muscle, at the back of the arm just above the elbow joint.

Work with a partner. Watch them doing a series of triceps dips and look at:

- how the elbow joint is used as they move
- what happens to the muscle as it extends and flexes.

Swap roles then describe the actions of the exercise to each other.

Preparing to complete a triceps dip

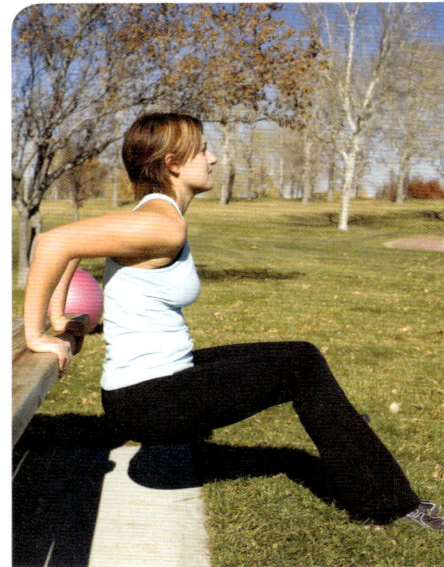

A triceps dip in action

Second class levers

In a second class lever, the load sits between the fulcrum and the effort.

A wheelbarrow is a good example of a second class lever. The wheel is the fulcrum, the handles take the effort, and the load is placed between them. The wheel helps to share the weight of the load, which means that it takes less effort to move a load in a wheelbarrow than to carry it.

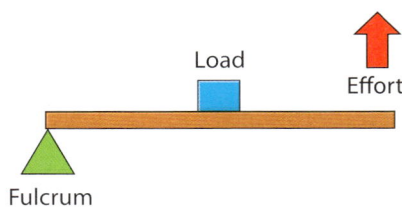

Figure 1.24 Diagram showing a second class lever

In your body

In physical education and sport, second class levers are also quite rare as they are less common in the body.

A calf raise is an example of a second class lever movement in training. The body weight (load) sits between the toes and balls of the feet (fulcrum), and the calf muscles apply the effort by pulling on the heel.

Figure 1.25 Diagram to show how a wheelbarrow is an example of a second class lever

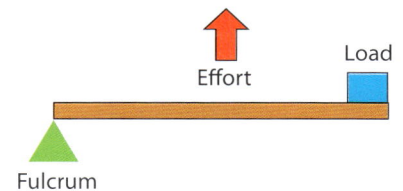

Preparing for a calf raise

A calf raise in motion

Third class levers

In a third class lever, the effort is applied between the fulcrum and the load.

A spade is a good example of a third class lever. When you use a spade, your first hand on the handle acts as the fulcrum, while your second hand applies the effort half way down the spade. Whatever the spade is picking up is the load.

In your body

Most of the levers in the body are third class levers, because the effort is applied between the fulcrum and the load. When you do a biceps curl, you are using a third class lever, as the force or effort is applied by the biceps muscle, which is between the fulcrum at the elbow joint and the weight in your hands.

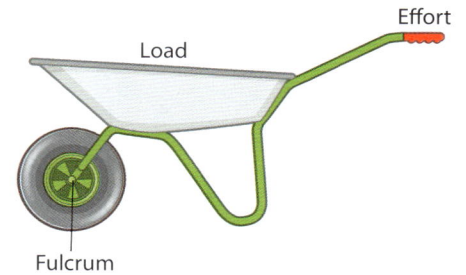

Figure 1.26 Diagram showing a third class lever

A spade is an example of a third class lever

Fitness and Body Systems

Preparing to complete a biceps curl

A biceps curl in action

Why your body has levers

Levers are the simplest type of machine. They help us do things we couldn't otherwise do – or do things more easily.

Understanding how levers work helps you to understand what is going on when you use your body's levers for sport and physical exercise.

Mechanical advantage and disadvantage

Using the proper scientific terms, a lever works at a **mechanical advantage** or **mechanical disadvantage**.

Mechanical advantage

This happens when the output of the lever is greater than the input – that is, when the load is greater than the effort, so you are getting more out than you are putting in. To calculate mechanical advantage, you simply divide the input by the output.

First class and second class levers both work at a mechanical advantage.

Mechanical disadvantage

This is the opposite of mechanical advantage. This happens when the effort and the load are both on the same side of the fulcrum, but the effort sits closer to the fulcrum than the load does. In this case, the input of the lever is greater than the output – the force you apply is greater than the load, so you are putting in more than you are getting out.

Third class levers work at a mechanical disadvantage.

How this applies to your body

As you saw earlier in this section, you do not have many first class and second class levers – the ones that provide mechanical advantage – in your body. However, there are two crucial ones.

- The head is a first class lever system. Your neck muscles provide the effort to move your head (the load) around the top of your spine (the fulcrum). With a small effort, you can move a larger load.
- When you plantar-flex your foot to raise your body up on your toes, you use the ankle as a second class lever system. The ball of your foot acts as the fulcrum. The ankle plantar-flexor muscles apply effort to the heel bone to lift your body (the load). Again, with a small effort, you can move a larger load.

Most of the levers in your body are third class levers, which means they work at a mechanical disadvantage. At first glance, this does not seem logical. Why would you have a system where you have to put in more than you get out?

However, there are two good reasons for having third class levers in your body.

- They enable you to convert small movements into larger actions. To lift something with your hand, your muscle only has to contract a few centimetres. You may be exerting more effort, but you are lifting the load a far greater distance. If your arm were designed with a mechanical advantage, your muscles would have to contract a much longer distance than you wanted to move the object. Your elbow would be dragging on the floor!
- You gain speed. With third class levers, the load travels much further than the effort. So when you use a rounders bat or a golf club, you can hit the ball harder with greater speed.

Apply it

If you want to increase the strength or weight you use for a biceps curl but cannot lift the weight over the full range of movement – from a straight arm to a fully bent arm – start with the arm bent, not straight. Then gradually straighten the arm to just below 90 degrees, and then bend it again.

If you start with the arm straight, you will be at a mechanical disadvantage. You can then gradually straighten the arm further as you get stronger until you can manage the weight over the full range, and then you can start with the arm straight.

Class of lever	Advantage	Disadvantage
First class	• Stable • Strong • Increasing the length of the lever arm increases the mechanical advantage	• Slow • Limited flexibility
Second class	• Stable • Strong • Increasing the length of the lever arm increases the mechanical advantage	• Slow • Limited flexibility
Third class	• Fast movement • Large range of motion • Increasing the length of the lever arm decreases the mechanical advantage	• The force applied must always exceed the load

Table 1.3 Advantages and disadvantages of different classes of lever

Fitness and Body Systems

2.2 Planes and axes of movements

Getting started

When you take part in sports or physical activities, your body moves in different ways depending on the type of sport or activity you are doing. Football, swimming, trampolining and gymnastics use quite different movements. For example, in football you move from side to side, in swimming your body is horizontal in the water, and in trampolining and gymnastics your body revolves as you twist and turn.

Learning objectives

By the end of this section you will know about:

- how the body uses a range of planes and axes to create movement patterns
- how planes and axes are used during sporting actions, such as somersaults, cartwheels and twist jumps on the trampoline.

Key terms

Plane: an imaginary flat surface that divides the body into sections.

Axis (pl. axes): an imaginary straight line around which something turns.

Sagittal plane: an imaginary line dividing the body vertically into left and right sides.

Frontal plane: an imaginary line dividing the body vertically from front to back.

Transverse plane: an imaginary line dividing the body horizontally from top to bottom.

To describe the direction and characteristics of movements used in different sports, we refer to **planes** and **axes** of motion.

Planes

Planes are theoretical divisions that divide the human body into sections. There are three **planes** of motion in the body.

- The **sagittal plane** divides the body from top to bottom (vertically), resulting in a left side and a right side.
- The **frontal plane** also divides the body from top to bottom (vertically), but giving front and back sections.
- The **transverse plane** divides the body across the middle (horizontally), giving a top section (also known as 'superior') and a bottom section ('inferior').

Different types of movement can be said to be 'in' a certain plane. For example, walking or squats are in the sagittal plane; a netball throw or a golf swing are in the frontal plane; and star jumps or side bends are in the transverse plane.

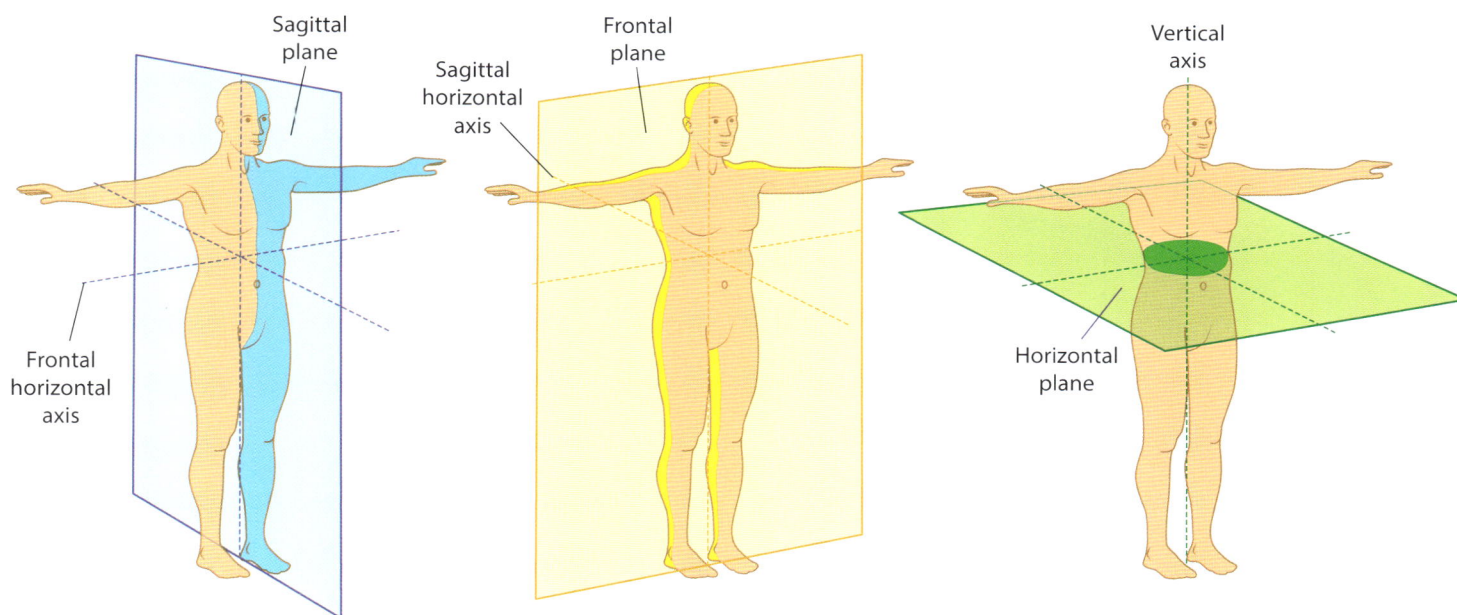

Figure 1.27 The sagittal, frontal and transverse (horizontal) planes of the human body

Axes

As well as referring to different planes when describing how the body moves, we talk about the extent and direction of rotation performed during movement. Our joints rotate around axes, and these axes allow movement to take place in one of the planes.

There are three different axes used to describe how the body can rotate.

- The **frontal axis** runs from side to side, formed by the intersection of the frontal and transverse planes.
- The **vertical axis** runs from top to bottom, formed by the intersection of the sagittal and frontal planes.
- The **sagittal axis** runs from front to back, formed by the intersection of the sagittal and transverse planes.

With axes, different types of movement are described as being 'around' a certain axis. For example, somersaults, forward or backwards, are around the frontal axis; twisting movements are around the vertical axis; and side somersaults are around the sagittal axis.

Top athletes in disciplines such as trampolining, gymnastics and diving can twist around more than one axis in a movement. For example, a barani in trampolining is a front somersault with half a twist.

Key terms

Frontal axis: imaginary line passing horizontally through the body from left to right, allows flexion and extension.

Vertical axis: imaginary line passing vertically through the body, allows rotation of the body in an upright position.

Sagittal axis: imaginary line passing horizontally through the body from front to back, allows abduction and adduction.

Apply it

Describe two axes of rotation a trampolinist rotates around when they perform a barani? Look at the photograph and discuss with a partner.

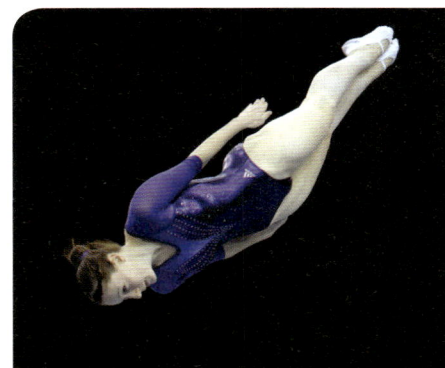

The barani, a twisting movement around more than one axis

Fitness and Body Systems

Exam-style question

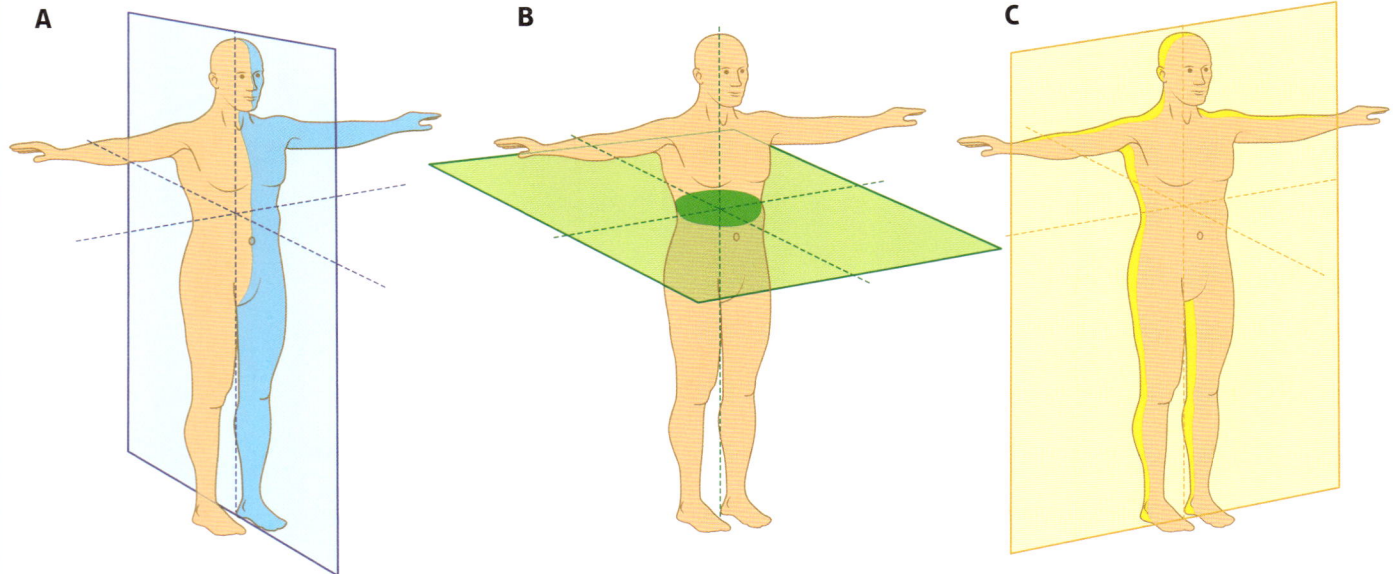

A

B

C

Which of the diagrams above shows the frontal plane and which of the diagrams shows the frontal horizontal axis? **(2 marks)**

Front and back tucked or piked somersaults

One of the first gymnastic moves most of us learn is the forward roll. This is a basic sort of somersault, and it is a movement in the sagittal plane around the frontal axis.

What are the characteristics of this type of movement?

- You move forward, with your left and right sides moving together in the same direction – in the sagittal plane, and
- Your body bends on a line that runs horizontally from side to side – around your frontal axis.

Jumped somersaults are similar. Front and back somersaults are whole-body movements in the sagittal plane, around the frontal axis.

Look at Figure 1.28. You can see the sequence of movements the performer makes as she does a tucked front somersault.

- She faces forward, with arms held upwards.
- She leans forward, lifts her seat and tucks it in tightly, holding the position with hands on her shins as she jumps.
- She releases her legs, extends them and stretching out her body.
- She raises her arms to slow down the rotation and lands.

All these movements are in the same plane, and around a single axis.

Figure 1.28 Discuss the movements of a tucked front somersault with a partner

Performing cartwheels

A cartwheel is done in the frontal plane around the sagittal axis.

What are the characteristics of this type of movement?

- You move sideways, from right to left or left to right – in the frontal plane
- Your body rotates around a line that runs from the front to the back of your body – around your sagittal axis.

Look at Figure 1.29 at the sequence of movements the performer makes as she does a cartwheel.

Figure 1.29 Describe the movements in a cartwheel to a partner

59

Fitness and Body Systems

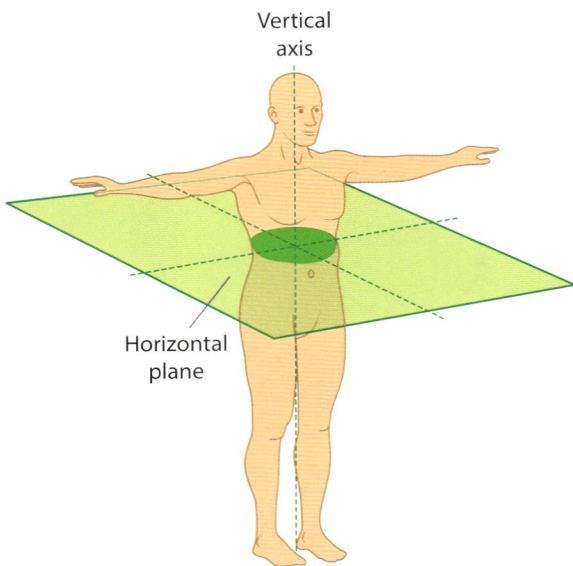

Vertical axis

Horizontal plane

Figure 1.30 Explain which axis is used in a twist jump

- She swings her chest and arms down.
- She moves into a straddled handstand.
- She puts down a landing leg, and lifts her arms and chest sideways and upwards.
- She returns to a standing position, with her hands and feet in a straight line.

Again, all these movements are essentially in the same plane, and around a single axis.

Twist jumps in trampolining

When a trampolinist does a twist, they travel in the transverse (horizontal) plane around the vertical axis.

What are the characteristics of this type of movement?

- The key movement is not up or down, or from side to side, but around one spot – in the transverse plane

- They twist around an invisible line that runs from head to toe – around the vertical axis.

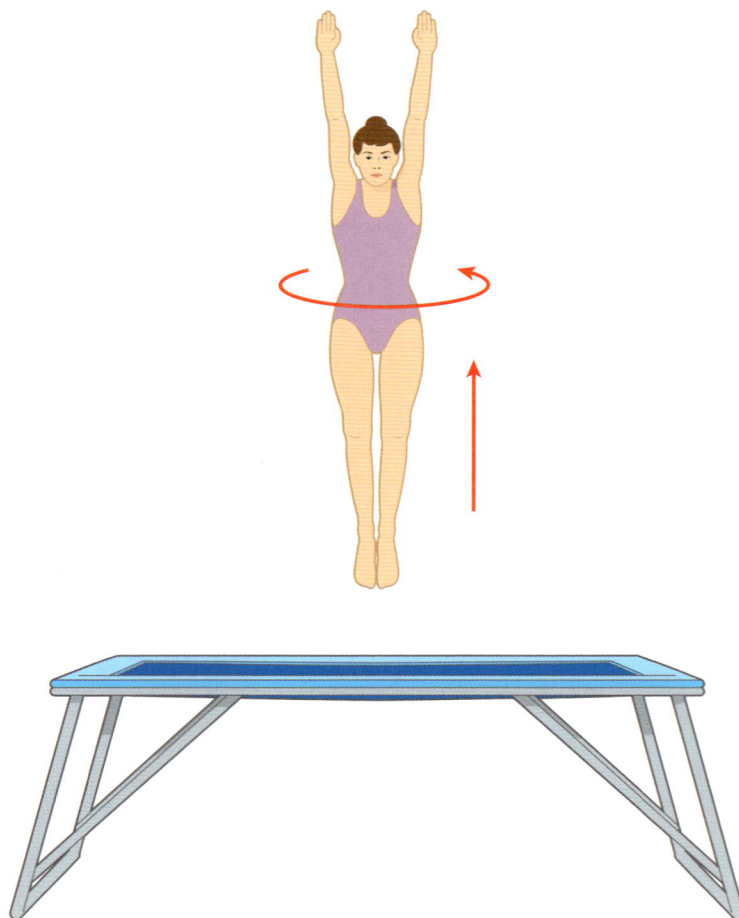

Figure 1.31 Twisting while jumping on a trampoline

In a full twist jump, the performer starts facing one end of the trampoline and spins either to the right or to the left and completes a full 360 degree spin in a straight position. They finish facing the same direction that they started in and still in a vertical position.

Practice

When you are working on your Personal Exercise Programme, know what planes you are working around when you exercise or in your warm up. Try to make sure you have at least one exercise in each plane and axis: for example, sit-ups = sagittal plane; astride jumps = frontal plane; more difficult but vertical twisting movements = vertical plane.

Exam-style question

Which axis do you turn around when you do a front somersault? **(1 mark)**

Exam tip

When you or one of your group do trampolining, discuss the rotations and twists you are doing, and the axes and planes that you are working around.

Summary

Key points to remember:

Body planes
- sagittal
  - top to bottom, left and right side
- frontal
  - top to bottom, front and back sections
- transverse (horizontal)
  - across the middle, top and bottom sections

Body axes
- frontal – runs from side to side
- sagittal – runs from front to back
- vertical – runs from top to bottom

Example movements
- somersault – in sagittal plane, around frontal axis
- cartwheel – in frontal plane, around sagittal axis
- vertical – in transverse plane, around vertical axis

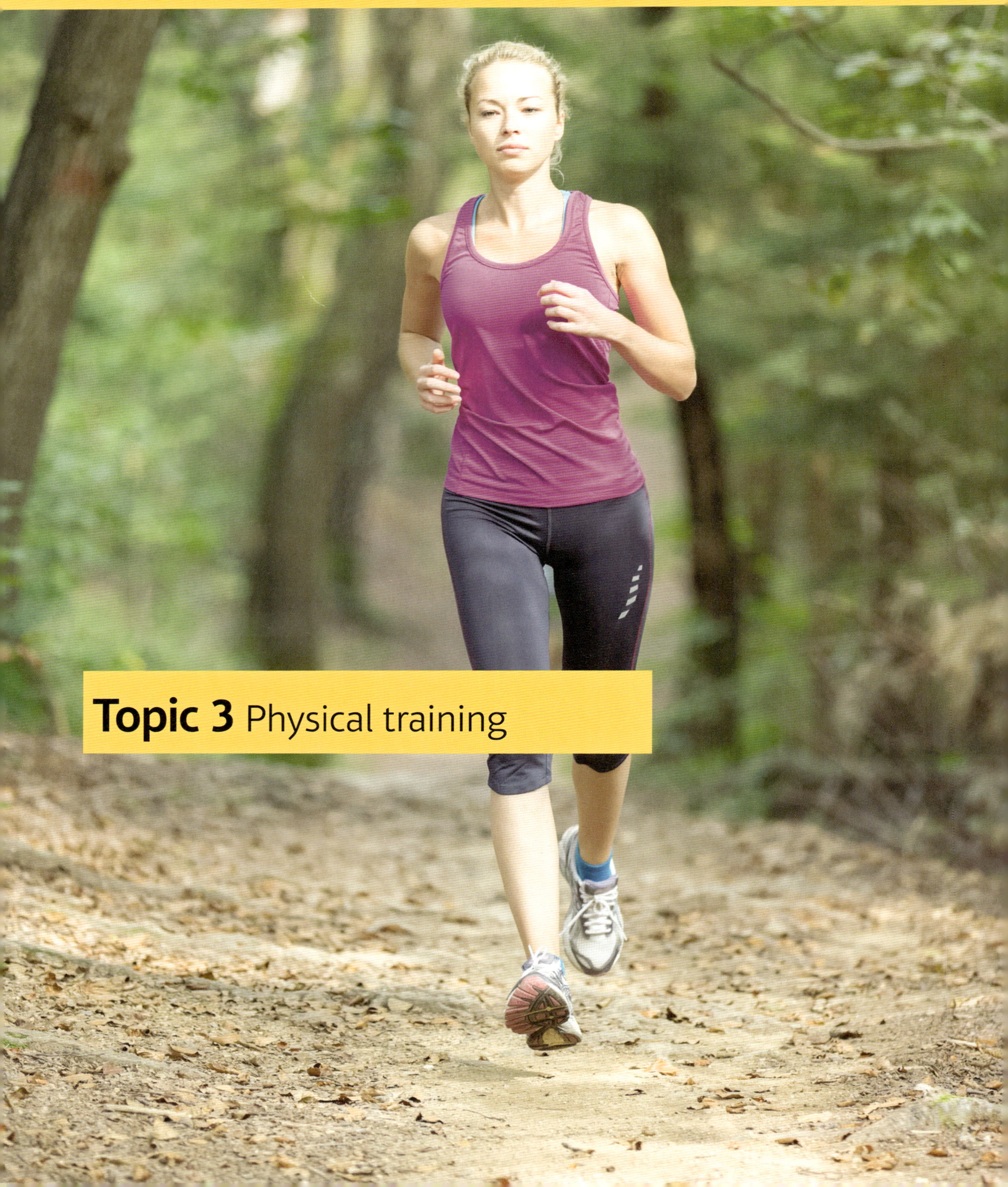

Topic 3 Physical training

3.1 The relationship between health and fitness and the role that exercise plays in both

Getting started

Health and fitness are key factors in exercise – but why?

- How do you think fitness affects sporting performance?
- Think about the types of training you have done and the sports you have played. What do you think they improve?
- Can you be fit but not healthy – or healthy but not fit?

Look at a range of health and fitness books. What differences are there between those that focus on health and those that focus on fitness?

Learning objectives

By the end of this topic you will understand:

- what the terms health, exercise, fitness and performance mean
- the relationship between health and fitness
- the role that exercise plays in keeping someone fit and healthy.

Health, exercise, fitness and performance

You will know that health and fitness are crucial if you are going to do exercise or perform a sport well – but what do these terms mean?

- **Health** is not as simple as just being well. Health is a state of complete emotional/psychological, physical and social well-being.
- **Exercise** is any activity that needs physical effort. Usually when you say 'exercise' you mean the sort of activity you do to keep yourself fit and healthy, or to improve your condition. However, activities like doing the housework or cycling to school are still forms of exercise, because they require physical effort.
- **Fitness** is the ability to meet the demands of an environment – so for a sportsperson, it means being in the right emotional/psychological and physical shape to be able to do what your sport requires of you.
- **Performance** is the action or process of doing something, but the term is also used to describe how you do something, or how well you do it.

Exercise

You can improve your health by taking part in exercise, as it builds up fitness levels, which in turn enables you to perform better.

Regular exercise also helps to keep you healthy by preventing illness. Although infectious diseases have become less widespread in the developed world, health problems caused by lack of exercise and a **sedentary** lifestyle have increased. Such conditions are called **hypokinetic diseases**, and include heart disease, high blood pressure and back pain. Hypokinetic diseases can be relieved by taking exercise.

Key terms

Health: a state of complete emotional/psychological, physical and social well-being, and not merely the absence of disease and infirmity.

Exercise: physical activity that maintains or improves health and fitness.

Fitness: ability to meet the demands of the environment.

Performance: how well a task is completed.

Sedentary: lacking in physical activity.

Hypokinetic disease: a disease caused by a lack of physical activity or sedentary lifestyle.

Fitness and Body Systems

Exercise also relieves stress and tension – for example, by distracting people from their everyday concerns. Taking part in exercise also increases fitness levels, which has a number of different benefits, detailed in Table 1.4.

Physical	Emotional/psychological	Social
• Increase cardiovascular fitness • Improve strength • Improve muscular endurance • Increase flexibility • Improve body composition • Improve performance	• Relieve or prevent stress and tension • Psychological challenge (can I do it?) • Increase self-esteem and confidence • Help the individual feel good • Appreciate an improved body shape/composition • Contribute to the enjoyment of life	• Mix with others • Make new friends • Develop teamwork/co-operation skills • Work with others

Table 1.4 The benefits of a healthy, active lifestyle

Link it up

Review Topic 1, Section 1.1 on the musculo-skeletal system and Topic 1, Section 1.2 on the cardiovascular system. As you review these sections, consider their relevance for fitness and health.

Fitness

To most people, being fit means being able to cope with the demands of everyday activities, such as school, college, work and home. People also exercise to improve their fitness. This can help them to lead an active life without too much strain on their health and, in some cases, to take part in sport and physical activity at a higher level.

Fitness also contributes to enhanced performance. For example, players who are fit can run further and faster, hold off more tackles, hit better shots and perform more advanced gymnastic positions.

Over recent years, people have become more aware of the importance of exercising and keeping fit.

Players at every level must exercise to keep themselves fit and enhance their performance

Performance

Performance is taking part in an activity to the best of your ability, whether it's Sunday afternoon football in the park or playing in the Premiership, playing tennis at school or competing at Wimbledon.

The benefits of a healthy, active lifestyle fall into three main categories: physical, emotional/psychological and social. Table 1.4 examines these benefits in detail.

The relationship between fitness and health

People often talk about being fit and healthy, as if the two always go together. However, it is possible to be fit but not healthy. Many sportsmen and women suffer debilitating injuries and illnesses, including emotional/psychological health issues.

Cricketer Jonathan Trott was physically fit to play, but decided to quit the 2013 Ashes series because of problems with anxiety. His emotional/psychological health was blocking his ability to physically perform.

Other sportspeople have long-running medical conditions that affect them physically, yet they still perform at the highest level. Footballer Lionel Messi has a growth hormone deficiency, and Barcelona paid for his treatment as part of his initial contract. Steve Redgrave was 35 when he was diagnosed with type 2 diabetes but still went on to win gold for rowing in the Sydney 2000 Olympic Games.

Sometimes, differences or variances in an athlete's genetic composition mean that they could be at a genetic advantage in some sports. Like many Jamaicans, Usain Bolt has a genetic variant called ACTN3 'sports gene', that can boost the performance of fast twitch muscle fibres – helping his muscle fibres to create greater force, speeding up his leg movements.

Exam-style question

Match the four terms **health**, **exercise, fitness** and **performance** to the correct definition listed below. **(4 marks)**

- How well a task is completed.
- The ability to meet the demands of the environment.
- A form of physical activity which maintains or improves health and/or physical fitness.
- A state of complete emotional/psychological, physical and social well-being and not merely the absence of disease and infirmity.

Exam tip

You should use these terms in your Personal Exercise Programme (PEP). Where you first use the term, put the definition in alongside it.

Fitness and Body Systems

3.2 The components of fitness, benefits for sport and how fitness is measured and improved

Getting started

There are many different ways to be fit. Consider the following questions:

- Have you ever done any fitness tests?
- What makes you fit for your favourite sport?
- What have you done to try to improve your fitness?

Imagine you are a personal trainer. What aspects of someone's fitness might you want to help them with? Make a list of these and explain how you might address each aspect.

Learning objectives

By the end of this section you will understand:

- basic components of fitness: cardiovascular fitness (aerobic endurance), muscular strength, muscular endurance, flexibility and body composition
- skill-related components of fitness: agility, balance, co-ordination, power, reaction time and speed
- the use and interpretation of different fitness tests.

The five components of fitness

There are five basic components that help you stay physically fit:

- **cardiovascular fitness** – your ability to exercise your whole body for long periods of time, sometimes called stamina or aerobic endurance
- **muscular strength** – your ability to exert force, such as when you lift a weight
- **muscular endurance** – your ability to use voluntary muscles repeatedly without getting tired
- **flexibility** – the range of motion of your joints or the ability of your joints to move freely
- **body composition** – the percentage of body weight that is muscle, fat or bone.

Cardiovascular fitness

Cardiovascular fitness is the efficiency of the cardiovascular system – the heart, lungs, blood and blood vessels – in getting oxygen to the muscles, so that the muscles can keep working for a long time. You need to have a strong heart and clear blood vessels to enable your blood to transport plenty of oxygen to your muscles. You can develop your cardiovascular fitness through training.

Cardiovascular fitness is the most important factor in being able to have a healthy, active lifestyle without getting tired. It also means you can carry on taking part in sport and being physically active throughout your life.

This is the fitness that sportspeople need to play long, hard matches in football, rugby, netball, tennis and many other sports.

Link it up

Review Topic 1, Section 1.2 to remind yourself how the cardiovascular system works and what role it plays in physical activity.

All athletes – from skiers to badminton players, from footballers to dancers – need a high level of cardiovascular fitness

Muscular strength

Muscular strength is the fitness that allows you to lift heavy weights, but it is also vital in any sport that involves the exertion of great force. You can develop your muscular strength by lifting heavy weights with few repetitions or through high-intensity muscular strength work with lighter weights.

Muscular strength is obviously important in activities such as weightlifting, where competitors have to make one massive effort. However, muscular strength is also required in games like rugby, where the two packs push against each other in the scrum, trying to drive their opponents backwards.

Muscular strength is sometimes associated with **steroid** use. Though these drugs can help an athlete develop their muscular strength and recover quickly – and so train harder– they have harmful side effects. Using unprescribed steroids is both dangerous to your health and illegal in competition. DO NOT take any drugs or medication that have not been prescribed to you by a doctor.

Muscular endurance

Muscular endurance is different from muscular strength. It enables you to exercise your muscles repeatedly without getting too tired. Muscular endurance is needed for many sports and physical activities, including distance running and swimming. Most exercise programmes you come across include some form of training to improve this area of fitness, such as press-ups or sit-ups.

Muscular endurance is often associated with games like tennis, which are played over a long period of time and where the muscles need to work hard throughout the match.

Muscular endurance is an important part of general fitness, and of everyday life. Doing the daily chores or working in the garden are examples of ordinary activities that need muscular endurance.

> **Key term**
>
> **Steroid**: a drug, which can have harmful side effects, that is sometimes used illegally by athletes to help them become stronger and more muscular.

Fitness and Body Systems

Link it up

Topic 1, Section 1.1 describes the different types of muscles in the body.

Apply it

Describe which muscles would be used in activities such as swimming or running that develop muscular endurance.

Investigate how different yoga positions can improve flexibility

Flexibility

Flexibility is an important aspect of fitness that is often overlooked. You may only think about flexibility when you can't do something, like bending over to tie your shoelaces, but in fact flexibility is important to all sorts of activity.

If you are not flexible, you have less range of movement and your joints get stiff more easily. Flexibility is obviously important in some sports where you need to perform particular skills, such as gymnastics or diving, but it is also important in other sports, like badminton, where you need to be able to stretch and move quickly. If you are flexible, you are also less likely to get injured.

Activities like yoga can help you improve your flexibility. Yoga is popular with people of all ages, many of whom do not take an active part in other sports.

Body composition

The way we are built is known as body composition – the percentage of body weight that is muscle, fat or bone.

Fat percentage is a particular issue for sportspeople. The amount of fat you carry varies from person to person, but on average a healthy level for a man is 15–18 per cent and for a woman it is 20–25 per cent. Keeping a healthy percentage of body fat is important because it can help protect you from diseases like cancer, heart disease and diabetes, and because too much fat puts added strain on your joints, muscles and bones, making you more prone to injury.

Different sports favour different body types. For example, heavy rugby players are more effective in the scrum than lightweight players, but in long distance running, lightweights will always beat heavyweights. Similarly, a rock climber's performance would be impaired with higher body-fat levels, but a heavyweight weightlifter might benefit from higher body fat because they can recover more easily.

Some aspects of body composition, such as height, are clearly genetic, but your body composition can still be improved by exercise and diet. A well-planned and effective Personal Exercise Programme (PEP) can help you enhance your body shape.

A player with this body type may not be so well suited to sprinting with the ball but would be able to put their bulk and strength to their advantage in the scrum

Body mass index

Weight is usually the first thing people think of in connection with their body composition. The most common and easiest way to get an idea of your body composition is by calculating your body mass index (BMI). Table 1.5 details degrees of obesity using BMI.

BMI is calculated by taking your weight in kilograms and dividing it by your height in metres squared (m^2). For example:

Weight = 60 kg

Height = 1.65 m

Height squared = 2.72 m^2

60/2.72 = 22

Classification	BMI (kg/m²)
Healthy weight	18.5–24.9
Overweight	25–29.9
Obesity I	30–34.9
Obesity II	35–39.9
Obesity III	40 or more

Table 1.5 Degrees of obesity in adults using BMI

Apply it

Measure your height and weight, then calculate your own BMI.

Source: Copyright © NCGC. Reproduced by permission.

Lean body mass

All our body parts add up to make the overall weight of our body. Our weight without fat is known as our lean body mass. This includes our muscles, bones and organs. If you work out your total body fat content and subtract this from your total body weight, you are left with the weight of your lean body mass.

Fitness and Body Systems

Calculate your desirable body weight and frame size.

- Measure your wrist around where you would normally wear your watch.
- Use Table 1.6 to work out your frame size.
- Use Figure 1.32 to work out your desirable body weight.

Frame	Men	Women
Small	6 inches or less	5.5 or less
Medium	6–7.25	5.6–5.9
Large	7.26 or more	6 or more

Table 1.6 Determining frame size using wrist size in inches

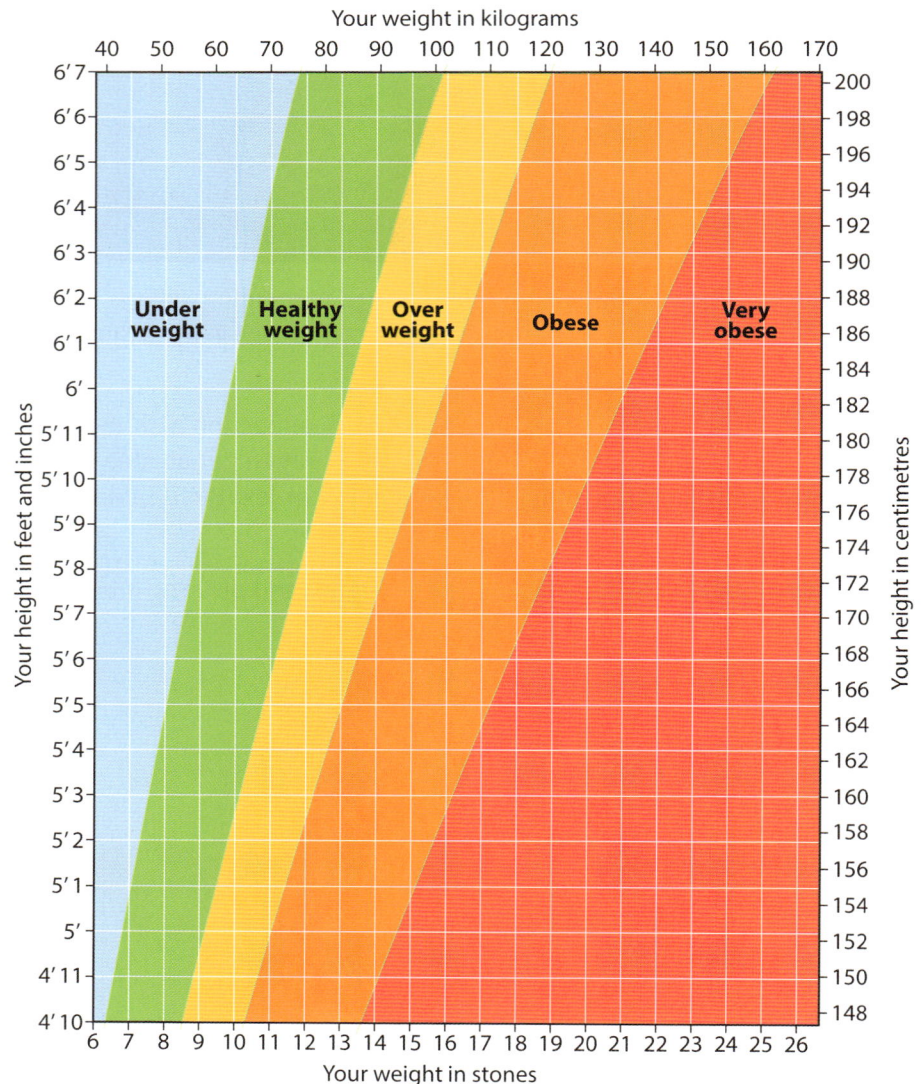

Source: NHS Choices

Figure 1.32 Height/weight chart

Choose an aspect of training in your PEP. List the relevant components of fitness (see the beginning of this section) that are being applied, in order of importance. Explain how each aspect is involved in the activity.

The elements of fitness are usually needed in combination, but not necessarily all at once or in equal amounts. Marathon runners do not need muscular strength but do need muscular endurance. Good flexibility in their lower body will help them to have a good stride length. They will also probably have slim body composition, but the main and essential feature is a high level of cardiovascular fitness to enable them to keep running (exercising) for a very long period of time and at a good pace.

As well as the five basic health-related components, there are six further fitness components that are skill-related:

- agility
- balance
- co-ordination
- power
- reaction time
- speed.

Skill-related fitness helps people to become good at physical activity. Different sports need different skills – or a different combination of skills. Being good at more technical activities and events requires more of the six skills. Fitness skills can be developed and improved with practice and training.

Agility

Agility means the ability to change position and control the body at speed. Running a 100-metre race does not require agility, but doing a floor work exercise in gymnastics does. Imagine a gymnast performing somersaults – they will need to be very agile. A rugby player running for the try line also needs agility to dodge tackling defenders.

Exam-style question

Agility means being able to change the body's position quickly and to have good control over the movement of the whole body.

Explain how balance can aid agility. **(2 marks)**

Balance

Balance means being able to keep the body stable, while at rest or when on the move.

There are two types of balance: static and dynamic.

- Static balance is keeping the body stable while stationary – for example, doing a handstand or the tree position in yoga. Archery is a good example of a sport in which static balance is needed.
- Dynamic balance is maintaining a controlled, stable position while moving. Hammer throwing and basketball are examples of sports where dynamic balance is essential.

In some sports, both types of balance are needed. For example, in gymnastics a gymnast could be holding a balance, such as a handstand, on the beam (static balance) or keeping balanced while on the move, as in a walkover (dynamic balance).

Exam tip

Make sure you remember all the components of skill-related fitness. The first three terms are easy to remember because they are the first three letters of the alphabet. To remember the others, you could make up a mnemonic such as Peter Power, Robert Reaction Time, and Sarah Speed. Then, during the exam, you could first put the six letters (ABCPRS) at the side of the question on skill-related fitness.

- **A** – Agility
- **B** – Balance
- **C** – Co-ordination
- **P** – Power
- **R** – Reaction Time
- **S** – Speed

Key terms

Agility: the ability to control the movement of the whole body and change position quickly.

Balance: being able to keep the body stable, while at rest or in motion.

Fitness and Body Systems

Practice

Pick one of your chosen practical performance activities. Give an example of static balance in that activity, and explain how you would use it. For the same, or another sport, give an example of dynamic balance and explain when you would perform it.

Key term

Co-ordination: the ability to use two or more body parts together.

Practice

Work with a partner to devise a practice in one of your practical activities to improve your co-ordination. This should be to improve your skill, not to test it.

After devising the practice, test it on another pair and let them test their practices on you. Discuss and compare the success of each practice and think and develop ways to improve them.

Apply it

Write down the names of two activities in which you participate and explain how co-ordination is used in each.

Co-ordination

Just as there are different types of balance, there are different types of **co-ordination**. Racket games require good hand-eye co-ordination in order to strike the ball or shuttle correctly. In football there are several types of co-ordination:

- hand-eye co-ordination for the goalkeeper to catch a shot on goal or catch or punch the ball when it is crossed, often under pressure from the opposition forwards, which makes it even more difficult
- foot-eye co-ordination to strike the ball to pass, shoot or control it
- head-eye co-ordination to strike the ball with the head in order to clear a corner or to aim at the target to score
- chest-eye or thigh-eye co-ordination to control the ball.

Left or right?

Most people are better co-ordinated on one side of their body than the other – they are better with their right hand than their left, or better with their right foot than their left. Generally, people who are right-handed are right-footed and *vice versa* – but not always. Some people may be naturally right-handed but left-footed. In some sports, such as cricket, they may even bat right-handed and bowl left-handed. For example, England cricketer Stuart Broad is a right-arm bowler but bats left-handed.

How do you use hand-eye co-ordination in your sport?

Power

Power is the ability to undertake strength performances quickly. It can be written as a formula:

power = strength × speed

So power increases as a result of an increase in strength or speed.

Athletes and sportspeople may use power to propel themselves or an object. For example, sprinters need power to drive their bodies out of the starting blocks when the gun fires to start the race. In athletics, discus throwers need power to throw the discus, but need to move fast across the circle. When a football player takes a long throw-in, they need power at the moment they throw the ball.

In many sports, athletes and players need to be able to jump high, either in a game or in a specific discipline such as the high jump or pole vault. Long jump and triple jump, although they are horizontal jumps, both require power at the moment of take-off.

Reaction time

Reaction time is the time between a stimulus and a movement in response to it. In sport, it is the time between the starting gun firing and the athlete beginning to run.

In most sports, the signal for a reaction is a sight stimulus: for example, a ball or shuttlecock is struck and the receiver has to react to the sight. Badminton players sometimes practise behind screens so they cannot see the shuttlecock and have to react as it comes over the screen.

You can improve your reaction times through practice. Anticipation from experience can also help reaction time.

Speed

Speed includes:

- leg speed – like sprinter Usain Bolt
- hand speed – like boxer Nicola Adams
- speed of thought – like tennis player Rafael Nadal.

If a sportsperson could choose one natural skill-related factor to have, it would probably be speed. Although a lack of speed can be overcome in some sports, it is an essential ingredient for most champions and it can sometimes make up for a lack of other skills.

You can improve your speed with practice: for example, by practising faster leg speed and arm movements when sprinting on the spot.

Key terms

Power: the ability to undertake strength performances quickly.

Reaction time: the time between the presentation of a stimulus and the onset of movement.

Speed: the rate at which an individual can perform a movement or cover a distance.

Apply it

Give an example from one of your sports activities where power is used and explain why and when it is used.

Apply it

Consider your own sports activities. How do you use reaction time? What is the stimulus?

Hand speed is one of the key factors in boxer Nicola Adams' success

Fitness and Body Systems

The relative importance of fitness components

Improving skill-related fitness can help improve our performance in normal daily work and leisure activities, and can help us to lead a full, healthy and energetic life. For example, a good reaction time is useful when driving a car, while good balance is helpful when standing on a step ladder painting a wall.

Also, it is important to remember how skills relate to each other. For example, in football foot-eye co-ordination is needed, but so is speed to get to the ball quickly; strength to hold off an opponent; power to get a hard shot on goal and, for goalkeepers, hand-eye co-ordination and agility to try to save the shot.

Think about the hammer throw. This is a technically difficult event where athletes:

- have to swing the hammer above their head while standing still in a controlled position
- rotate on one foot while accelerating across the circle, getting quicker with each turn while maintaining the movement and position of the hammer
- on reaching the front of the circle, launch the hammer with great force at exactly the right moment.

Apply it

In the series of movements listed for the hammer throw, indicate where each skill-related factor is being used.

Practice

Make a list of the skill-related fitness aspects of a sport you take part in. Create a table with the skill-related aspects in the left-hand column. In the right-hand column explain how you use these components when playing or practising.

The hammer throw requires several skill-related fitness factors

Fitness tests

Whatever your sport or physical activity, fitness is key to success. Without fitness for your sport you cannot hope to reach your full potential. Different sports require different types of fitness. For example, Mo Farah, a 5k and 10k runner, and Tom Daley, a diver, have very different fitness needs and completely different training programmes.

In some sports, fitness may be the difference between the success achieved by top players and those who are less successful.

You can use a single fitness test or a number of fitness tests to measure and assess your current fitness level in a specific area. You can then apply the principles and methods of training in your PEP to improve your fitness for your chosen sport. At the end of your PEP re-test yourself, using exactly the same protocol to see how well you have done with your training and to evaluate your PEP.

Identify your strengths and weaknesses

You can compare your results to other athletes in a training group, people involved in the same sport, or against the standards for your gender and age group in national **norms** or scoring tables. This will help you see which areas you are fine in and which need improvement, so that you can change your programme to achieve this.

Monitor your progress

Once you know where your fitness levels are, you have a baseline against which you can check your progress. If you repeat tests at regular intervals, you can then get an idea of how effectively your training is working.

Give yourself an incentive

Doing a fitness test can let you set yourself the goal of reaching a particular standard or level. You could even set yourself a deadline by which you will achieve it, to motivate yourself further.

Choosing the right fitness test

Before starting any training programme (including a PEP), you should decide what aspect of fitness you are aiming to improve.

You could look at the components of fitness and use this knowledge to help you to decide on your aims. It is important to remember that, in this case, fitness is the main purpose of the programme rather than skill, but you could aim to improve more than one component.

When you have decided which component or components of fitness you want to improve, you can choose the appropriate tests. You should do the tests before starting your programme and at the end of your programme. You may also choose to re-test at intervals during your training, to check on your progress.

Practice

1 Which components of fitness would you assess before planning your training programme, and how would you test them?
2 How could you assess your results for your age?
3 Why do you train? Why do you think other people train?

Key term

Norm: a pattern or standard.

Fitness and Body Systems

In a group, discuss the tests you have undertaken in your own training

Here are some examples of appropriate tests to meet different aims.

A netballer wanting to improve their cardiovascular fitness might use the Cooper 12-minute run test.

A hurdler wanting to improve their speed might use the 60m sprint test.

A gymnast wanting to improve their flexibility might use the sit and reach test.

It may be that you want to improve more than one aspect of fitness. In this case, you might use a number of tests side-by-side, working them in at the beginning, end and key stages of your training programme.

Collection and interpretation of data

By using a specific fitness test before the start of an exercise programme and again at the end, you can accurately measure any improvement in your fitness or performance.

The process of gathering data in this way is known as **quantitative** analysis. For example, if you use the Cooper 12-minute test, you can compare the distance run during the first test with the distance achieved in the second test. Without this data you might be able to compare how you felt each time you ran, but you would not have the facts to back up your opinion. Analysis based on opinion with no data is known as **qualitative** analysis.

Use of data

It is important to follow what is known as the correct **protocol** – the set way of doing the test. If you do the test one way at the start of your programme and a different way at the end, the test will not be valid and your scores will not be accurate.

Types of fitness test

There are two groups for fitness tests:

- tests for basic health-related fitness.
- tests for skill-related fitness.

Some people may only choose to do the ones related to the aspects they want to improve. Other people may do them all and then after comparing their results to norms decide which aspects they need to improve in their programme.

For each test you will find out:

- the purpose of the test (what it is testing)
- the test protocol (how to do it).

Components of fitness tests

Cooper 12-minute run test

Purpose

Tests cardiovascular fitness and estimates VO_2 max.

Protocol

Run for 12 minutes around a course, normally marked by cones at, for example, 50-metre intervals. Measure the distance you cover and your VO_2 max, and calculate your score against a table of normative data. Use the same course when you do your re-test run.

Harvard step test

Purpose

Tests cardiovascular endurance as the score is based on heart rates; good muscular endurance in the legs is helpful but not measured.

Protocol

Step on and off a 45cm-high bench every two seconds for five minutes. Keep to a regular pace so that you step on and off once every two seconds, making 150 steps in five minutes. It may help you to count 1 – 2 – 3 – 4 for a complete step on and off the bench. Measure your heart rate at one, two and three minutes into recovery. The fitter you are, the quicker your recovery will be.

If your heart rate has not recovered to your resting heart rate after three minutes, continue every minute until it has fully recovered and note that time too.

Practice

If you decide to use this test for your PEP, carry it out by following the protocol. Search online for 'Cooper 12-minute run test normative data' to analyse your scores.

Step-ups

Figure 1.33 The Harvard step test

Fitness and Body Systems

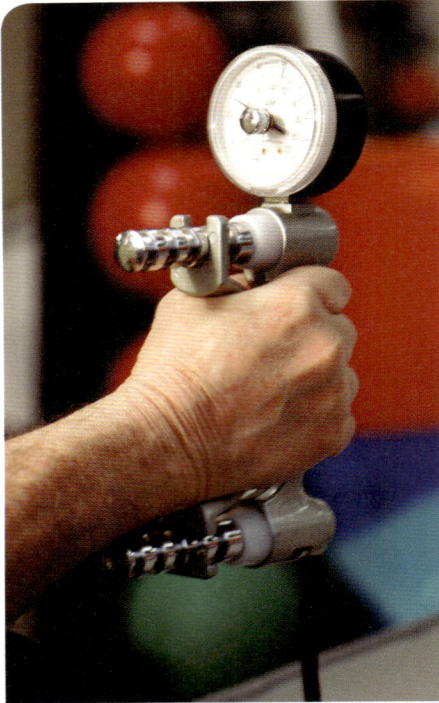

Using a hand grip dynamometer, record your own scores. Compare these with a partner. What might account for the differences?

Hand grip strength test

Purpose

Tests muscular strength in the hand.

Protocol

Use a hand grip dynamometer. With your strongest hand, squeeze as tightly as possible. Take three recordings. Record the best score.

Practice

If you decide to use this test for your PEP, carry it out by following the protocol, then search online for 'hand grip strength test normative data' to analyse your scores.

One-minute press-up test

Purpose

Tests muscular endurance.

Protocol

Perform each press-up with your hands on the ground, level with your shoulders. Then straighten your arms to get into the starting position. Bend your arms and lower your body until your elbows form a 90 degree angle, then return to the starting position to complete one press up.

Work with a partner.

Your partner starts the clock as you start your press-ups and continue with good form for one minute. Your partner records the number of correctly completed press-ups. If you cannot do a full press-up, perform kneeling press-ups instead.

One-minute sit-up test

Purpose

Tests abdominal muscular endurance.

Protocol

Perform each sit-up with your knees bent and your hands on your ears. Sit up and touch your knees with your elbows.

Work with a partner. Your partner starts the clock as you start your sit-ups and continue with good form for one minute. Your partner records the number of correctly completed sits-ups.

Apply it

In a group, investigate and discuss the most appropriate test for each of these athletes.

- A gymnast wanting to monitor their lower back.
- A netballer wanting to check their cardiovascular fitness.

An average female aged 16-19 would be expected to perform 9-14 sit-ups in this test

30m sprint

Purpose

Tests a person's speed.

Protocol

Work with a partner. Mark out a 30m distance. When your partner signals you to start, run as fast as you can while your partner records your time.

Vertical jump/Sargent jump test

Purpose

Tests leg power.

Protocol

Chalk your fingertips then reach up and touch the wall as high as you can. Bend your knees and jump, touching the wall at the highest point of the jump. Measure how high above your standing reach mark you jumped and record your result. Score the best of three attempts.

Sit and reach test

Purpose

Measures the flexibility of the hamstrings and lower back muscles.

Protocol

Either use a standard sit and reach box or sit down with legs straight and feet against a bench set on its side. Measure how far beyond your toes you can reach. If you cannot reach your toes you score a minus total. If you just reach your toes you score zero, which is average.

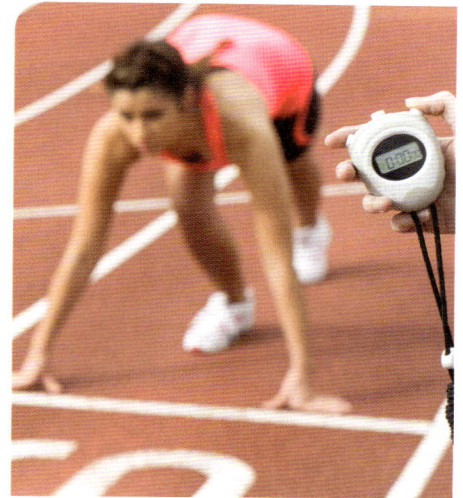

Over the time of your PEP you would expect to score a faster time on the completion of each test

Try the sit and reach test. Discuss with a partner how you could train to improve your results.

Apply it

In a group, investigate and discuss the most appropriate test for each of these sportspeople.

- A diver wanting to be as flexible as possible in dives involving twists and turns.
- A long jumper wanting to improve their run-up speed.
- A high jumper monitoring their ability to launch into a jump.

Fitness and Body Systems

Practice

After performing all of these tests or the ones you have chosen to include in your PEP you will have a list of results. You can use your PEP to work towards improving your results and re-test at the end of the programme. You can then discuss the results in your PEP evaluation.

Exam-style question

Name an appropriate test that a shot putter could use before starting a training programme. Explain why it is appropriate. **(3 marks)**

Exam tip

Use your PEP to apply the knowledge that you have learned in your theory lessons: for example, in the tests that you choose, and the aspects of fitness that you want to improve. Before the exam, when you go over your PEP, you should be revising the knowledge you have applied too.

How fitness is improved

Link it up

In the next section we will look at how fitness is improved through training.

3.3 The principles of training and their application to personal exercise/ training programmes

Getting started

Think about the training people do for a particular sport or activity.

- How much do you think success depends on natural talent, and how much on good training?
- Why do some people go to particular places to train?
- What different types of training can you think of?

Choose three of your favourite athletes or sportspeople and research their training plans on the internet.

Learning objectives

By the end of this section you will understand:

- the principles of training, including individual needs, specificity, progressive overload and FITT
- how to use these principles when planning a personal exercise programme (PEP)
- overtraining and how to prevent it
- reversibility and its impact on performance
- training thresholds and how to calculate maximum heart rates using two different formulae
- what to consider when deciding which training methods to use for different activities
- how to use different training methods to improve specific components of fitness.

The principles of training

In Topic 3, Section 3.2 you learned how to assess your personal levels of fitness through fitness testing before starting an exercise programme. Here you will look at the principles of training, how to use them and how they are relevant to your PEP.

You will know that different athletes prepare in different ways. Perhaps you think of sprinters practising their start from the blocks, boxers skipping or long-distance runners gradually extending the length of their practice runs.

When looking at any training programme, you need to start from some basic principles. The first four key principles are:

- individual needs
- specificity
- progressive overload
- FITT (Frequency, Intensity, Time, Type).

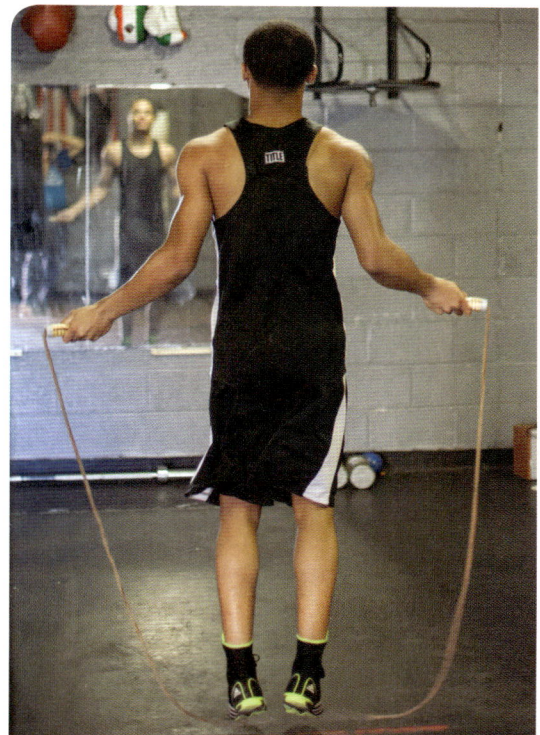

How do you decide on the right training programme for you?

81

Fitness and Body Systems

Individual needs

When planning a PEP, the needs of the individual athlete come first. Using someone else's programme will not work because every athlete has different needs – and a different starting point – and training should focus on these. For example, athletes starting a programme with a very low level of fitness should not follow the programme of someone who has been training for a long time. They may find this too difficult and give up, or they may even sustain an injury.

An extreme example would be a first-time marathon runner using an experienced marathon runner's training programme. The first-time marathon runner would not have the level of fitness, experience or motivation to benefit from it, and could potentially cause themselves injury.

Specificity

Specificity means matching training to the requirements of an activity. Every sport has its own specialist needs; divers and long-distance runners obviously train in different ways. Specificity in football might mean concentrating on cardiovascular fitness (health-related fitness) or speed (skill-related fitness). Cardiovascular fitness enables players to keep going for longer, while speed helps them to move quickly during a game. Goalkeepers, on the other hand, have different training needs (such as agility) – so different, in fact, that Premiership football clubs have specialist goalkeeper coaches to help with this.

The need for specificity is clear in a game such as rugby. All the players must be very fit and strong. However, the forwards need to train for strength when pushing in the scrum while the backs need to be fast and agile to get past the defenders.

Practice

In your PEP, you will need to take into account your body build, your sport (and position played), your aims and, most importantly, your current level of fitness.

Key term

Specificity: the particular requirements of an activity.

Practice

In your PEP you could use the principle of specificity by training to improve your cardiovascular fitness, and choosing particular methods of training to do this. This should be made clear in your PEP and you will need to highlight exactly where you are using the principle of specificity.

Apply it

1   In some team sports different positions call for different fitness requirements. Give an example of a sport where this is the case and describe which health-related and skill-related fitness components need to be trained.

2   Select three different physical activities that have similar fitness needs. Use specific positions where this is relevant. Evaluate how the principle of specificity applies to these activities.

Exam tip

The word is **specificity**. Some students use specify, special, specific or even specification. You must use the correct word and spell it correctly. One way to remember it is: **specific + ity**.

Exam-style questions

1   Oliver is a swimmer. What principle of training should he use to make sure that his training is going to improve his performance in his sport? **(1 mark)**

2   Oliver decides to use circuit training to get fit for his swimming. How can he use this principle to make sure that his circuit is getting him fit for his sport? **(2 marks)**

Learning to be a good goalkeeper takes specific training

Progressive overload

The term 'overload' is used to describe when an athlete trains more than they normally do. This is the only way athletes can improve their fitness. It is often mistaken for training too much, or training too hard, but this is not correct. It means working at a higher range of intensity than the minimum required to improve fitness (the minimum threshold of training) while staying below the maximum (the maximum threshold of training). The area between the minimum threshold and the maximum threshold is known as the **target zone**.

Progressive overload means gradually increasing the amount of overload so as to gain fitness without the risk of injury. The principle of progressive overload applies to all areas of health-related fitness. For example:

- for strength, overload training may mean lifting a weight at 60 to 80 per cent of maximum effort
- for muscular endurance, overload training might be between 60 and 80 per cent of maximum repetitions
- to improve flexibility, overload training means that the stretch must reach or pass the end of the full range of movement to bring about improvement.

Improving cardiovascular fitness can be shown by reducing your resting heart rate over a period of training (for example, a six-week PEP).

Exam-style question

Give an example of how overload could be used in a PEP.
(2 marks)

Key terms

Target zone: the range within which an individual needs to work for aerobic training to take place (60-80 per cent of maximum heart rate).

Progressive overload: gradually increasing the amount of overload to improve fitness but without injury.

Practice

You should apply the principle of progressive overload to your own PEP. Review and evaluate your six-week programme after two weeks, and gradually increase the overload. Then review and evaluate after another two weeks, and adjust again. In this way, you can gradually adjust training loads using progressive overload.

Exam tip

Overload does not mean training too hard or too much. This is a common mistake in the exam. Make sure you understand (and use) the correct definition of progressive overload – gradually increasing how hard you train in order to improve fitness without injury.

Fitness and Body Systems

The FITT principle

The **FITT** principle enables you to plan an exercise programme to get the most out of it as safely as possible. FITT stands for:

- frequency (how often)
- intensity (how hard)
- time (how long)
- type (method).

The FITT principle works with the principle of progressive overload because, as you get fitter, you can train more frequently, train at a higher intensity and for longer periods of time at a given type of activity.

Frequency means how often to train. Frequency can be adjusted to help you manage progressive overload. For example, a training exercise could be planned for a minimum of three times a week, but could be increased to four times a week. Frequency overlaps with the principles of rest and recovery, and can be used to make good use of these. For example, training every other day would allow a rest to recover on the days between training. This would give the body time to adapt and gain the benefits from the training session.

Intensity means how hard someone trains. Intensity might vary depending on the aims and type of training. For example, intensity for a runner would mean getting a little breathless and raising your heart rate in the target zone. However, whatever the type of training, it must be carried out at a worthwhile level of intensity, as part of progressive overload. Planning the intensity of training correctly is very important.

Time means how long each training session must last in order to be of any benefit and to achieve improvement. For example:

- At least 20 minutes per session should be spent in the target zone. This does not mean five minutes to warm up, five to train, five to cool down and another five to shower and change back again!
- In terms of cardiovascular fitness, at least 20 minutes should be spent training with the heart rate in the target zone after a good warm up and before a proper cool down.

Professionals will train for much longer than this to reach their required levels of fitness. They will spend more than 20 minutes warming up, and marathon runners are likely to spend over two hours running on a Sunday morning, in addition to all the other training they do during the week.

Type means the method of training to achieve particular goals. Type overlaps with the principle of specificity; training should be chosen according to what needs to be improved and what the end goal is. If strength needs to be improved by training, is it muscular strength or muscular endurance?

Many people may want to improve their overall fitness without having a particular goal in mind. This could be achieved through a wide variety of activities that raise the heart rate into the target zone to maintain a healthy, active lifestyle – including dancing (from hip-hop to line to ballroom), swimming, cycling, brisk walking, jogging, aerobics to using the cross-trainer.

The type of training is more important for sportspeople who specialise in one event and want to compete at a high level. For example, sprinters train specifically to improve their speed, so focus on particular training methods.

Rest and recovery

Rest and **recovery** are now recognised as important parts of any training programme.

The human body reacts to a hard training session by increasing its ability to cope with future punishing training sessions. This process is called **adaptation**, but it only happens when you rest.

As you rest, your body has time to recover, repairing and strengthening itself between workouts. Your body can adapt to the stress associated with exercise, replenish its stores of energy (muscle glycogen) and repair body tissue.

Including rest and recovery in a training programme is vital. For example, someone training five times a week would probably train on three days, take a day off to recover (and allow adaptation to take place), then train on the next two days and rest again on the seventh. Professionals may follow a programme where they train more often than this, but they may rest different parts of their bodies on different days.

Overtraining

Hitting a good level of training is sometimes a delicate balance for sportspeople, but it is important to get it right.

Overtraining happens when you train beyond your body's ability to recover. Athletes often exercise longer and harder so that they can improve. However, without adequate rest and recovery, this can backfire and actually make your performance worse. Not only will your training be ineffective, but you may also suffer injury or illness, which may mean you have to stop training altogether.

Reversibility

Reversibility means gradually losing fitness instead of progressing or remaining at the current level. This happens when a person is ill or injured. Some people keep their fitness longer than others; this may be related to how long they have taken to build up their fitness or how serious their illness or injury was. However, anyone will lose fitness if they stop training.

Practice

One way to measure both progression and reversibility is to take your heart rate after completing your training programme, and then measure how long it takes for your heart rate to return to normal. If you miss training for a couple of weeks (through injury or sickness) you may see reversibility taking place as your heart rate takes longer to return to normal.

Practice

Rest must be included in your PEP to allow time for recovery and adaptation. Make sure that you allow for this as an integral part of your plan, rather than just as an add-on.

Link it up

It is important to have a well-planned training session which includes a warm up and cool down. Many muscle injuries are caused because the person has not warmed up all their muscles properly or adequately. For more information on warm ups and cool downs see Section 3.6 later in this topic.

Key terms

Rest: the period of time allotted to recovery.

Recovery: repair of damage to the body caused by training or competition.

Adaptation: your body's response to training and how your body changes to cope with new activity.

Overtraining: training beyond your body's ability to recover.

Reversibility: gradually losing fitness instead of progressing or remaining at the current level.

Fitness and Body Systems

Thresholds of training – how do we train safely?

As you have seen, effective training needs to involve progressive overload, which puts the body's systems under stress – but there is a danger that someone can overtrain too, putting too much stress on the body.

This is where **training thresholds** apply. Thresholds set levels for people to train at that are effective but still safe. Work done below the threshold will have little or no impact on improving fitness, but work done above the threshold could damage fitness and cause injury.

There are two main ways to establish what your training thresholds should be: calculating your aerobic target zone and using the **Karvonen formula**.

Target zones

Your **aerobic target zone** is the range within which you want your heart rate to be as you exercise, to achieve the best impact on your cardiovascular system. You work it out by finding out your maximum heart rate, then setting lower and upper limits to your zone.

For aerobic training (for example, for a long-distance runner), these limits are usually at 60 per cent and 80 per cent of your maximum heart rate; for anaerobic training (for example, for a sprinter), they would usually be at 80 per cent and 90 per cent. The higher into the target zone, the higher the intensity of the exercise session.

Example

A 16-year-old athlete who wants to do aerobic training.

Find their maximum heart rate, using the formula:

MHR = 220 – the person's age

In this example:

MHR = 220 – 16 = 204

To find the aerobic target zone, work out 60 per cent and 80 per cent of this figure:

$$60\% \times 204 = \frac{60 \times 204}{100} = 122.4$$

$$80\% \times 204 = \frac{80 \times 204}{100} = 163.2$$

So the aerobic target zone for this person to aim for is a heart rate of between 122 and 163 rounded to the nearest figure.

Karvonen formula

Calculating the aerobic target zone is useful, but it doesn't take into account individual needs or differences. A more sophisticated way of working out an individual's optimum heart rate uses the Karvonen formula.

This formula uses your resting heart rate (RHR), which is a good indicator of your general fitness.

To measure your RHR, <u>before you get out of bed in the morning</u>:

- find your pulse on your wrist (radial pulse) or on the side of your neck (carotid pulse)
- count the number of beats, starting with zero, for one full minute, this is known as beats per minute (bpm).

Once you know your RHR, you can take it away from your maximum heart rate (MHR) to find your heart rate reserve (HRR).

Now you use your RHR, MHR and your HRR to find your target heart rate when training at a maximum percentage.

Here's how the formula works (220 is used as a base figure):

Step 1: 220 – the person's age = MHR
Step 2: MHR – RHR = HRR
Step 3: (HRR × training %) + RHR = target heart rate

Example

Let's take an example a 50-year-old athlete with a RHR of 65 bpm who wants to train at a maximum of 70 per cent.

MHR = 220 – 50 = 170 bpm
HRR = 170 – 65 = 105 bpm
(105 × 70%) + 65 = 73.5 + 65 = 138.5 bpm

Using the formula this person would have a target heart rate of 138.5 beats per minute.

Exam-style question

In the graphs on the right, the red and blue lines show the thresholds of training. Here they are set at 123 and 164 beats per minute for someone aged 15. The heart rate is represented by a black line.

Carl and Zoe are both in year 11 and are very good athletes. Zoe runs the 3000 m, and Carl runs the 100 m. At their last training session, their coaches gave them heart rate monitors to wear, to record their heart rates during their training so that they could analyse their results.

The graphs of their heart rates are shown in Figure 1.34. Use the information to answer the questions.

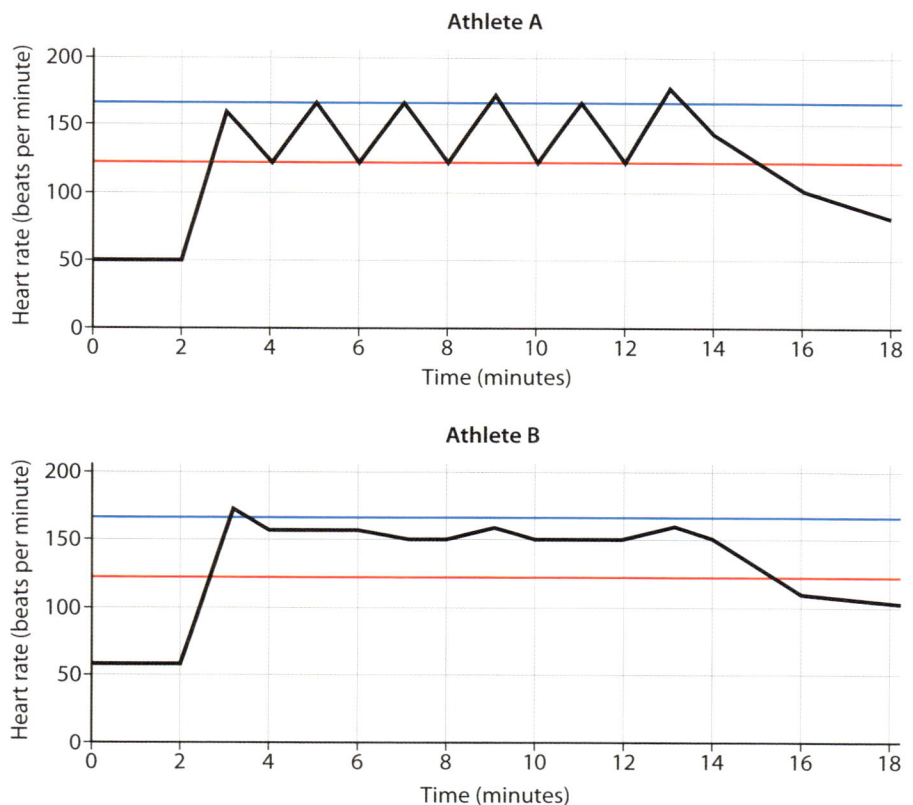

Figure 1.34 Graphs showing the heart rates of two athletes during training

Fitness and Body Systems

Exam-style questions

1 From what you know of Carl and Zoe, which is athlete A and which is athlete B? **(1 mark)**

2 What do the horizontal red and blue lines on the graphs indicate? **(1 mark)**

3 Explain how the positions of these lines are calculated. **(2 marks)**

4 How long did athlete A train with their heart rate in this area? **(1 mark)**

5 How long did athlete B train with their heart rate in this area? **(1 mark)**

6 Explain Carl and Zoe's working heart rates in relation to each other's graphs. **(2 marks)**

7 Who has the lower resting heart rate? **(1 mark)**

Use of data

You may need to work out more complicated formulae on a calculator – but a calculator only helps if you know how to use it. Practice calculations like this before the exam day, and check the results to make sure you are using your calculator correctly.

Choosing the right method of training

There are a number of factors to think about when deciding which training methods to use. The main factors are:

- the requirements of the particular sport or activity
- the facilities available in the local area
- the individual's current level of fitness.

Requirements of the sport

The need for fitness and the need for skill are balanced differently in different sports, and this needs to be reflected in training programmes. For example, a marathon runner will train (by running) for many hours each week, to improve their fitness, but they will not spend too much time on skill. Tennis players, on the other hand, need to maintain fitness but also have to practise their skills for many hours a week.

Athletes and their coaches must consider the needs of the specific sport before deciding on the best training methods. Most tennis players train in a similar way and most marathon runners train in the same way but there will probably be slight variations introduced by their particular coaches.

Programme for a marathon runner

Distance runners will spend most of their training running, but they also need to train to improve and to keep their muscular endurance, so that their muscles can keep going for a long time. They will also need to be able to run at a fast pace for the whole race and outsprint their rivals at the finish so they will do some **interval training**.

Key term

Interval training: physical training involving alternating stages of high- and low-intensity activity.

A programme for an elite marathon runner could include:

- 135 miles of running in a week
- shorter runs at a faster pace using interval training, such as:
  - a one mile warm-up jog
  - 10 x 200m intervals (with 200m recovery jogs) on grass
  - 10 x 200m hill sprints at equal effort, walk back down to recover
  - four mile cool-down run.
- strength and conditioning sessions (1 hour).

Programme for a tennis player

Tennis players need to be very fit. They don't have to run 10 kilometres or a half marathon faster than their opponents, but it is estimated that may run over 8 kilometres in a tough, five-set match with long rallies. At the same time, they have many skills to practice and refine to keep on top of their game.

A programme for a tennis player could include:

- short sprints with short rests for explosive power and speed
- strength training for greater power and core stability
- drills to improve co-ordination, such as ladder drills for footwork
- skills practice for specific shots – for example, service, forehand and backhand shots.

Facilities available

When planning your training programme (PEP) you will have to take into account what resources you will need. For example, if you want to do weight training do you have your own equipment or are you going to need to use the local sports centre? If you are going to use the local sports centre what facilities do they have? When are they available to you and what will it cost?

At your local sports centre there may be different classes that you can join, for example, yoga or spinning. If these facilities are not available to you or are too expensive, you will have to plan around it and develop your programme to suit your own situation. For example, you could design a circuit training programme using your own body weight in some exercises, such as press-ups or step-ups on the stairs. Alternatively, you could add a weight when doing sit-ups to make the resistance greater, such as a litre water bottle. Walking and running are effective ways of staying fit without needing to visit a gym or sports centre. You will need to plan your training around what you have got and what is available.

Current level of fitness

Before creating any training programme, it is essential that you fully understand the current level of fitness. If you do not, your programme may well be ineffective, but more importantly it could be dangerous or damaging for the person involved.

Fitness and Body Systems

Checking your heart rate is one key element of understanding your own level of fitness

Apply it

Learn these training methods by trying out each one. This will help you to apply your knowledge.

For example, if someone wants to improve their muscular strength by weight training, they need to have a clear understanding of the weights they should use to start with. Choosing a weight that is too heavy could injure them. Someone who wants to improve their cardiovascular fitness needs to pace themselves; if they overestimate their current fitness and run too far, too often and too soon, they too could injure themselves, which could create problems with their training plan and target or even take them out of sport completely.

It is very important to choose the most appropriate test, then perform and record the test correctly to establish your current fitness level before starting to train. Many people follow this with re-tests, to check on progress and alter their training in a measured way.

Practice

Before planning your PEP you must know your own fitness levels. Remember that you can assess these using appropriate fitness tests.

Methods of training

A number of training methods can be used to improve fitness. Each designed for a specific purpose, to improve a specific aspect of fitness, and each suits different sports and activities.

The main training methods are:

- continuous
- fartlek
- circuit
- interval
- plyometrics
- weight/resistance.

Continuous training

Continuous training is steady training. Your working heart rate will not be very high but will be in the target zone for aerobic fitness. There are no rest periods, and a session usually lasts for at least 15 minutes.

Continuous training is appropriate where high-intensity exercise may be unwise, so it would be the most suitable to improve cardiovascular fitness for a sedentary adult who has not trained for some time and is quite unfit. It may take various forms and could start with brisk walking, graduating to jogging.

Even with sports that involve short bursts of activity followed by slow walking or jogging (such as football), where interval training is usually the most useful, continuous training may be more appropriate at the start of the season or during the off-season. Long-distance athletes, cyclists and swimmers may use some continuous training as it resembles their actual competitive activity. However, they are more likely to use a combination of interval, continuous and **fartlek**. Table 1.7 show the advantages and disadvantages of continuous training.

Key term

Fartlek: a method of training for runners where the terrain and speed are constantly changing.

Apply it

1   Walk briskly for 15 minutes, on your own or with a partner whose fitness level is similar. Note your starting and finishing points. How far do you think you walked? This is a good way to start training after injury or after a long lay-off.

2   On your own or with the same partner, start from the same point and try to jog continuously for seven minutes over the same course. How close are you to the finishing point of your walk? How far do you think you have run? You can download an app so that you will know how far and how fast you ran.

3   Which session did you find the hardest?

Advantages	Disadvantages
• Improves aerobic fitness, as it includes long, comparatively slow activity • Inexpensive (apart from cost of suitable footwear for running) • Can be done individually or in a group • Suitable for improving health and fitness • Can be done in a variety of places and times • Can be adapted to individual needs • A wide range of activities can be used, including running, jogging, swimming, cycling, as well as exercise machines such as rowing machines, exercise bicycles, treadmills, cross-trainers, and skiing machines • Can be adapted to use the FITT principle	• Does not improve anaerobic fitness so games players would need other training as well • Some people find it boring • Outdoor training can be dependent on the weather

Table 1.7 Advantages and disadvantages of continuous training

Fartlek training

Fartlek training originated in Sweden. The word fartlek is a combination of the two Swedish words for 'speed' and 'play'. Fartlek is a combination of fast and slow running and pre-dates interval training.

Fartlek training is suitable for games such as football, netball and hockey, because it includes the short bursts of activity – such as starting and stopping, or fast sprinting followed by a short rest – which are typical of these games.

In many ways, fartlek resembles interval training; like interval training, it includes periods of work followed by periods of rest (or lighter work). However, fartlek sessions include sprints of varying distances, not necessarily measured distances as in interval training. So a session might include a sprint of 200 metres from one tree to another, or up a hill of no measured distance. Table 1.8 shows the advantages and disadvantages of fartlek.

Advantages	Disadvantages
• Can be done over a variety of terrain, e.g. sand dunes near a beach, parkland and forests • Can include hill work, both up and down hills • Can include repetitions, e.g. up the same hill several times • Programmes can be very flexible • Rest periods can be included or the session can be continuous with intermittent hard and easy running • It is suited to most games such as rugby and netball, as well as general fitness programmes	• There may not be suitable terrain nearby, or only limited options, which could be boring • The individual needs to be highly motivated • The coach may not be able to monitor the training unless they run with the athlete • Outdoor training can be dependent on the weather

Table 1.8 Advantages and disadvantages of fartlek training

Circuit training

Circuit training primarily improves muscular endurance, cardiovascular fitness and circulo-respiratory fitness.

Circuit training involves a number of exercises, arranged so as to avoid exercising the same muscle groups consecutively. For example, a press-up station could be followed by a step-up station, which is then followed by a sit-up station.

Circuit training develops general fitness, working both the muscles and the cardiovascular system. It is therefore suitable for a wide range of activities including football and boxing. It is also excellent training for badminton and tennis players: many professional players use circuit training as part of their Personal Exercise Programme.

Repetitions and circuit training

Exercises at each station may be carried out for a set length of time, for example, as many repetitions as possible in 30 seconds. Alternatively, the exercises may be carried out a set number of times, for example, 30 repetitions. This will be determined according to the fitness level of the participant. After completing each set of repetitions, the person moves on to the next exercise until a whole circuit has been completed. Then the circuit is repeated. Usually three circuits are completed in a session with a 30-second rest between each station and two minutes rest at the end of each circuit.

Advantages	Disadvantages
It can combine muscular endurance, power, speed and cardiovascular fitness effectively within one session	The circuit needs to be well planned out so that there are not too many people waiting to exercise at the same station
A good source of training for all-round fitness	It is important to work hard on each circuit but it is easy to put a lot of energy in to the first circuit rather than pacing yourself for the remaining circuits
Includes both aerobic and anaerobic activities	Skill stations may be included but if the aim of the circuit is to improve fitness then it should not include skill stations such as coordination and balance or shooting for netball, as they normally allow the heart rate to fall below what you would expect in a fitness circuit. Power and speed, for example, may be included

Table 1.9 Advantages and disadvantages of circuit training

Interval training

Interval training is defined as high-intensity periods of work followed by defined periods of rest. It is possible to train individually, with a partner, or in a team or group. The aim of interval training is to have a high-intensity, high-quality workout, always done at a fast pace. Interval training is mainly designed to improve speed, but will also improve cardiovascular fitness.

Interval training is suitable for many different sports, from individual activities, such as swimming and athletics, to team games, such as football and hockey. It is good for team players, as it fits the style of many games, with short bursts of activity followed by slow walking or jogging or stopping, but it is also good for athletes who run long distances and individual sports players.

The 'work' period, or interval, may be a distance to run, such as 60 metres, or a time to run, such as 10 seconds. This will probably be linked to the particular activity, using the principle of specificity.

The 'rest' period, or interval, may be a walk back to the starting point, or simply not working (rest). The duration of this should be at least 30 seconds to allow recovery and preparation for the next work interval. Otherwise the quality, or intensity, of the work is not likely to be good enough.

In interval training, the number of repetitions is important. One repetition is equal to one work period plus one rest period – for example, one repetition could be one run of 200 metres followed by a 30-second rest period. A set of repetitions may be six, eight or ten runs of 200-metre, each with a 30-second rest period. An athlete may perform a number of sets with longer rest intervals between the sets: for example, four sets, with each set consisting of six repetitions of 200 metre sprints with a walk back as the rest interval between repetitions, and then three minutes rest between sets. Table 1.10 shows the advantages and disadvantages of interval training.

Link it up

Sprinters who use interval training to improve their speed are also using the principle of specificity, since they have chosen this specific training method to improve their performance. See Section 3.3 earlier in this topic to review the principle of specificity.

Link it up

This links with Topic 1, Section 1.2 on cardiovascular fitness.

Advantages	Disadvantages
• Includes repeated sprint running or swimming, which is anaerobic • Includes a rest period (interval) that allows recovery • Heart rates can be measured and shown in graphic form, so they can be evaluated and the quality of the sessions compared • Takes place over short periods or bursts • Includes repetitions of high-quality work that raise the heart rate to near maximum, which improves cardiovascular fitness	• Can be very intense so needs full commitment and motivation • Some people find repeating intervals boring • Outdoor training can be dependent on the weather

Table 1.10 Advantages and disadvantages of interval training

Apply it

In a group, write a short paragraph or make a table comparing interval training, continuous training and fartlek training, or discuss the similarities and differences. Make sure you are clear about the differences.

Exam tip

Fartlek and interval training are very similar, so make sure you show in your answer that fartlek takes place over different terrain and can include hills.

Fitness and Body Systems

Plyometrics

Plyometrics are exercises in which muscles exert maximum force in short intervals of time. The exercises aim to increase your muscle's elastic strength and **explosiveness**, which increases your power, in order to enhance your performance as an athlete. Remember that the two components of power in sport are speed and strength, and plyometrics aims to improve both of these.

Plyometrics can help many sorts of athletes to improve their power. For example:

- a high jumper might want to improve the power in their legs to improve their take-off
- a javelin thrower might want to improve the power in their arms, for the moment of release
- a rugby forward in the scrum

Table 1.11 shows the advantages and disadvantages of plyometric training.

Advantages	Disadvantages
• Improves explosive fitness, e.g. power • Does not need expensive equipment • Exercises can be designed for the specific performance, e.g. for the high jumper	• Need to be fit before you start plyometrics • Need knowledge of your event or a coach • Need to progress gradually, as rest and recovery are important

Table 1.11 Advantages and disadvantages of plyometric training

Weight/resistance training

Weight/resistance training uses progressive resistance, either in the form of the actual weight lifted or in terms of the number of times the weight is lifted (repetitions). It is used to:

- increase muscular strength
- increase muscular endurance
- increase speed
- develop muscle bulk (size)
- rehabilitate after illness or injury.

Weight/resistance training is suitable for people who take part in strength events in athletics and speed and jumping events, such as sprinting and long jump. It also builds muscular endurance of sportspeople (e.g. distance runners).

Constructing a weight/resistance training schedule

A number of factors need to be taken into account in the design of an effective weight/resistance training schedule.

- **Number of exercises**

  For someone just starting, six to eight exercises would make a suitable core training programme. After this, the number of exercises for specific muscles could be varied.

- **Exercises for each muscle group**

  In the early stages of weight/resistance training, it would be advisable to follow a core programme before concentrating on particular muscle groups.

- **Weight used**

  The safest amount is about 40 to 50 per cent of the five repetition maximum (RM). One RM is the maximum a person can lift once; five RM is the most a person can lift five times.

- **Number of repetitions**

  In the 'sets method', it is usual to do ten repetitions per set. Experienced athletes might do fewer repetitions for strength or more repetitions for muscular endurance.

- **Number of sets**

  Normally three sets of ten repetitions are performed, but for a six-week programme it is probably best to start with two sets and move up to three sets after two weeks.

- **How fast the exercise is done**

  It is more important, when starting out, to be in control of the weights than to work too quickly. Each repetition should be done in 1.5 to 2.0 seconds.

- **Length of rest between sets**

  Recovery between sets is normally about 1–2 minutes. If working with a training partner or partners, taking turns is normally about the same amount of time.

- **Frequency of training**

  The 'sets method' of weight/ resistance training is not as demanding or intensive as pure strength training, so does not need the same amount of rest between sessions. However, at least one rest day between sessions is advisable for novice weight trainers.

Weight training schedules need careful planning to be effective while avoiding injury

Fitness and Body Systems

Table 1.12 shows the advantages and disadvantages of weight/resistance training.

Advantages	Disadvantages
• Can be used to improve muscular strength, muscular endurance or power depending on how the programme is organised • Wide variety of exercises to choose from • Programme can be created to improve specific muscle groups – for example, bench press develops the pectoral muscles • Easy to monitor progress and overload	• Need suitable facilities • Need special equipment • May need spotters (another person supporting) • Need knowledge of safety and technique

Table 1.12 Advantages and disadvantages of weight/resistance training

Link it up

This section links with Section 3.2 on muscular strength and muscular endurance, and the earlier part of this section on rest and recovery.

Practice

Using the information on weight/resistance training, construct a weight/resistance training schedule of six suitable exercises for your six-week PEP.

Make work cards with diagrams or pictures for each exercise. Explain which muscle groups are being trained. Are you working to improve muscular strength or muscular endurance?

Exam tip

Always make sure you read questions like these carefully. You need to consider which two athletes you choose, making sure that:

• they use very different training methods
• you can explain why these training methods work well for that type of athlete.

Exam-style question

Choose two athletes who would train in very different ways: for example, a sprinter and a marathon runner. For each athlete, choose two training methods they would use from the list below, and explain how these would help them prepare for their sport. **(3 marks)**

• Continuous training
• Fartlek training
• Circuit training
• Interval training
• Plyometrics
• Weight/resistance training

Fitness classes

Many people attend fitness classes, at their gym, as part of a club or in another local venue. Classes have advantages and disadvantages. For example, some classes are expensive or involve payment in advance for a whole course; sometimes the only classes are some distance away, and transport facilities to get there are poor; and sometimes the classes are on at times that are difficult for someone to make.

However, if you find the right class for you, a fitness class can play an important role in your health and well-being. A huge range of general and specialist fitness classes are available. Table 1.13 shows just a few of the more common classes you will find.

Exam-style question

Some training activities can be adapted to suit different performance activities. Explain how a cross-country runner and a footballer might adapt fartlek training to suit their own activity? **(2 marks)**

Exam tip

Make sure you read the question carefully. Don't just describe the different training methods – make sure you say how the training sessions would be adapted and applied.

Class	What you do	Component of fitness
Aerobics	Mainly aerobic exercise to music, covering a variety of exercises	• Mainly cardiovascular fitness • Develops some strength, muscular endurance and flexibility • Impacts on body composition
Body pump	Exercise to music normally using low weights with many repetitions and a variety of exercises, such as lunges and squats	• Mainly cardiovascular fitness and muscular endurance, toning the body • Develops some strength and flexibility • Impacts on body composition
Pilates	A series of core stability exercises focusing on the quality of the exercise rather than the quantity – so less vigorous but working on a range of movement. Also focuses on correct breathing, relaxation and stress reduction	• Works on the body and the mind – like yoga does • Develops a range of fitness, but not vigorous such as aerobic and anaerobic • Develops muscular endurance and flexibility, with some strength
Yoga	Ancient form of exercise that focuses on postures or poses (to increase strength and flexibility), breathing and sometimes meditation, to boost physical and emotional well-being Emphasis on quality of exercise, holding the correct position with full range of movement and balance, and breathing correctly	• Works on the body and the mind • Develops muscular endurance, flexibility and balance • Develops strength and, to some extent, cardiovascular fitness
Spinning	Aerobic and anaerobic cycling on a stationary bike to music	• Mainly aerobic fitness • Also develops muscular endurance, mainly in the legs

Table 1.13 Fitness classes offer a variety of exercises

Fitness and Body Systems

3.4 The long-term effects of exercise

Getting started

Exercise can make you out of breath, make you sweat and give you muscle pain – but what about the long-term effects?

- For what reasons do people exercise?
- How might your reasons for doing exercise change as you get older?
- Do you think all sports bring the same long-term benefits?
- Are some sorts of exercise bad for you in the long-term?

Write a list of what you think the long-term effects of exercise are. Explain each effect.

Learning objectives

By the end of this section you will understand:

- the long-term effects of aerobic and anaerobic training and exercise
- the benefits to the musculo-skeletal system, including:
  - increased bone density
  - increased strength of ligaments and tendons
  - muscle hypertrophy
- the importance of rest and recovery
- the benefits to the cardio-respiratory system, including:
  - the heart
  - the blood
  - the respiratory system
- the benefits to performance.

Long-term effects of aerobic and anaerobic training

Regular or long-term participation in physical activity has many benefits, the most important of which is that the heart becomes more efficient.

The main areas that benefit are:

- the musculo-skeletal system
- the cardio-respiratory system
- performance.

Long-term training effects

The long-term effects of training will depend on what methods of training you have used.

For example, in your PEP, if you have used continuous training or interval training, this will improve your aerobic fitness and anaerobic fitness. As a result:

- your lungs will work more efficiently
- your body will be better able to cope with the carbon dioxide produced by exercise, because the lungs are removing it more efficiently
- you will be able to work harder for longer than before – so you can train for longer and at a higher intensity
- water – another by-product of aerobic exercise – is more efficiently used by the cells or more likely lost as sweat or through moisture in exhaled air.

In terms of anaerobic exercise, the effect of training over the long term will be an increase in the ability to move in quick bursts. In practice, this could apply to:

- sprinting for the ball in football
- running to the try line in rugby
- improved times over the shorter/sprint distances in athletics and swimming.

Effects and benefits for the musculo-skeletal system

When someone is fit, you can often see that their muscles are toned and they look strong. Exercise brings a number of benefits for your musculo-skeletal system – some of which you can't see.

Increased bone density

Weight-bearing exercise, such as weight training and running, puts your bones under stress. In response your body produces more cells that build new bone, making the bones stronger and denser. This helps to prevent osteoporosis, which is when the bones get weaker and can result in breaking a bone from a fall (mostly in older people).

Increased strength of ligaments and tendons

Weight-bearing exercise also increases the strength of ligaments, which attach bone to bone, and tendons, which attach muscles to bone, and this helps to reduce the chances of injury to these ligaments and tendons.

Muscle hypertrophy

The method of training you use will affect the muscle fibres. Strength training will therefore result in an increase in both the size (muscle hypertrophy) and the strength of the muscle, for example, biceps curls will increase both the size and the strength of the biceps. If you use light weights and many repetitions you will increase your muscular endurance, but heavier weights and fewer repetitions will result in an increase in muscular strength. Though both methods will result in an increase of some strength and some endurance.

Rest for adaptation and recovery

The body reacts to the training loads imposed on it by increasing its ability to cope with those loads. Adaptation occurs during the **recovery** period after the training session is completed.

Link it up

This links with Topic 1, Section 1.1 the structure and functions of the musculo-skeletal system and Topic 1, Section 1.4, the short-term and long-term effects of exercise.

Key terms

Recovery: the time required for the repair of damage to the body caused by training or competition. Alternatively, the period between sets of a given exercise or between intervals in an interval training session/workout.

Fitness and Body Systems

How do you build rest and recovery into your training?

Link it up

This section links with Topic 1, Section 1.4, the structure and functions of the cardio-respiratory system.

Practice

You should monitor your heart rate recovery when performing your PEP to assess your fitness level.

Key term

Coronary heart disease: when your coronary arteries are narrowed by a slow build-up of fatty material within their walls.

Effects and benefits for the cardio-respiratory system

The cardio-respiratory and musculo-skeletal systems work together to enable any athlete to perform at their best. Taking part in exercise brings many long-term benefits for the heart, blood and respiratory system too.

Your heart

Decreased resting heart rate

Your resting heart rate (RHR) gives an indication of your fitness. This is because the heart gets bigger and stronger with training, so it can supply the same amount of blood with fewer beats. So the heart of a fit person beats fewer times, which is more efficient and results in less stress on the heart.

A trained athlete, such as Olympic heptathlon champion Jessica Ennis-Hill, could have an RHR as low as 40 bpm, while an average person might have an RHR of 72 bpm. Your RHR can also be affected by age, sex, size, posture, eating, emotion, body temperature, environmental factors and smoking.

Faster recovery rate

Heart recovery rate is the speed at which your heart returns to RHR after you exercise. The faster your recovery rate, the fitter you are. As you get fitter, your heart gets back to its RHR faster, so a faster heart recovery rate is another long-term benefit of exercise.

Increased resting stroke volume

Stroke volume is the amount of blood pumped by your heart per beat. When you exercise regularly, your stroke volume increases, both at rest and at work. This is because your heart becomes more efficient and stronger as a result of regular training. At rest, stroke volume may be 85 ml, but when exercising it could be up to 130 ml.

Maximum cardiac output

Cardiac output is the amount of blood ejected from your heart in one minute. It is governed by the heart rate (pulse) and the stroke volume, which both change when you participate in exercise over a long time. The equation to calculate cardiac output is:

cardiac output (CO) = stroke volume (SV) × heart rate (HR)

Size and strength of your heart

Regular training and exercise will have an effect on your heart. The stroke volume of your heart will increase – both at work and at rest – and your heart rate will decrease, meaning that it is working more efficiently. Training increases the heart muscle in size, thickness and strength; the chambers increase in volume and the whole heart gets bigger.

So if a trained athlete is training at the same heart rate as an untrained athlete, the trained athlete will have a bigger stroke volume and cardiac output than the untrained athlete.

Because of these effects, regular aerobic exercise can also lower the risk of **coronary heart disease** (CHD).

Your blood
Increased capillarisation
Capillaries are the smallest of the blood vessels. They play a key role in circulating blood between the arteries and the veins, because they:

- take oxygenated blood from the arteries to the tissues of the body
- take deoxygenated blood from the tissues back into the veins.

Improved fitness increases the number of capillaries in your heart muscle and helps make blood vessels more elastic, flexible and efficient.

Increase in the number of red blood cells
Another benefit of aerobic fitness training is an increase in the number of red blood cells. These are the cells that carry oxygen to the muscles, so having a higher red blood cell count can help an athlete improve their performance.

Drop in resting blood pressure
Regular exercise reduces blood pressure due to the muscular wall of the veins and arteries becoming more elastic. It also makes your heart stronger, and a stronger heart can pump blood with less effort. If your heart doesn't have to work so hard, the force on your arteries decreases, which lowers your blood pressure.

Exercise can help with weight loss, which can also reduce blood pressure. Being overweight can cause or add to the risk of having high blood pressure.

It is possible to have high blood pressure without knowing; it can lead to a stroke or heart attack. Factors that can affect blood pressure include age, sex, muscular development, stress and tiredness. Altitude can also affect blood pressure, as the body reacts to the low oxygen pressure that can occur at high altitudes.

Blood pressure is a useful starting point for assessing the long-term benefits of exercise

Your respiratory system
Increased lung capacity/volume and vital capacity
After a sustained period of regular exercise your lung volume will increase. Because your lungs are more efficient, they will be better at delivering oxygen to your working muscles, so your body will be able to cope better during exercise. Carbon dioxide will be removed more efficiently, so your body can cope with a greater increase in the production of carbon dioxide during exercise. Your vital capacity will increase too, as the whole system – particularly the lungs – becomes more efficient.

Increased number of alveoli
More **alveoli** become available for gaseous exchange after regular exercise, so more oxygen can be absorbed by the capillaries and more carbon dioxide taken from them. As a result, VO_2 max (aerobic capacity) increases too.

Increased strength of the diaphragm and external intercostal muscles
Exercise also increases the strength of the **diaphragm** and the external intercostal muscles – the muscles that work to increase airflow during physical activity. At rest, you breathe at about 12 breaths per minute, but this rises to up to 48 breaths per minute during exercise.

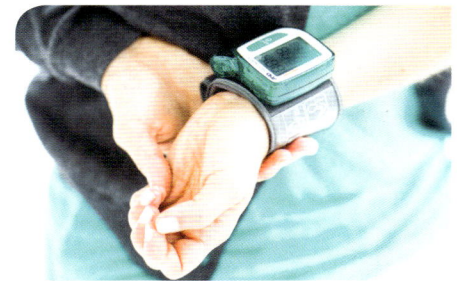

> **Key terms**
>
> **Alveoli**: tiny sacs within our lungs that allow oxygen and carbon dioxide to move between the lungs and bloodstream.
>
> **Diaphragm**: the primary muscle used in the process of inspiration, or inhalation. It is a dome-shaped sheet of muscle that separates the chest from the rest of the body cavity.

Fitness and Body Systems

3.5 How to optimise training and prevent injury

Getting started

Consider the impact injury can have on you and on your ability to play sport or exercise.

- What are the worst sporting injuries you have heard about?
- How do you think you can prevent injury?
- Will some sports always have a greater risk of injury?

Investigate the changes in training practice over the past 100 years that have a) improved training, and b) helped to prevent injury.

Learning objectives

By the end of this section you will understand:

- what a PAR-Q is, and how it is used in training
- how to prevent injury through correct training, warming up and cooling down, wearing appropriate clothing, checking equipment and facilities, and playing to the rules
- some common injuries in sport and how to treat injuries: RICE (rest, ice, compression, elevation)
- performance-enhancing drugs and their positive and negative effects.

Key term

PAR-Q (Physical Activity Readiness Questionnaire): a self-screening tool that can be used by anyone who is planning to start an exercise or training routine.

PAR-Q (Physical Activity Readiness Questionnaire)

Before starting an exercise programme you must make sure you are ready to do so. Being physically active is safe for most of us, but some people need to check with their doctors before they increase their activity or start a new programme – but how can you tell if you are one of these people?

The physical activity readiness questionnaire (**PAR-Q**) was devised to help you do this. It is a screening tool that anyone can use on themselves. There are several standard questions – a questionnaire – which you need to ask yourself.

Trainers and coaches also use PAR-Q to check that the individuals they are working with are safe and not at risk through exercising.

The PAR-Q has been designed to identify the small number of adults for whom physical activity may be inappropriate or those who should have medical advice concerning the type of activity most suitable for them.

Before you can complete the questionnaire you need to be sure about your medical history: any medical conditions, respiratory problems or other concerns. You should also be clear about your previous sporting or exercise history. The questions you should consider are:

1. Have you any medical conditions, e.g. a heart condition?
2. Do you experience chest pains?
3. Do you have any ongoing injuries?
4. Do you have high or low blood pressure?
5. Do you have diabetes?
6. Do you have asthma?
7. Have you had a cold or flu or a virus in the last four weeks?
8. Is there any other reason why you should not do physical activity?

If you honestly answered NO to questions 1–8, and you're happy with your current medical condition, then you can start – and then gradually increase your level of – physical activity.

If you answered YES to any question you should go to see your doctor and have a medical examination – especially if you have been in poor health, had an injury or a viral infection, or if you are getting over a cold or flu.

Preventing injuries

Most physical activities and sports have some element of risk attached to them, although this will be higher in some cases than others, both in terms of an accident happening and the severity of the possible injury. However, much can be done to minimise the risk.

Correct use of the principles of training

If you are planning a PEP you should make sure that it is for you and planned for you to meet your 'individual needs'.

The second principle is FITT. Your training should not be too often (Frequency). If you are just starting your programme then three sessions a week should be appropriate, gradually increasing as you get fitter. You should not push yourself too hard too soon (Intensity), for example, a run should not be too far or too fast. Start with 20 minutes with your heart rate in your target zone (Time). Finally, choose the best method of training for you, and your current level of fitness (Type).

Specificity is vital. Training for your particular activity and using the most appropriate training methods for you will allow you to achieve the best results. In your PEP work, remain within the thresholds of training, for example, 60 to 80 per cent of your maximum heart rate. As you get fitter you may work for some of the time at a higher rate but do this gradually using the principle of progressive overload to make your training harder. Do not suddenly lift weights which are much too heavy and that you cannot lift correctly and safely. You must build time for rest and recovery into your programme. This is when training adaptations take place and you recover from your training sessions. You will always want to avoid reversibility and to avoid overtraining causing injury and illness. Overtraining can lead to an **overuse injury** which is an injury caused by repeated action, such as repetitive strain injury. **Acute injury** happens in an instant, for example, a leg broken in a tackle.

> **Key terms**
>
> **Overuse injury**: sustained from repeated action, such as shin splints caused by running.
>
> **Acute injury**: a sudden injury that is usually associated with a traumatic event, such as crashing into another player during sport, causing your bone to crack, muscles to tear or ligaments to snap.

Fitness and Body Systems

Warming up/cooling down

One of the main reasons for warming up is that warming the muscles gradually helps to prevent injury and makes your workouts more effective. Cooling down after exercise or sport gradually lowers your body temperature, heart rate and breathing rate. This helps to slowly return your body to its resting state. If exercise ends sharply, blood pressure also drops, which could cause dizziness. Remember that cooling down serves not to prevent injury but to disperse lactic acid – preventing soreness and aches.

Protective equipment and clothing

Many activities call for protective equipment and clothing and some, such as football, hockey, sailing and riding, have the need for such equipment built into the rules. The clothing may also vary according to the position you play. Hockey goalkeepers wear more protective clothing than the rest of the team and the same is true of a batsman in cricket. It is quite easy to explain why these players need extra protection, as they play in positions where they are vulnerable to being hit by a very hard ball which is travelling at speed.

It is also important not to wear clothing that might injure an opponent (or teammate).

Jewellery should be removed or taped over if it cannot be removed.

Checking equipment and facilities

Organisers and officials, as well as participants, need to check for safety before an activity or competition. Organisers should check that the facilities are safe and secure, and that any equipment is in good condition. The specific checks needed will of course vary considerably according to the activity. Before a football match, for example, officials must check that the pitch is suitable to play on and that the markings are clearly visible.

Playing to the rules of competition

All games and sports have rules so that there can be fair competition. Rules help to ensure safety and help games to flow. If rules are broken participants are punished. This could be a red card in football or a lifetime sanction for an athlete found to have taken banned substances.

Occasionally in sport 'professional fouls' – where players deliberately act to stop or affect play – are used, particularly in team games. Behaviour like this goes against

Give three examples of protective equipment used in sport

the spirit of 'fair play'. Over-aggression or professional fouls can cause serious injuries which could threaten a player's career. Players can be heavily fined and/or banned for over-aggressive play outside the rules and 'spirit of the game'.

Injuries that can occur in physical activity and sport

It is in the nature of sport that people will sometimes be hurt or hurt themselves, even when every possible precaution has been taken.

Concussion

Concussion is an injury normally caused by a blow to the head and can happen in many sports. Rugby is the sport mostly associated with this injury due to the full-contact nature of the game. There are many symptoms of concussion and they include: headaches, weakness, loss of co-ordination and/or balance, confusion and slurred speech.

Fractures

A fracture is a broken or cracked bone. Fractures can occur from a blow, e.g. to the tibia, or from a severe twisting or wrenching of a joint, e.g. at the fibula. The tibia and fibula are the long bones between knee and ankle.

The symptoms are likely to include pain at the site of the injury and, if the injured part is a limb, an inability to move it. The point of injury will be very tender and swelling might occur with bruising later. Another obvious symptom might be deformity (a misshapen bone at the point of the break); a broken clavicle (collarbone) is a good example of this. Sometimes, the bone can be heard breaking.

There are several types of fracture. In closed fractures, as the name implies, the skin over the break is not damaged. In compound fractures, the broken bone protrudes through the skin. These fractures are generally more serious, as there is a risk of infection.

Simple fractures take place in one line, with no displacement of the bone. They include greenstick fractures, where the bone is only partly broken. These are common at the wrist joint, and, for example, can occur when running relays and using the walls to turn in the sports hall. Greenstick fractures are particularly common in children, whose bones are soft and less likely to break completely.

Stress fractures are often referred to as overuse injuries. They can happen as a result of muscles becoming fatigued and unable to absorb shock. Stress fractures can also occur when increasing the amount or intensity of exercise too rapidly or by playing on unfamiliar surfaces, for example, switching from a soft grass tennis court to a hard court. Stress fractures of the foot can be caused by wearing ill-fitting or poor quality shoes, for example, running on hard roads and not wearing good quality running shoes. Most stress fractures happen in weight-bearing parts of the body, such as the bones of the lower leg and the lower back.

Link it up

You can review the structure and functions of the musculo-skeletal system in Topic 1, Section 1.1.

It has been shown that people who take part in repetitive activities which are often performed on hard surfaces, such as tennis, basketball and road running, are susceptible to stress fractures. Rest between exercise sessions is essential to allow bones and especially joints to recover before the next training session.

Stress fractures are also linked with osteoporosis in old age and the eating disorders anorexia nervosa and bulimia.

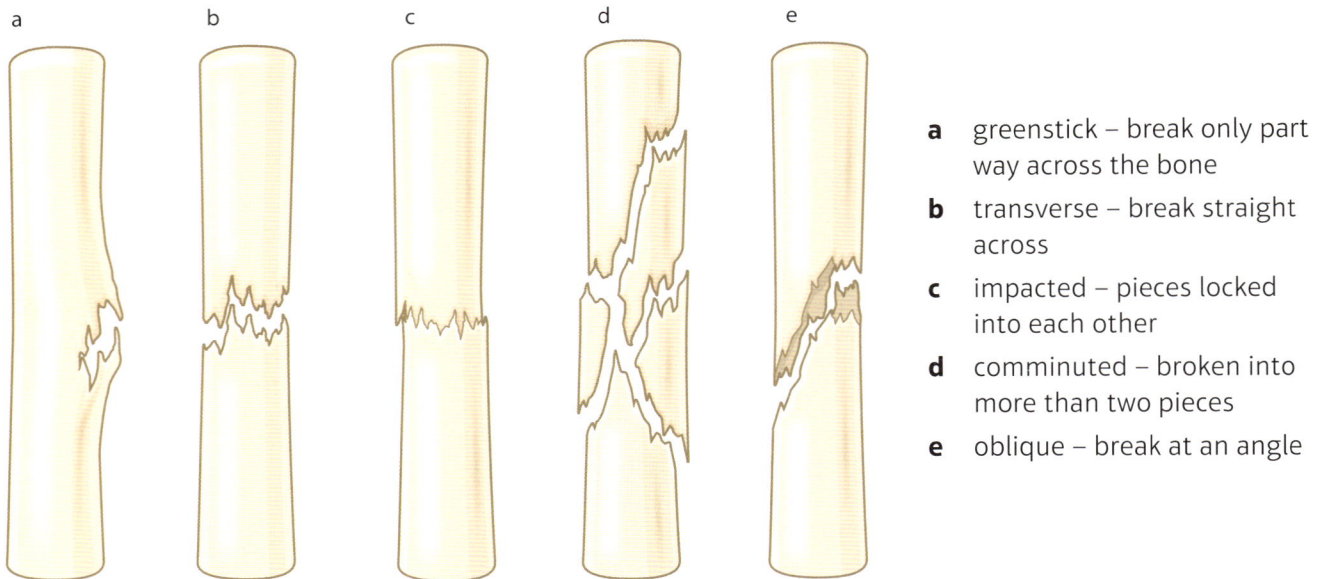

a greenstick – break only part way across the bone

b transverse – break straight across

c impacted – pieces locked into each other

d comminuted – broken into more than two pieces

e oblique – break at an angle

Figure 1.35 Injuries to the bone

Dislocations

A dislocation is when a bone at a joint is forced out of its normal position, often as a result of a hard blow which causes one of the bones to be displaced. The most obvious sign is deformity and swelling of the joint, which is locked out of position. Dislocations are very painful. There may also be an associated fracture of one of the bones; if there is any doubt, the injury should be treated as a fracture.

Sprains

A sprain is a damaged ligament. One of the most common sprains in sport is a twisted ankle, which is often sustained in invasion games such as hockey, netball, football and rugby. A sprained ankle means that the foot has been inverted or turned inwards, tearing the ligaments which hold the bones of the ankle joint together.

Sprains often occur when stretching too far past the normal range of a joint, but can also be caused by falling, twisting or colliding with another player. Sprains of the ankle and knee are the most common, but sprains can also occur at the wrist or elbow as a result of falling and landing awkwardly. Finger sprains are very common in netball, basketball and volleyball.

Torn cartilage

Cartilage is a firm elastic substance which lines adjoining bones. It absorbs the impact on the bones while reducing the friction in sports and general activities. Damage to cartilage is often due to wear and tear from long-term overuse.

Soft tissue injury

Joints are where two or more bones meet. They are particularly prone to injury because movement past the range allowed can tear or pull tendons and ligaments. Frequent repetitive exercise can also often result in injury to joints.

Strain

A strain is a twist, pull or tear of a muscle or a tendon (while a sprain is an injury to a ligament).

The most common places for sportspeople to get strains are in the back and the hamstring (at the back of the thigh) – and these can easily happen in sports such as football, hockey, netball, boxing and wrestling. Arm and hand strains are also quite common, so performers doing gymnastics, tennis, rowing or golf may often get them.

Tennis and golfer's elbow

Both of these injuries are strains that happen by stretching or tearing muscle or tendon. A tendon is a fibrous cord of tissue that connects muscles to bones.

Both these conditions are overuse injuries to the tendons at the elbow joints. The main symptom of tennis elbow is pain on the outside of the elbow; it is often caused by using a racket with the wrong sized grip. Golfer's elbow involves pain on the inside of the elbow. These injuries can happen to people who do not play tennis or golf but may occur because of repetitive action in their everyday life, for example, a carpenter.

Abrasions

Abrasions or grazes can be caused by friction of the skin against a rough surface, e.g. a concrete playground, artificial pitch or road surface. They are less likely to happen when playing on a grass surface. These can happen from a fall or as a result of a tackle, for example, but most grazes are quick to heal. The injured areas should be kept clean to prevent infection and cleaned with a sterile wipe and antiseptic cream applied to the injured area.

RICE (Rest, Ice, Compression, Elevation)

The RICE (Rest, Ice, Compression and Elevation) process is followed to treat minor injuries. If minor injuries are treated in this way as soon as they occur, they can often be prevented from getting worse. Obviously, if a major injury such as a fracture or dislocation is suspected, medical help should be called.

Link it up

This links with Topic 1, Section 1.1 and the role of tendons and ligaments, and their relevance to sport.

- Rest – stop playing or training.
- Ice – using a bag of peas from the freezer, cold water or ice cubes, apply pressure to the injury. Be careful not to do this for too long as it can damage the skin. The cold can provide some pain relief and limits swelling by reducing blood flow to the injured area.
- Compression – use pressure to hold the ice pack on the injury. This also limits swelling and may sometimes provide pain relief.
- Elevation – raise the injury, e.g. often the ankle or knee, and keep it raised. If possible keep the area at or above the level of the injured person's heart as this will help minimise the swelling.

Performance-enhancing drugs (PEDS)

A drug is a substance that can be taken in a variety of ways to produce expected and welcome physical and/or psychological effects on the person taking it, but may also cause some effects that are both unpleasant and unwanted. These are known as side effects.

All drugs have side effects. A side effect of some drugs is that they are addictive; this is as true of nicotine (cigarettes) and alcohol as it is of heroin and cocaine. If a person becomes addicted to using drugs it is very difficult to give up. Most drugs have physical side effects, which can range from high blood pressure to insomnia.

Performance-enhancing drugs can enhance a person's performance in some way, either in physical activity and training, or in daily life. They include some drugs that are socially acceptable and many that are illegal.

Performance-enhancing drugs include:

- anabolic steroids
- beta blockers
- diuretics
- narcotic analgesics
- peptide hormones, including erythropoietin/EPO
- growth hormones
- stimulants.

In addition, **blood doping** is a process which aims to boost performance.

Why do people take performance-enhancing drugs?

Some people take drugs to enhance or improve their performance, or are encouraged to do so by their coaches or fellow athletes. The temptation to do this is great as the rewards of success can be high; winning an Olympic gold medal in some sports is said to be worth a million dollars in endorsements.

Key term

Blood doping: an illegal attempt to improve performance in sporting events. This happens by artificially increasing the number of red blood cells in the bloodstream, boosting the blood's ability to bring oxygen to the muscles.

Professionals who compete at the highest levels can make a lot of money. Some athletes might take drugs so they can compete at a higher level than they would otherwise have reached.

Another incentive is that the competitive life of a professional sportsperson is comparatively short, and so they must become well known enough and earn enough money to be able to live comfortably after their competitive life has finished.

In recent years it has been proven or alleged that competitors in athletics, cycling, swimming, association football, weightlifting, American football, basketball, skiing and the World's Strongest Man competition, as well as other sports, have taken banned substances.

Anabolic steroids

Anabolic steroids are reputed to be the drugs most commonly used to enhance performance in sport. They mimic the male hormone testosterone and have the effects of deepening the voice and causing the growth of facial hair – side effects that are, of course, most noticeable in women. Anabolic steroids increase muscle mass and develop bone growth, therefore increasing strength while at the same time allowing the athlete to train harder and recover quicker. The other attraction is that they produce results quickly. Some people believe that over a long period of time the same effects can be gained legally using good training methods and correct nutrition.

Dwain Chambers, a British 100m sprinter lost his European relay gold medal in 2002 after being found guilty of taking steroids. When he returned to athletics after being banned for two years, many experts debated whether his performance was still being enhanced as a result of the steroids he had taken, giving him an unfair advantage.

Steroids also increase aggression.

The side effects of anabolic steroids include:

- increased risk of heart attacks and strokes
- high blood pressure
- liver disease
- increased risk of muscle injury
- infertility in women
- death.

It is important not to take any restricted drug that has not been specifically prescribed for you by a doctor.

> **Key term**
>
> **Anabolic steroids:** drugs that mimic the male sex hormone testosterone and promote bone and muscle growth.

> **Apply it**
>
> Identify three different sports in which the development of muscular strength is very important. Explain the reasons for your answer to a partner.

Fitness and Body Systems

Beta blockers

These drugs are commonly prescribed for people with heart problems as they maintain a low heart rate and lower blood pressure. As a result, stress levels and anxiety are reduced.

Beta blockers can help in target sports where steadiness and precision are required, because they reduce the heart rate. They are banned in many sports where steadiness is essential, such as snooker, archery, shooting and curling, as well as in sports such as gymnastics and ski jumping, and control sports such as motor cycling. Beta blockers can reduce a fit person's heart rate to a dangerous level.

The side effects of beta blockers include:

- nausea and diarrhoea
- tiredness
- depression
- insomnia and nightmares.

Diuretics

Diuretics are used to increase the amount of urine produced and to increase kidney function, so speeding up the elimination of fluid from the body. This can help performers who need to lose weight, for example, boxers or jockeys. Diuretics may also be taken in an attempt to reduce the concentration of any other banned substance that may be present in the urine.

The side effects of diuretics include:

- dehydration, which can cause dizziness, muscle cramps, headaches and nausea
- long-term effects, such as kidney problems.

Narcotics and analgesics

Injuries can be a problem for many sportspeople. They want to compete, not sit and watch from the sidelines. As a result, many are prepared to take drugs so they can return to competition as quickly as possible. **Narcotics** and **analgesics** help them do this. Drugs in this category include heroin, methadone, pethidine and, the powerful painkiller, morphine.

These drugs act by depressing the central nervous system and give relief from painful injuries, but by allowing the injured player to take part, they can increase the risk of severe or long-lasting injury. This is one reason why they are banned; the other is that they can have dangerous side effects. Some are only available on prescription whereas some narcotics/ analgesics are not legally available at all.

The side effects of narcotics/analgesics include:

- loss of concentration
- loss of balance
- loss of co-ordination
- emotional effects, including hallucinations (morphine).

Peptide hormones, including erythropoietin (EPO)

We all produce hormones naturally but they can also be produced unnaturally by drugs. High doses are sometimes taken by athletes to increase muscle development. Human growth hormone (HGH) is now used by some athletes for this reason. Athletes are tested at regular intervals for the use of steroids, but HGH is a comparatively new drug that is being used to gain advantage. It is also thought to have fewer side effects than steroids. Although there is no urine test for HGH it can be detected through a blood test.

Peptide hormones are often used to produce the same effects as anabolic steroids, namely, to increase muscle growth, and to assist in recovery from injury and heavy training sessions. The specific performance-enhancing quality of these drugs is that they increase the number of red blood cells, allowing the body to carry extra oxygen, and disperse waste products and lactic acid.

Erythropoietin (EPO) is used to treat people with anaemia as it increases the production of red blood cells and therefore the amount of haemoglobin available to take up oxygen. This effect increases aerobic capacity, which is useful in, for example, long-distance running and cycling events.

One of the problems with EPO is that it thickens the blood, a condition which also occurs as a result of dehydration. This makes it much more difficult for blood to pass through the small capillaries and increases the risk of a heart attack or stroke. An accurate urine test has been in use since the 2004 Olympic Games in Athens to detect synthetic EPO.

Growth hormones

Growth hormone (GH) is used by some athletes to increase their muscle development. Athletes are tested at regular intervals to check for the use of steroids, but GH is used to gain the same advantage. There are also thought to be fewer side effects with GH than if an athlete uses steroids. Although there is no urine test for GH, it can be detected by a blood test.

> **Exam tip**
>
> Remember that GH stands for growth hormone. It is important that you understand the reasons why some sportspeople may use it – to build muscle – and the reasons why sportspeople should not use it – banned substances, possible side effects, unfair competitive advantage.

> **Exam-style question**
>
> Give an event other than shot putting at which athletes using GH would be at an advantage. **(1 mark)**

Fitness and Body Systems

Stimulants

Stimulants are the second most commonly used drugs in sport. This group of drugs includes amphetamines, ephedrine and cocaine, as well as nicotine and caffeine.

The latter two drugs are very common, and many people take them regularly. They increase alertness, enabling people to think more quickly by stimulating the **central nervous system** (CNS). Using these drugs helps to overcome tiredness. They are especially useful to offset the effects of lactic acid on muscles.

The side effects of stimulants include:

- insomnia
- irritability
- irregular heart beat
- increased heart rate
- high blood pressure
- addiction – some stimulants, such as amphetamines, are highly addictive.

Blood doping

Blood doping is a banned process – not a banned drug. Blood doping involves boosting the number of red blood cells in the bloodstream in order to improve your performance. Because red blood cells carry oxygen to the muscles, having a higher concentration of these cells in your blood can improve your VO_2 max (your aerobic capacity) and so increase your endurance.

For many years, people have known that if an athlete trains at high altitude the oxygen-carrying capacity of their blood increases. For this reason, athletes born – or raised – at high altitude have had a distinct advantage in the endurance events such as the 10,000 metres.

Knowing this, some athletes train at high altitude for a time, then have as much as two pints of blood taken from their body (rather like a blood donor) and their red blood cells frozen. The body's system soon recovers, and the normal eight pints of blood is restored. When it is getting close to the time for a big competition, the red blood cells are unfrozen and put back into the athlete's bloodstream – a process thought to increase their performance by as much as 20 per cent.

Blood doping is banned by the International Olympic Committee (IOC) and a number of other sports organisations.

3.6 Effective use of warm up and cool down

Getting started

It is vital that you should warm up before exercise and cool down afterwards.

- Have you ever done exercise from cold, without warming up?
- Why do you think body temperature is important?
- What sorts of exercises have you used in warm ups and cool downs – and for which parts of the body?

Investigate two warm up and two cool down programmes for different fitness classes. What are the similarities and the differences?

Learning objectives

By the end of this section you will understand:

- the purpose and importance of warm ups and cool downs to effective training
- the phases and activities included in warm ups and cool downs.

Purpose and importance of warm ups and cool downs

A training session, match or competition should always be split into three sections, performed in the same logical order:

- warm up
- main activity
- cool down.

Warm up – purpose and importance

The warm up gradually raises body temperature and heart rate and improves the delivery of oxygen from haemoglobin. A warm up is essential to:

- prevent injury
- improve performance
- practise skills before the event, match or game
- prepare psychologically for the event.

A warm up should provide a smooth transition from rest to the intensity of the main activity or competitive situation. For example, in football the first sprint should be during the warm up, not the match! This applies equally to all games, players and athletes.

Cool down – purpose and importance

As the warm up gradually raises heart rate and body temperature to the level necessary for the activity, so the cool down gradually returns the body to its normal resting heart rate and temperature.

Fitness and Body Systems

Link it up

Topic 1, Section 1.3 covers the production of lactic acid.

Every training session and competitive situation should finish with a cool down, but this is especially important after an anaerobic workout. Cooling down properly is important as it disperses lactic acid – the poison produced during exercise – and the cool down helps to prevent stiffness and soreness in the muscles.

Phases and activities for warm ups and cool downs

Warm up – phases and activities

Cardiovascular

Every training or exercise session or competitive situation should start with a cardiovascular warm up, to gradually raise the heart rate towards the working heart rate. The cardiovascular warm up can take various forms, depending on the main activity, but can include cycling on a static bicycle (often used by rugby teams), skipping, swimming or, more usually, easy jogging and walking.

Apply it

What warm up rituals do you use? Investigate other rituals used by athletes or teams. Discuss your findings in a group.

This part of the warm up usually takes between 10 and 15 minutes depending on the person and the activity. International athletes preparing for a competition usually take much longer. During this time they also prepare psychologically for the competitive situation they are about to take part in. Many use music to help their motivation.

Warm up routines and rituals help you prepare for the main event, physically and psychologically

Stretching

Stretching forms the second phase of the warm up.

There are two main sorts of stretching:

- static stretching – easy, on-the-spot stretches that are held without straining
- dynamic stretching – stretches that use movements specific to a sport, gradually increasing your reach and speed.

Dynamic stretching will also help you with your emotional/psychological preparation for the game/competition ahead and will also help to prevent injury as they are more like the game situation.

Athletes and swimmers may prepare on their own, and a tennis player may have their coach to warm up with them, but footballers and rugby players normally warm up as a team

Some people start with static stretching, but warming up with dynamic stretches will prepare your body for the movements you are about to experience in the game situation. Some athletes like to follow the same ritual every time they compete.

Stretching is usually done starting at the top of the body and working down to the ankles and feet. You should pay extra attention to the areas used in your particular sport – for example, neck and shoulders for some positions in rugby.

It is recommended that your stretching should be related to the activity and your role. For example, if the game is football, most players would stretch the gastrocnemius, hamstrings and quadriceps, but the goalkeeper would also need to include some specialist exercises, of a gymnastic nature. A swimmer would include stretches specific to the stroke or strokes that they are about to perform, so they would do more specific upper body stretches than a midfield player in football or a netball shooter.

Specific skills practices

The final phase of the warm up will be to practise the skills of the activity, such as:

- sprint starts for a 100-metre runner to get used to driving out of the starting blocks
- practice throws for a discus, shot, hammer or javelin thrower
- take-off practice runs for the pole vaulters, high jumpers, long jumpers and triple jumpers.

Apply it

Investigate further examples of cardiovascular exercises used in warm ups.

Apply it

Investigate two further stretches used in warm ups.

- volleys, forehand and backhand shots for racket players
- catching, bowling, throwing and batting for cricketers
- catching crosses and shots and throwing the ball out for goalkeepers in football.

Cool down – phases and activities

Activities similar to those used in the warm up, such as jogging, can be used to return the heart rate gradually to its resting level. The cool down takes about 5–10 minutes to return the heart rate to normal, depending on the activity. This is usually followed by 10–15 minutes of stretching, although, as with the warm up, many athletes take much longer than this. The static stretches in the cool down are held for about 30–35 seconds, and they should start at the top and work systematically downwards.

Relaxation exercises should finish the session, especially if the main activity has been of high intensity. This relaxation should last for 10–15 minutes; quiet music is sometimes used during these exercises. Relaxation exercises could start in a sitting position, with legs crossed as in yoga, with some breathing exercises, and continue lying down flexing and relaxing muscles for 20 seconds, again in sequence starting from the neck and shoulders.

In some exercise classes, particularly yoga, participants may be asked to imagine they are on a nice sandy beach on a lovely sunny day listening to the waves rippling on the beach, feeling heavy, relaxed, calm and peaceful. This helps to relieve stress and tension and leads to a sense of well-being – one of the most important benefits of exercise for many people.

Exam tip

Make sure that you include example activities that are relevant to the game given here – basketball.

Exam-style question

Complete the table below, giving an example of an activity associated with each phase of a warm up that would be suitable before a basketball game (or a game of your choice). **(3 marks)**

Phase	Example activity
Increase heart rate	
Stretching	
Drills (more intense exercise)	

Summary

Key points to remember:

Health and fitness

- Health – a state of complete emotional/psychological, physical and social well-being
- Exercise – physical activity that maintains or improves health and fitness
- Fitness – ability to meet the demands of an environment
- Performance – how well a task is done

Components of fitness

- Five basic health-related: cardiovascular, muscular strength, muscular endurance, flexibility, body composition (measured with **BMI**)
- Six skill-related: agility, balance, co-ordination, power, reaction time, speed (**ABCPRS**)
- Fitness tests – different tests measure different fitness components

Principles of training

- Four key principles:
  - individual needs – first point for planning a programme
  - specificity – match training to the requirements of an activity
  - progressive overload – gradually increase overload to gain fitness safely
  - FITT – frequency, intensity, time, type
- Rest and recovery – vital for adaptation
- Thresholds of training help you improve without injury, calculated by:
  - target zones
  - Karvonen formula
- Choose right method:
  - requirements of sport
  - local facilities
  - current fitness level
- Methods of training
  - continuous
  - fartlek
  - circuit
  - interval
  - plyometrics
  - weight/resistance

Long-term effects of exercise

- Musculo-skeletal system – higher bone density, stronger ligaments/tendons, muscle hypertrophy
- Cardio-respiratory system – heart, blood, lungs, diaphragm

Optimising training

- Before starting, do a PAR-Q – physical activity readiness questionnaire
- Prevent injury – train correctly, warm up and cool down, use protective equipment/clothing, check equipment, play to the rules
- Understand and avoid common injuries
- Understand and avoid performance-enhancing drugs

Effective warm up and cool down

- Warm up can:
  - prevent injury
  - improve performance
  - practise skills
  - prepare you psychologically
- Phases for warm up and cool down
  - cardiovascular
  - stretching
  - (skills practice for warm up)
  - (relaxation for cool down).

Preparing for your exam: Component 1 Fitness and Body Systems

The Edexcel GCSE (9–1) Physical Education consists of two externally examined papers. This section of the book has been designed to help you prepare for the exam paper covering Component 1.

Overview of the exam paper

Component 1 covers all the topics related to Fitness and Body Systems. The written exam will be 1 hour and 45 minutes and will be out of 90 marks. This component will be worth 36 per cent of your final marks.

The assessment will include multiple-choice, short-answer and extended writing questions. Short-answer questions will be worth two, three or four marks each. You must answer all questions.

There will be two nine-mark extended writing questions. You should make sure you allow enough time to complete these – try to spend at least 15 minutes on each of these questions to plan and write your answer as well as checking over all your answers at the end.

Exam strategy

You will be assessed in this written paper against three objectives. The questions will target one, two or even all three of these assessment objectives. Short answers, or questions that carry fewer marks, tend to focus on AO1. The higher value questions, particularly the essay questions will include a mixture of AO1-3 content. Table 1.14 explains what you need to focus on to succeed in meeting each objective.

A01	Demonstrate knowledge and understanding of the factors that underpin performance and involvement in physical activity and sport. *This could be simple recall of facts, definitions or descriptions relating to the question.*
A02	Apply knowledge and understanding of the factors that underpin performance and involvement in physical activity and sport. *This is where you need to link your knowledge and understanding specifically to the question. This may mean providing an appropriate example.*
A03	Analyse and evaluate the factors that underpin performance and involvement in physical activity and sport. *This is where you will demonstrate higher order thinking – you may make a judgement about the question or draw a conclusion based on the facts you have discussed.*

Table 1.14 Assessment objectives

You should aim to develop all the skills required in these objectives at the start of your course. The nine-mark questions, in particular, will require **linkage** of points to show the required level of development.

Preparing for your exam

Table 1.15 shows a selection of words and phrases, called '**connective words**', which you can practise using in your answers. Using these kinds of words indicates to the examiner that you are carefully linking your thoughts to make a well-argued point.

Look out for examples of these connective words and how they are used in the student responses later in this section. They are highlighted in yellow.

Connective words	When to use?
also, equally, likewise, similarly	To compare and discuss
after a while, at once, firstly, next, since, while, finally, later, last, now, eventually, subsequently, then, when, soon, thereafter, meanwhile, ultimately, presently	To show time or sequence
in other words, for example, for instance, in order to, to illustrate, as a result, that is to say, to be specific, such as, moreover, furthermore, just as important, similarly	To explain
and, also, another, besides, further, furthermore, too, moreover, in addition, then, equally important	To add another idea to your point
accordingly, as a result, so, as a consequence, consequently, since, therefore, for this reason, because of this, in case	To show results
to this end, for this purpose, therefore, with this in mind, for this reason(s)	To show cause
first, firstly, second, secondly (etc.), finally, next, then, from here on, to begin with, last of all, for one thing, after, before, as soon as, in the end, gradually, to conclude	To show order or sequence
alternatively, anyway, but, by contrast, conversely, however, still, nevertheless, yet, and yet, on the other hand, on the contrary, or, in spite of this, actually, in fact, although, whereas	To talk about the differences between ideas
in summary, to sum up, in summation, briefly, finally, on the whole, therefore, as I have said, in conclusion, as you can see	To summarise

Table 1.15 Connective words

Look at a practical example of how the connective words can help you build an answer. In the example shown in Figure 1.36 you are asked to explain how safety equipment can reduce injury.

Think of your answer like building blocks.

Using the building blocks and connective words you may then come up with an answer like this:

Hockey is potentially a dangerous sport played with a hard ball and stick. A hockey player wears a gum shield **in order to** protect their teeth and gums **in case** the ball strikes their mouth or the hockey stick is raised too high. **As a result**, the player will be protected from losing teeth or bleeding gums.

Now let's look at examples of some questions and responses of the kind you may find in your exam paper.

Hockey

High stick/hard ball

Gum shield

Protects teeth

Figure 1.36 How can safety equipment reduce injury?

Component 1, Question 4

Explain the importance of reaction time for the performers competing in the two types of activity below.

(4 marks)

Badminton

200-metre runner

Exam tip

There are two marks available for each sport in the question. Make sure you give an example of when reaction time is needed in each sport and a reason why. The command word in the question 'explain' tells you this is what is needed. 'Explain' will always expect some linked reasoning in your answer. For more information about 'command words' in exam questions, see Preparing for your exam: Component 2 Health and Performance on page 176.

Average answer

Badminton
❶ *A badminton player needs fast reaction time to return the shuttle when it is smashed at him.*

200-metre runner
A 200-metre runner needs good reaction time at the start of the race.

❶ *Identifies an example of when reaction time is used by a badminton player and when it is required by a 200-metre runner.*

Verdict

This question targets assessment objectives A01 and A02. It is an average answer because while two valid examples are given there is no explanation of why they are necessary.

A01. The student **knows and understands** the need for reaction time and provides a valid example.

A02. The student **has not applied** the knowledge. There is no link between the example provided and why this is important.

Connective words have been highlighted in the sample answer to demonstrate how they help the student structure and develop their points.

Strong answer

Badminton
❶ *A fast reaction time is vital in badminton because the shuttle travels at high speed, for example, when defending a smash, ❷ so there is little time to make an effective decision.*

❶ *200-metre runner*
A 200-metre runner needs to react quickly to the starter's gun in order to ❷ get a head start in the race and not be left behind.

❶ *Identifies a valid example for both badminton and running and also an explanation of ❷ its importance in each activity.*

Verdict

This is a strong answer because both parts contain a valid example and an explanation of why it is important.

A01. The student **knows and understands** the need for reaction time and provides a valid example.

A02. The student **has applied** the knowledge. There are clear links between the examples provided and why these are important.

Component 1, Question 18

The ability to identify and reduce risks associated with physical activities is essential to minimise injuries.

Discuss how to reduce a variety of risks associated with team game activities in order to maintain physical health. **(9 marks)**

Exam tip

Read the question! This sounds obvious but the question is related to **team game activities** so avoid reference to individual sports, e.g. wearing a helmet when skiing or cycling. Look for the 'command' word – in this case 'discuss'. This means you should explore the issue that is being assessed in the question, expressing different or contrasting viewpoints.

Again, some of the connective words used in the sample answer have been highlighted.

Student answer

❶ There are many ways that risks associated with games activities such as football can be reduced although in a contact sport these can never be eliminated altogether.

❷ Firstly, protective clothing and equipment can reduce injuries. For example, wearing shin pads will protect the tibia bone at the front of the shin from any late, 'over the top' or forceful tackles where the studs from football boots could inflict a fractured tibia without this protection. In cricket, batsmen wear helmets in order to protect the cranium and minimise the risk of concussion from being struck by a bouncer by fast bowlers. In spite of this, the equipment can only provide limited protection,

❸ as can be seen from the tragic death of Australian cricketer Phillip Hughes. He was struck by a ball which missed the helmet behind his neck. Helmets have since been redesigned to give further protection at the neck. There is also a thought that wearing protective equipment can sometimes make players take more risks as they believe they are invincible.

❹ Secondly, rules are often put in place with safety in mind. In football, tackles from behind are outlawed to protect players from damaging or tearing their Achilles tendon or fracturing their fibula from strong tackles from this position.

❶ Good introduction – draws the reader in.

❷ Accurate examples and descriptions of how protective equipment can prevent injury.

❸ There is some very good analysis of the issue here. This is AO3 material. Excellent example provided of how risks cannot be totally eliminated.

❹ More relevant material from a different angle supported again with developed points.

High feet are also not allowed to protect players from head injuries such as gashes to the forehead following studs being raised for the ball or a fractured cranium from high challenges with boots.

5 In addition, referees should also check the playing surface before a game. If it is frozen then players could easily fall under a challenge, hit their head on the frozen ground and sustain concussion. Objects may also be on the pitch such as glass which could inflict a gash to the knee during a slide tackle or if the player fell to the ground.

6 Finally, warming up can reduce the chance of injury. A three-stage warm up comprising a pulse raiser followed by stretches and then some skill-based practices such as passing, dribbling and shooting can increase the temperature and elasticity of muscles. This will help reduce injuries such as a torn hamstring following a sprint down the wing in the early stages of the game because the muscles are warm and stretched and should not pull with the sudden change in pace. However, sometimes a sportsperson such as a rugby player can be so psychologically prepared and motivated during the warm up that they put themselves at risk in the early stages of the game with reckless tackles and this can cause unnecessary injury as well as reduced performance levels.

Games activities will never be 100% safe but these measures will help reduce the number of injuries.

5 More accurate valid points and good use of connective words to structure the argument.

6 Further analysis and evaluation worthy of AO3 credit here – how warming up and being over motivated could have negative impact on safety and performance.

Verdict

This is a high level response.

AO1. The student **knows and understands** the different safety measures designed to reduce injury. The ability to recall them, define them and describe them are evidenced with many accurate examples provided.

AO2. The student **applies** the different safety measures in different contexts and settings. The student has clearly **linked** their knowledge and understanding to the question. Each risk has been linked to an injury or possible scenario showing good understanding of the question.

AO3. The student has **analysed and evaluated** the question. For example, recognising that protective equipment cannot always fully protect players, and that protective clothing can make players more reckless. It provides a good example of how protective clothing cannot always eliminate the risks. There is also some analysis of warming up and how being over motivated can be detrimental to performance. Although not essential there is also a brief conclusion.

2 Health and Performance

Topic 1 Health, fitness and well-being

1.1 Physical, emotional and social health, fitness and well-being

Getting started

Think about what people get out of doing sport, apart from feeling physically fit.

- Why do interviewers always ask sportspeople how they feel after an event?
- Which famous sportspeople can you think of who seem happiest with their achievements?
- What can happen when someone gets too 'into' their sport?

Research three sportspeople who say sport is the most important thing in their life. What reasons do they give for this?

Learning objectives

By the end of this section you will understand:

- how increasing physical ability can improve health and reduce health risks
- how taking part in sport can improve emotional health
- how taking part in sport can improve social health
- the impacts of fitness on well-being – both positive and negative
- how to use a Personal Exercise Programme (PEP) to promote personal health
- lifestyle choices and their impact on health, fitness and well-being.

Exercise and physical activity help to improve cardiovascular fitness, increase muscular strength and muscular endurance, improve body composition and flexibility and tone muscles, all of which can:

- increase fitness
- contribute to good health
- help the individual feel good
- help relieve stress, and prevent stress-related illness
- increase self-esteem and confidence
- contribute to enjoyment of life
- provide an emotional/psychological challenge.

Recent research has discovered a clear link between physical activity and increased brain function. Higher levels of aerobic fitness in children have been found to benefit brain function, and improve children's levels of achievement at school. Evidence also suggests that physical activity has an impact on the physical structure of the brain.

Some of the benefits of improving fitness are physical (for example, increasing cardiovascular fitness or contributing to good health), while others relate to our psychological or emotional well-being.

Health and Performance

The benefits of increased fitness on our physical health

You have seen how taking part in sport and physical activity can improve each aspect of Health Related Exercise (HRE), cardiovascular fitness, body composition, muscular strength, muscular endurance and flexibility. A programme of planned, well thought-out exercises, resistance training and sport participation is a good way to achieve increased fitness. Muscles can be strengthened, becoming more toned in the process.

Practice

You will have to plan your PEP and decide which aspects of HRE to include in your programme.

Your physical health will improve in different ways according to what you plan in your training programme. For example, if your programme has a lot of cardiovascular work, such as running, swimming or cycling this will improve your cardiovascular health, which is the most important aspect of fitness.

Cardiovascular fitness

Exercise improves the cardiovascular system, and helps to reduce resting blood pressure. Improving cardiovascular fitness will reduce the risk of cardiovascular disease, including coronary heart disease (CHD) and stroke. It should also make it easier for you to cope with your normal, daily routine.

The number of times your heart beats per minute (bpm) is related to your fitness level; for an average adult this might mean a resting rate of 72–75 bpm but an elite marathon runner could have a resting heart rate as low as 35–40 bpm. A lower resting heart rate is more efficient and places less stress on the heart.

With training, the heart muscle increases in size, thickness and strength, the chambers increase in volume, and the whole heart gets bigger, allowing it to work harder for longer.

Link it up

For more information on cardiovascular fitness see Component 1, Topic 1, Section 3.2

Physical activity such as hockey can help to improve cardiovascular fitness

Body composition

For some people, physical activity helps with weight control. Maintaining a healthy body weight reduces the risk of obesity and type 2 diabetes.

Exercising and playing sport expends energy, which uses up calories. This can contribute to weight control, although this is most effective when combined with a calorie controlled diet.

Muscular strength and muscular endurance

Strength training can also help to improve general health and fitness by building strength or muscular endurance – or both. Strength training and weight-bearing exercise, including walking, have been shown to strengthen the muscles and prevent loss of bone density or low bone mass. Both men and women can suffer from this which is a symptom of **osteoporosis**, where the bones become brittle. Those with osteoporosis – especially older people – have a greater risk of fractures, especially of the hip, spinal vertebrae and wrist.

When you do weight training – the main way to increase strength – you can use heavy weights and few repetitions to increase your muscular strength, and you can use light weights with many repetitions to increase your muscular endurance.

Other health benefits

People who are physically fit may also be able to fight off illness more effectively than those who do little exercise. This applies not only to a common cold or flu, but also, many scientists believe, to serious illness such as a heart attack, stroke and conditions such as type II diabetes. Some research has shown that exercise can reduce the risk of some cancers.

The ability to withstand and recover from illness is related to fitness, so exercise and sport contribute to good health, increasing your chances of living a healthy and active life for longer.

> **Exam-style question** ⬤
>
> Taking part in physical activity on a regular basis can reduce the risk of heart disease and high blood pressure.
>
> Explain one other health risk that can be reduced through long-term physical activity.
>
> **(3 marks)**

Effects of physical activity on emotional health

There are many examples of how taking part in sport or other physical activity can improve your emotional health.

Feeling good

Many people take part in physical activity, play sport or embark on an exercise programme because they want to feel good. Exercise produces

> **Link it up**
>
> Consider linking your PEP to your diet: for example, limiting the amount of fat you eat but eating more protein and carbohydrates.

> **Key term**
>
> **Osteoporosis**: a condition causing the bones to become brittle and fragile from loss of tissue, resulting from hormone changes, or a deficiency in calcium or vitamin D.

> **Apply it**
>
> Research how people with diabetes can benefit from physical activity and sport.

> **Exam tip** ⬤
>
> When you have a question like this, think of the sports that you play and the health benefits they give you. This can prompt ideas for your answer.

Health and Performance

Many people enjoy fitness classes because they boost their mood and help them to unwind

serotonin – a 'feel-good' chemical in your body – so exercise is not just 'physically' beneficial but also emotionally good for you. Regular physical activity improves fitness and body shape, and helps you to feel better about yourself; for people with low self-esteem this can be a real boost.

Relieving stress and tension

Physical activities can provide a distraction from the problems of daily life, and can relieve stress and tension caused by work, school and family pressures. Although exercise itself cannot solve problems or remove pressures, it can make them easier to deal with. When we exercise our brains produce **endorphins**. These are chemicals in the brain that, like serotonin, are another of your body's natural 'feel-good' chemicals.

Increasing self-esteem and confidence

Many activities provide a physical challenge. Overcoming such a challenge gives a sense of achievement, which can lead to an increase in self-esteem and confidence.

For example, it is difficult to train for and complete a triathlon. If you succeed, the sense of achievement improves your self-esteem. You are then likely to have more confidence taking on other challenging tasks.

For enjoyment

Most people who exercise and play sport do so because they enjoy it. Take a look at the players at your local sports centre or tennis courts – they are there because they want to be. Playing for a team, or exercising in a group can be social and a chance for you to spend time with friends.

How you enjoy exercise or physical activity can be affected by the reason why you are taking part. It may be compulsory to take part in PE at school or there might be sports you do not enjoy playing. Others are highly competitive and want to win; some take part because they know it is good for general health and well-being.

For an emotional/psychological challenge

Many sporting activities provide an emotional/psychological as well as a physical challenge. For example, the Yorkshire Three Peaks Challenge involves climbing three mountains in the Pennines in Yorkshire. It is a tough physical challenge, but it is an equally tough emotional/psychological challenge – the thought of covering a large distance with over 2000m of ascent and descent can be daunting, especially for someone who has not completed such a challenge before.

Challenging yourself can boost your confidence

For aesthetic appreciation

Aesthetic appreciation means enjoying something because it is pleasing to look at: for example, as an observer rather than a participant.

Moments in sport are sometimes beautiful, although this aspect of sport may not always be appreciated as much as winning. Beauty may be seen in a brilliantly executed goal or a save in football, a try in rugby, a jump shot in basketball, a smash in badminton, a cover drive in cricket or a delicate chip in golf.

Often it is the observer who appreciates the performer, although hitting a cover drive in cricket can feel brilliant. Sports such as figure skating or gymnastics are often thought of in these terms.

Apply it

In a small group, each choose a different example of a physical activity, and use it to explain the benefits of taking part in sport. Make the case for your chosen activity, using images, video or news stories to illustrate your points.

Exam-style question

Which of the following statements describes an **emotional/psychological** benefit of exercise?

(a) Playing in a team with all your friends.

(b) Running to improve your fitness.

(c) Praise and support from your coach.

(d) A goalkeeper needs to be agile.

(1 mark)

Exam tip

If you are not sure of the answer straight away work out what each statement describes to try to eliminate each one until you get the correct answer. For example, (a) playing in a team with all your friends is a 'social' benefit.

Health and Performance

Effects of physical activity on social health

As well as having benefits for you as an individual, taking part in physical activity can bring benefits that come from working as a team, competing and being with others. These aspects relate to **social health** – the ability to interact with others, adapt to social situations and form relationships.

These benefits include:

- co-operation
- developing friendships and mixing socially
- gaining a good attitude to competing, learning how to win and lose.

Most activities offer an opportunity to gain one or more of these benefits.

Co-operation

Many sports are played in teams. Working in groups helps to improve teamwork and co-operation, which are often necessary in everyday life. Netball, football, rugby and hockey are all good examples of team sports where it is important to support and encourage your team mates, and work together for a common purpose.

Team members often spend a lot of time together – for example, on tours or when taking part in competitions – so it is important for them to get along with each other. This is also true at your local club, where you train together as well as play as a team.

Developing friendships and mixing socially

Taking part in exercise or sport at school or at a club means involvement with other people, including fellow participants, coaches, trainers and officials. Participants get to know more people, make new friends and often develop lasting friendships.

Consider your own team experience and how your team works together

How many of your friends have you met through playing sport?

Most activities also offer you the opportunity to mix with each other off the sports field – for example, through club and social events.

Gaining a good attitude to competing

To compete well in sport, you need to have a strong sense of self, but there is a social aspect to competition too. When you are competing against another team or player, you need to learn to respect your opponent and to cope with both success and failure graciously. Doing this well can help your social health, as it helps you manage relationships with others better.

> **Apply it**
>
> Think about a sport or activity that you do with other people. List the social health benefits you have gained from this.

> **Exam-style question** ⬤
>
> Which of the following is not a social benefit of taking part in sport?
>
> (a) Joining the local kayaking team.
>
> (b) Becoming a volunteer for the local diving club.
>
> (c) Always being able to see the beauty of the performance.
>
> (d) Competing in a local charity run to raise money.
>
> **(1 mark)**

> **Exam tip** ⬤
>
> 'Social' usually means doing something with others.

The impact of fitness on well-being

Fitness is our ability to meet the demands of the environment, while **well-being** can be defined as being comfortable, healthy and happy, so impacting on emotional/psychological health and happiness.

How does fitness contribute to your well-being? Table 2.1 shows that there are both positive and negative effects.

> **Key term**
>
> **Well-being**: the state of being comfortable, healthy or happy.

Health and Performance

Positive effects	Negative effects
• Helps you cope with the physical side of life • Even moderate exercise improves **longevity** – how long you will live • Lowers risk of psychological illness • Lowers risk of eating problems • Makes you less likely to use drugs or smoke • Means you are less likely to be off work with sickness • Gives you a lower resting heart rate and lower blood pressure • Can help weight control • Gives you stronger bones • Improves your body composition	• Puts you at risk of sport-related injury • Time off to recover from injury can lead to psychological problems • Competition pressure can lead to psychological problems • Early specialisation in one sport can reduce other opportunities • Stresses and needs of a particular sport can lead to long-term health problems • Can lead to obsessive interest in body shape or composition

Table 2.1. Effects of fitness on well-being – positive and negative

Promoting personal health through a Personal Exercise Programme

So far in your course you have learned a lot of the theory of physical education. Much of the theory is related to human anatomy and physiology, fitness and training and improving fitness levels and performance in your sports.

Another important part of this course is understanding how to apply that knowledge to improve your personal fitness levels with a specific purpose in mind. You will need to demonstrate that you can plan, perform, monitor and evaluate a Personal Exercise Programme (PEP).

A PEP is a training programme designed to improve your personal fitness. This may be associated with any of the components of fitness, but for this exam it is more likely to be planned to improve one or more of the basic components. It should also be related to one or more of the basic components for the exam. For example, if you are playing football or netball, improved cardiovascular fitness is likely to improve your performance in the game situation; if you are doing the shot put in athletics, it will improve your strength. Your PEP could also include a diet plan, as well as how you plan to achieve a work-rest balance, to make sure you recover well before your next training session.

Creating your PEP is also a life skill, which should enable you to plan your fitness requirements for the rest of your life.

Link it up

For more information on how to plan, carry out, monitor and evaluate your PEP see Component 4.

Lifestyle choices

Apply it

Consider the following questions.

- How would you describe a balanced lifestyle?
- Do you think you have a balanced lifestyle?
- In what ways do you think your diet is healthy or unhealthy?

People often talk about having a healthy lifestyle, or making good or bad lifestyle choices. What sort of things does 'lifestyle' cover – and which areas are most important for people taking part in sport and physical activity?

Diet, activity level, work/rest/sleep balance, recreational drugs, smoking and alcohol all have a part to play in shaping your lifestyle. Making good choices in each of these areas will help to ensure your happiness and well-being, as well as keeping you physically fit.

Diet

Diet is an essential part of providing our bodies with the energy we need to work and exercise, and the nutrients required to repair body tissues. Getting the right energy balance is important: the number of calories in your diet should be the same as the number of calories you use through metabolic processes and physical activity.

Active people use more energy so they need more calories in their diet and more of the foods that provide them. A balanced diet is not just about calories and energy: it is about providing the body with all the nutrients it requires to work as effectively as possible.

Diet is a big and complex subject, but anyone interested in sport needs to know this topic and understand it well.

Activity level

People give different reasons for not doing exercise – or not doing enough. There are of course restrictions and excuses that can make it difficult to take part in physical activity on a regular basis. These include location and travel requirements, lack of access or facilities, the availability of particular sports, the cost of classes or equipment, involvement of friends and time.

These are all valid reasons but they can be overcome. Your activity level has a huge impact on your health and fitness.

Perhaps the most important factor is choice; choosing to be active and choosing your activity. You may want to play sport on a regular, yet informal basis or you may want to train to play at a competitive level.

Recording what you do and when helps maintain your activity level. When you plan your lifestyle choices, you can choose how you build exercise into the time you have available – for example, by doing sport with friends. You can also look at how you can overcome barriers such as location and time rather than letting them get in your way.

Health and Performance

Sleep should be an integral part of any training programme

Work/rest/sleep balance

Exercise should help you to sleep better and let your body recover, so that you will be ready to tackle what you have to do the next day. Exercise should help you to get to sleep faster when you go to bed and have a deeper, more productive sleep. However, it is important to make sure you do not exercise too late in the day or you may be too energised to fall asleep.

Rest is also an important aspect of training, as it allows your body time to recover and helps to build muscle.

Link it up

For more information on why rest and recovery are an important part of training and performing see Component 1, Topic 3, Section 3.3.

Recreational drugs

Recreational drugs are split into two categories. Firstly, **legal drugs** including:

- caffeine, found in tea, coffee, energy drinks and some fizzy drinks
- nicotine from smoking
- ethanol, more commonly known as alcohol.

Even though each of these can have negative effects on our bodies or our behaviour, these are all legal and accepted (smoking to a lesser extent) in our society.

Secondly, other forms of recreational drug, such as heroin, cocaine, LSD, amphetamines, barbiturates, cannabis or ecstasy are not accepted in society. These drugs have negative and harmful effects and can be highly dangerous, in some cases leading to death.

Smoking and nicotine

Most smokers take up the habit early in life.

As a teenager it is easy to think that you can try smoking and then stop. However, smoking is highly addictive. Within a short time, people who smoke start to develop cravings for cigarettes and experience withdrawal symptoms if they go too long without a cigarette. Because of these feelings, the amount they smoke increases.

The addictive ingredient in cigarettes is nicotine. Nicotine is a **stimulant** that raises alertness. As nicotine is an addictive drug, the more cigarettes people smoke, and the longer they smoke for, the harder it is for them to stop.

Key terms

Legal drugs: found in everyday products, such as caffeine, nicotine or alcohol.

Stimulant: a substance that raises the level of physiological or nervous activity in the body.

While nicotine creates addiction, smoking is extremely harmful. Not only will it impact on, and damage the respiratory system, it also increases the likelihood of diseases, such as cancer and heart disease.

Because of the damage that smoking can cause to others as 'second-hand smoke' it has been banned in all enclosed public places and within the workplace since 2007. In efforts to reduce the number of people smoking, the government increased the legal age for buying tobacco products from 16 years old to 18 years old.

Alcohol

While caffeine is a stimulant, which makes you more alert, alcohol is a **depressant**: it slows your reactions down and alters the way you see, hear, move and respond to things. A small amount of alcohol can make you feel more relaxed and less anxious; larger amounts can make you drunk, as it causes greater changes in your brain. Drinking alcohol before sport or exercise and directly afterwards is not advised because of the effect it has on your body.

Alcohol is banned in sports, such as shooting or archery, where it may be used as a **sedative** to produce a calming effect. It is also banned in sports where it is considered a safety risk, such as motor sports, because it slows down your reaction times and impairs your judgement.

Positive and negative impacts of lifestyle choices

All the **lifestyle choices** you make – from what you have for breakfast to when you go to bed – have an impact on your health and well-being. It is important that you think about the positive and negative impacts of your choices, so that you can maintain as healthy a balance as possible.

The effects of smoking

As you would expect, there is no positive impact of smoking, but there are many harmful effects on your health. Stopping smoking does reduce the risk of these, and the earlier a person stops, the better it is for their health. Cardiovascular exercise and improvements in cardiovascular fitness can also reduce the risk of these factors.

Shortness of breath/reduced lung capacity

Taking oxygen into the body and expelling carbon dioxide through gaseous exchange are the vital requirements of the respiratory system. Smoking can have serious adverse effects on this process. Smoke damages the lungs and especially the alveoli, making them less stretchy and less efficient. As a result, it becomes more difficult to get oxygen in and carbon dioxide out, and smokers may become short of breath. Their hearts have to work harder to get the oxygen their bodies need and as a result they feel tired.

Heart disease

Tobacco smoke is a major risk factor of heart disease. Smoking lowers the levels of **high-density lipoprotein cholesterol** (HDL), sometimes known as 'good' cholesterol, and increases the tendency for blood to clot, which can lead to acute illness, such as a heart attack or stroke.

> **Exam tip**
>
> Remember that it is nicotine that is the drug, not cigarettes.

> **Key terms**
>
> **Depressant**: a substance that lowers the level of physiological or nervous activity in the body.
>
> **Sedative**: a drug that has a calming or sleep-inducing effect.
>
> **Lifestyle choice**: the choices we make about how we live and behave that impact on our health.
>
> **High-density lipoprotein cholesterol (HDL)**: high-density lipoprotein cholesterol, sometimes known as 'good' cholesterol, which removes 'bad' cholesterol in the body.

> **Link it up**
>
> For more information on the respiratory system, the process of gaseous exchange and the function of the alveoli see Component 1, Topic 1, Section 1.2.

Health and Performance

Key terms

Adrenaline: a hormone that increases rates of blood circulation and breathing.

Bronchitis: inflammation of the lining of the bronchial tubes.

Passive smoking: breathing in the smoke from other people's cigarettes.

E-cigarette: electronic cigarette; battery-powered vaporiser that simulates the feeling of smoking.

Coronary heart disease (CHD) is the most common cause of death related to smoking. Smoking damages the cardiovascular system, in particular the heart, the oxygen-carrying capacity of the blood, and the blood vessels. This has a negative effect on fitness, especially aerobic fitness, and often results in poorer performance.

Increased blood pressure

The nicotine in cigarettes raises blood pressure because it releases **adrenaline**. Adrenaline constricts the arteries and causes the heart to beat faster. Smoking just one cigarette can raise the heart rate.

Bronchitis and lung disease

Smoking is known to be the main cause of chronic **bronchitis** – long-term inflammation of the lining of your bronchial tubes, which carry air to and from your lungs. Chronic bronchitis makes you short of breath, making you wheeze and cough, and severely limits your ability to do physical exercise.

Smoking is also the main cause of lung cancer. Figures show that:

- the more you smoke, the more likely you are to get lung cancer
- the longer time you have been smoking, the more likely you are to get lung cancer.

Some people get lung cancer by exposure to other people's smoking; this is called **passive smoking**.

High risk of death during medical operations

Medical operations carry a higher risk for smokers. Even if an operation goes smoothly, a smoker's heart and lungs will have to work harder. Smokers who undergo surgery risk a higher chance than non-smokers of blood clots developing in their legs; these clots may travel to and damage the lungs, heart and brain. As smoking decreases the oxygen-carrying capacity of the blood, it decreases the amount of oxygen that reaches the cells in your surgical wound. This means that a wound will take longer to heal and will be at more risk of infection.

E-cigarettes

E-cigarettes, or electronic cigarettes, are growing in popularity, as an alternative to cigarettes or to help smokers to quit. E-cigarettes are battery-powered vaporisers that simulate the feeling of smoking. Although they do not burn tobacco, so do not have harmful chemicals like tar and arsenic, e-cigarettes still contain nicotine.

E-cigarettes don't burn tobacco, but still use nicotine

The effects of alcohol

Drinking too much – over time – can have a serious impact on your health. It can:

- affect the way the brain works, changing your behaviour and making it harder for you to think clearly – which can put you at risk
- damage your heart and circulatory system, causing problems like a stroke and high blood pressure
- lead to liver damage, such as cirrhosis
- cause your pancreas to produce toxic substances that can lead to dangerous inflammation
- increase your risk of developing some cancers, including mouth, liver and even breast cancer
- weaken your immune system, making your body an easier target for disease.

Most people who have these health problems are not alcoholics, but just drink more than the recommended levels on a regular basis. The health impact of alcohol is not always immediate, but can develop over a number of years.

Alcohol can also offset the work you have put in to your training sessions. For example, if you train and work off a few pounds of weight, drinking alcohol can soon put those pounds back on again, and it can also make you dehydrated.

Exam-style question

Tom wants to join his local street dance group. However, while some of his friends think this is a great idea, others respond differently.

Explain how his friends can influence Tom. Give two examples: one a positive influence and one a negative influence. **(3 marks)**

Exam tip

Questions in this section are likely to be open questions, which require a longer answer – not just a 'yes' or 'no', or a single fact response. You will need to evaluate the positive influences and the negative influences before starting to write your answer.

1.2 The consequences of a sedentary lifestyle

Getting started

Many people take part in sport literally without thinking about the physical benefits. There are, however, people who do not take part in any sport or physical activity leading to what is known as a sedentary lifestyle.

Discuss with your group:

1 What may be the physical implications of a sedentary lifestyle?

2 What simple, cheap and easy activities can people take part in that will help them to develop a healthy active lifestyle, for example, walking their dog?

Learning objectives

By the end of this section you will understand:

- what a sedentary lifestyle is
- the consequences of a sedentary lifestyle for health
- how to interpret and analyse graphs showing health trend data.

Key term

Sedentary lifestyle: where there is little, irregular or no physical activity.

A sedentary lifestyle

Many people follow a **sedentary lifestyle** – a lifestyle that is seriously lacking in physical exercise or activity. This means that they do little exercise, training or taking part in sports activities.

You don't have to do sport to be active; what other ways can you build moderate intensity activity into your daily routine?

Having a sedentary lifestyle goes against all expert advice. You should aim to be active, exercise or play sport at a moderate intensity for at least 30 minutes five days a week.

There are many risks and consequences associated with having a sedentary lifestyle, including long-term health risks, obesity and depression.

Issues to do with weight

There are a number of different terms used to describe weight issues, including overweight, obese and even overfat. Be careful: these words do not mean the same thing!

- If someone is overweight, they have more weight than is considered healthy by medical professionals.
- If someone is obese, they are extremely overweight – usually more than 20 per cent above normal for men and 35 per cent above normal for women.
- If someone is overfat, too high a proportion of their body composition is fat – usually more than 19 per cent of total body composition for men, and more than 26 per cent for women.

For sportspeople, being overweight is not necessarily a problem. For example, a rugby player may be overweight because they have a lot of muscle, which they need to perform well. However, sportspeople who are overfat or obese usually find it hard to perform well. One rare exception is sumo wrestling, where many competitors are overfat or obese, as absolute weight is a requirement for success.

Depression

Studies have shown that there is a clear link between sedentary behaviour and **depression** – a persistent feeling of sadness and loss of interest in life. If you don't do much exercise, you are more likely to become depressed; and if you have depression, doing exercise can help to reduce, or even cure it.

Coronary heart disease

When you are sitting down, your muscles burn less fat and blood flows more sluggishly, which allows fatty deposits to clog the heart more easily. People who sit for eight hours a day or more are more than twice as likely to have cardiovascular disease as those who sit for less than four hours.

Key term

Depression: a persistent feeling of sadness and loss of interest in life.

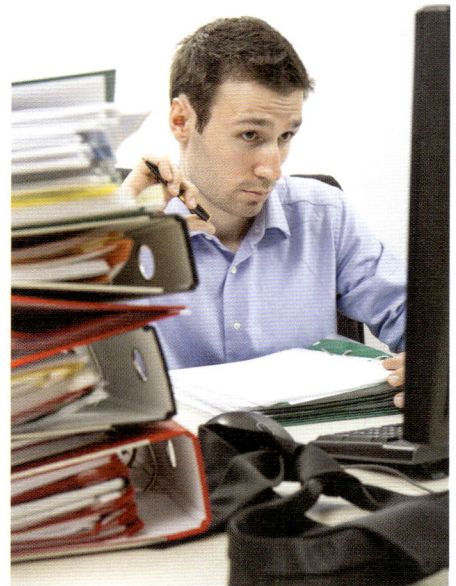

Apply it

The link between a sedentary lifestyle and coronary heart disease was made in the 1940s. Do some research to find out about Jerry Morris and his study of working people, including London bus drivers and conductors. What impact did that study have on public health policy?

Office workers should now be encouraged to take regular breaks to stand and walk

High blood pressure

As you have seen, blood pressure is the force of the blood pushing against the walls of the arteries as the heart pumps. If your blood pressure rises and stays high, it can damage your body in many ways.

There is growing evidence to suggest that, even if you take the recommended levels of exercise but spend the rest of your time sitting down, you could still suffer from high blood pressure – putting your health at risk.

Diabetes

Diabetes is a condition where the amount of glucose in your blood is too high because your body can't regulate the levels in the blood correctly. Diabetes develops when:

- your pancreas does not produce any insulin – a hormone that regulates your blood sugar levels – this is type 1 diabetes
- your pancreas does not produce enough insulin, or the body's cells do not react to insulin – this is type 2 diabetes.

Insulin is a hormone that carries glucose to our cells to give us energy. If we are inactive the cells in our muscles don't respond as readily to insulin, so the pancreas produces more and more which can lead to diabetes and other diseases. A study in 2012 by Dunstan et al. found a declined insulin response after just one day of prolonged sitting.

A study in 2015 by Biswas et al. suggested that a sedentary lifestyle is linked to a 91 per cent increased risk of developing type 2 diabetes. People who exercised were at slightly less risk, but exercise was not enough on its own to make up for the impact of sitting for a long time.

Many office workers now have desks that they can work at while standing up to try to prevent this happening.

Increased risk of osteoporosis

In recent years, there has been a rise in the number of cases of osteoporosis – the medical condition in which bones become brittle and fragile. Scientists think this is partly due to people's increasing lack of activity. Weight-bearing activities like walking and running encourage your hip and lower body bones to become thicker, denser and stronger.

Loss of muscle tone and poor posture

When you are standing or moving, you have to use your abdominal muscles to keep you upright. If you sit for a long time, your back muscles get tight and your abdominal muscles lose tone and soften.

Sitting down for long periods of time can give you bad posture, leading to back and neck pain. When your spine doesn't move, it gets less flexible and is more likely to get damaged when you do use it. When you move around, the soft discs between your vertebrae expand and contract, soaking up blood and nutrients. However, when you are sitting, these discs can get squashed and lose their ability to soak up what they need.

All of this can damage your spine and cause you pain.

Impact on components of fitness

Because of its link with so many factors of health, a sedentary lifestyle has an impact on all the basic components of fitness: cardiovascular fitness, muscular strength, muscular endurance, flexibility and body composition.

Trends in physical health issues

Understanding trends in physical health issues can be helpful for many people. People providing health services, like doctors and health workers, will be more aware of health issues to look out for. The Government will understand what provision it needs to make, or what public awareness issues it should highlight. People in the sports industry may see opportunities to help people with new health needs, or tap into new trends.

Various regulatory bodies monitor health trends and produce statistics and analysis. Often these are illustrated with graphs and charts to show current, historical and possible future trends or predictions.

The most common graphs you will find on physical health trends are:

- bar charts.
- line graphs.

Example one: bar chart

Look at Figure 2.1. This bar chart provides figures which show how BMI relates to high blood pressure.

There are three groups of data. Read along the horizontal axis – the x-axis – and you will find that this shows data for people with normal BMI, people who are overweight and people who are obese. Follow the line from each bar across to the vertical axis – the y-axis – and you can see the percentage of people in that group who have high blood pressure.

You will see that the bars are in pairs: one for men and one for women – so you can easily compare the results by gender.

The first bar shows that, out of men with normal BMI, 17 per cent have high blood pressure.

Using this bar chart you can do a number of things, including:

- find the percentage of men and women with high blood pressure for each age group
- compare the figures across the groups
- compare the figures for men and women

Practice

Show and explain how your PEP will help you overcome one aspect of a sedentary lifestyle.

Apply it

Investigate current health trends in the news or in magazines. What do these trends focus on? Where is the information coming from? Are they backed by proven research?

Health and Performance

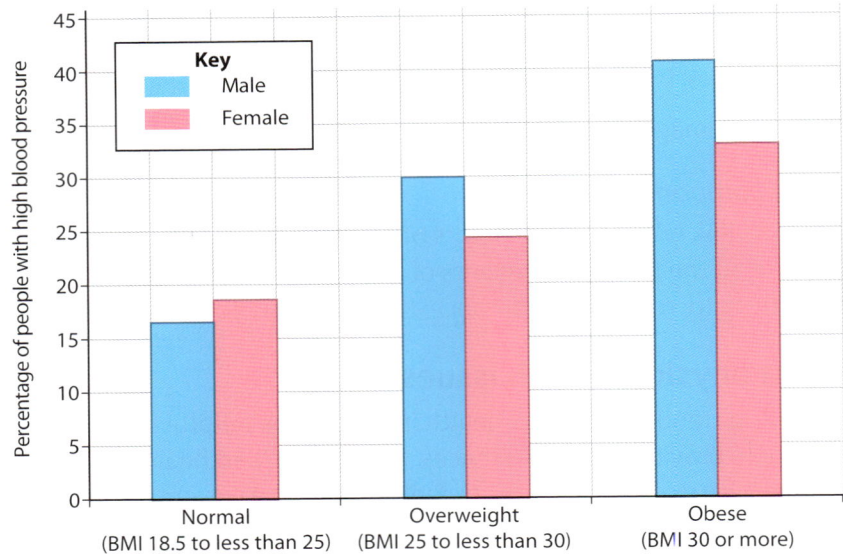

Figure 2.1 Percentage of people in different BMI ranges who have high blood pressure, by gender

Exam tip

Always take time to read the figure caption and the information on the axes carefully. Surprisingly, lots of people don't do this, so they cannot properly understand what the chart is showing – and the numbers involved. This means they can easily give the wrong answer because they do not fully understand the information.

Exam-style question

Look at the bar chart shown in Figure 2.2.

1   Which age group has the most cases of diabetes? **(1 mark)**
2   Which age group has the lowest number of cases of diabetes? **(1 mark)**
3   How many people were admitted to hospital because of diabetes in total in 2013? **(3 marks)**

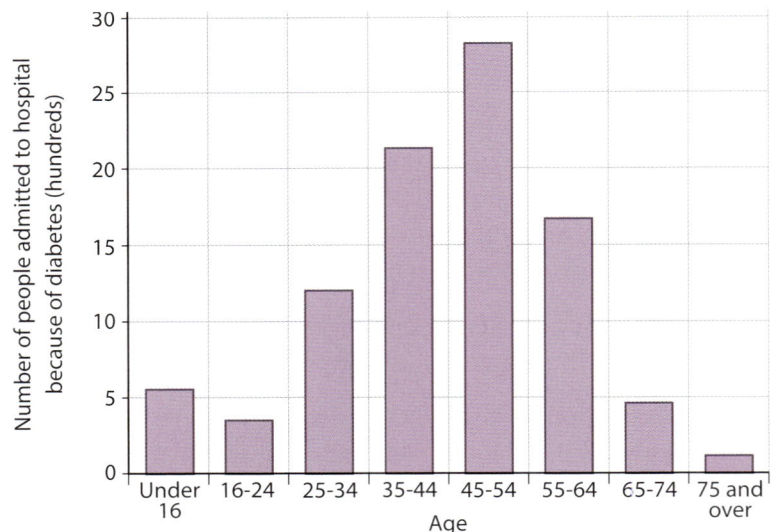

Figure 2.2 People admitted to hospital in 2013 because of diabetes, by age group

Example two: line graph

Line graphs are a useful way to show patterns and trends over time. Look at Figure 2.3 and you'll see that the x-axis shows dates, from 2003/04 to 2013/14, while the y-axis shows thousands of people. So from the caption you can see that these lines are showing how many thousands of people went to hospital because of diabetes between 2003 and 2014.

142

Again, data is shown separately for men and for women, using two different coloured lines.

For the final year on the graph, you can see that around 6800 women and around 2700 men went to hospital with diabetes in between 2003 and 2014.

You can use the line graph to do a number of things, including:

- read simple figures for any given year, for men or women
- compare figures for men and women at a glance, by comparing the height of the line
- compare the figures for different years
- follow the trend or pattern for men or women, by tracking along the line and seeing how it fluctuates.

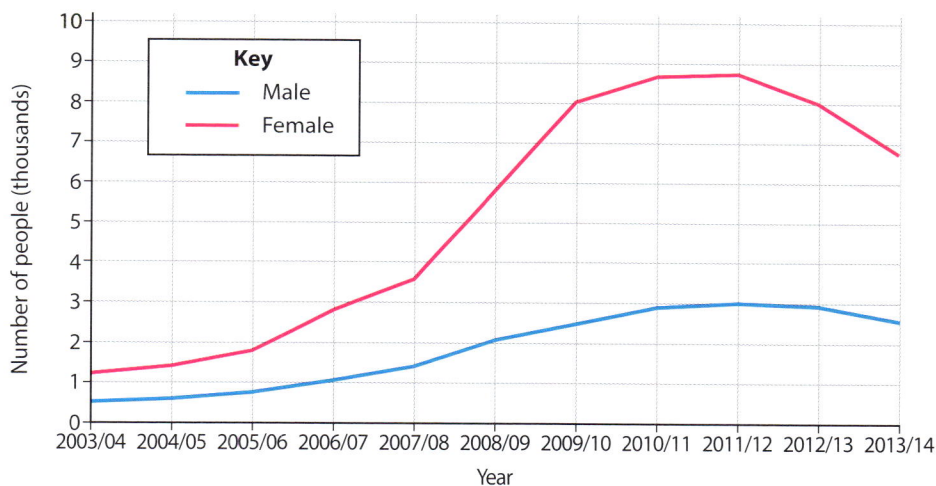

Source: Health Survey for England, 2013.

Figure 2.3 Numbers of people going to hospital because of diabetes from 2003/04 to 2013/14, by gender

Exam-style question

Look at the line graph shown in Figure 2.3.

1   In which year did the highest number of women go to hospital because of diabetes? **(1 mark)**

2   Give one reason why the figures for men and women might be different. **(1 mark)**

3   Describe the broad trend in people going to hospital because of diabetes from 2003/04 to 2013/14. **(3 marks)**

Exam tip

Sometimes there can be several lines on a line graph, and they can overlap and look confusing. Use your finger to trace along the line you are looking at, or use a coloured pen to make that line stronger and easier to pick out.

Health and Performance

1.3 Energy use, diet, nutrition and hydration

Getting started

Think about what you eat and drink, and how this links to the exercise you do.

- Do you always know when you need water?
- Which physical activities make you most hungry?
- Do different sportspeople need different food?

List the different elements that make up your diet. What foods do you typically eat each day?

Learning objectives

By the end of this section you will understand:

- what makes a balanced diet
- the roles of macronutrients and micronutrients for physical activity
- factors affecting weight, variations in weight for different sports and energy balance for weight control
- hydration and physical activity.

A balanced diet

Having a properly balanced diet is important for all of us, but is especially important for sportspeople wanting to perform as well as possible.

When balancing your diet, there are seven elements you need to consider:

- carbohydrates
- fats
- proteins
- vitamins
- minerals
- water
- fibre.

Macronutrients, carbohydrate loading and protein intake

Macronutrients

Macronutrients are the types of food that you need in large amounts in your diet: carbohydrates, fats and proteins.

Carbohydrates

Carbohydrates are important because they give you energy. There are two types of carbohydrates, complex and simple.

- **Complex carbohydrates** (starch) are found in natural foods, such as bananas, brown rice, wholemeal bread, wholemeal pasta, nuts and potatoes. Foods of this type help to provide energy for exercise and should form about half of your daily intake.
- **Simple carbohydrates** (sugars) are found in their natural form in fruit and vegetables, and in their refined form in biscuits, cakes, chocolate and confectionery.

Carbohydrates are stored in the muscles and the liver as glycogen, which is quickly converted into glucose and used to provide energy.

The energy needed to work and exercise should come from complex carbohydrates because they provide a slower and longer-lasting release of energy than simple carbohydrates, and can contribute to good, long-term health.

What did you have to eat yesterday? Were your meals healthy and balanced? How could you improve your diet?

Fats

Fats are important because they provide energy and, together with glycogen, help muscles to work. Fats are found in butter, margarine and cooking oils. They can also be found in foods such as bacon, cheese, oily fish and nuts. The daily intake of fats to provide energy should be about 30 per cent of the total diet.

Proteins

Proteins are important to help build muscles and to repair damaged tissue. Proteins are particularly important to strength athletes, such as rugby players and shot and hammer throwers. Proteins are also used to provide energy during extended periods of exercise, such as marathon running, when all the carbohydrate has been used up.

Protein comes from two types of food: animal protein and plant or vegetable protein.

- Animal protein is found in meat, poultry, fish and dairy products such as milk, cheese and yoghurt. Eggs are also a good source of protein.
- Plant or vegetable protein is found in pulses (lentils, peas and beans), nuts, bread, potatoes, breakfast cereal, pasta and rice. Some of these foods are also a source of carbohydrate.

People who follow a vegan diet eat no animal products, so have to get their protein from cereals, nuts and pulses.

Apply it

Food labels now appear on all packaged foods in the UK. Research the red, amber and green coding used on some labels. How is this code used to tell us what is in the food we are buying? Develop this research by comparing this information on four or five popular breakfast cereals. Present your findings to a small group or your class.

Health and Performance

People doing different sports require a different balance of the three macronutrients. For example:

- sumo wrestlers need more fat, for weight
- sprinters need more protein, for explosive strength and muscle
- marathon runners need more carbohydrates to allow them to run further and faster.

Carbohydrate loading for endurance athletes

From what you have learned so far, you will know that carbohydrates are the main source of fuel for endurance athletes. Carbohydrate loading – also known as carb-loading or carbo-loading – is a strategy these athletes use to maximise the stores of glycogen (or energy) in their muscles and liver.

Imagine you are a distance runner preparing for a race in a week's time. In the early part of the week before the race, eating more protein will help your muscles to repair after high-intensity training sessions. Later in the week, eating high levels of carbohydrates will help you to pack in and store as much carbohydrate as possible, which will in turn increase the glycogen stores in your liver and muscles, ready to use in the race itself.

It is also important to take in food in the first two hours after a race, event or training session, to restock on carbohydrates used up during the activity. Isotonic drinks have a similar carbohydrate electrolyte concentration to the body's own fluids and can be used in the recovery process to boost energy intake.

Research a protein-based diet for a power athlete. How does this protein intake differ from your own diet?

Timing protein intake for power athletes

All athletes, but particularly power athletes, see protein as a key part of their diet, because of the role it plays in stimulating muscle growth. The timing of intake – when you eat protein – seems to be the main factor in getting the best results from it. Current research says that the ideal time to have protein is immediately after exercise, when it does most to:

- minimise protein breakdown – exercise breaks down muscle
- stimulate muscle protein synthesis – this process repairs and grows muscle after exercise
- help build muscle – because less muscle is broken down and more is grown, total muscle increases.

Micronutrients, water and fibre

Micronutrients

Micronutrients are the parts of your food that you need for normal growth, but only in small amounts – what we usually call vitamins and minerals.

Vitamins

A balanced supply of vitamins is essential for the body to function properly. Vitamins are essential for:

- good vision
- good skin
- red blood cell formation
- healing
- healthy bones and teeth
- blood clotting.

Vitamins come in two groups; water-soluble vitamins (that can be dissolved in water) and fat-soluble vitamins (that can be dissolved in fat). This is one of the reasons you need fat in your diet.

- Vitamin A (found in milk, cheese, egg yolk, liver and carrots) is necessary for vision and helps to prevent night blindness.
- Vitamin B1 (found in wholegrains, nuts and meat) is needed to release carbohydrate for working muscles.
- Vitamin C (found in fruit and vegetables) helps healing, fights infection and helps to maintain the bones, teeth and gums.
- Vitamin D (found in milk, fish, liver and eggs, as well as from sunshine) is needed for the absorption of calcium, which is necessary for healthy bones.
- Vitamin E (found in vegetable oil, wholemeal bread and cereals) is needed for growth and development.

Minerals

Minerals are essential for a healthy body. Two key minerals you need as a sportsperson are calcium and iron.

- **Calcium** (found in milk, cheese and cereals) is important in the formation of bones and teeth, and helps to make the bones strong – something that is crucial for many sports. Bones are at their strongest when you are around 30–35 years old, then they get weaker. It is important to keep up your calcium intake as you get older to reduce the likelihood of osteoporosis.
- **Iron** (found in many foods, including meat) is linked with haemoglobin, the oxygen-carrying capacity of the blood and the formation of red blood cells. Without it, the blood would not be able to carry oxygen around the body – so iron is important to any athlete. Lack of iron can lead to anaemia, which causes tiredness, shortness of breath and palpitations (irregular heart beat).

Other minerals include:

- **Sodium**, which is needed for maintaining blood pressure and balance of body fluid content. It is also needed for the transmission of nerve impulses.
- **Potassium**, which has many important functions including: the balancing of fluids in our bodies and maintaining the correct functioning of our heart muscle.
- Trace elements, such as **zinc** (promoting healing and cell growth) and **selenium** (protecting our immune system function), which are needed in very small amounts, but are still important minerals for our health.

Water

Water accounts for around half of your body weight. It holds oxygen and is the main component of many cells. It transports nutrients, waste and hormones around the body and controls the distribution of electrolytes (or body salts).

During exercise, your body sweats and loses electrolytes. Some isotonic drinks claim to replace these, but a balanced diet will also do this naturally. Water is also essential to control temperature.

Most athletes and sportspeople need water when competing in order to improve their performance and to offset **dehydration**. In most sports, players take on water or **hydrate** at regular intervals. For example, tennis players take on water at the change of ends.

Fibre

Fibre (roughage) adds bulk to food and aids the functioning of the digestive system. It is important to have a healthy, active lifestyle because your digestive system does not operate properly without it and cannot get rid of waste products, which could lead to disease.

> **Key terms**
>
> **Dehydration**: the loss of water and salts essential for normal body function.
>
> **Hydrate**: take on water.

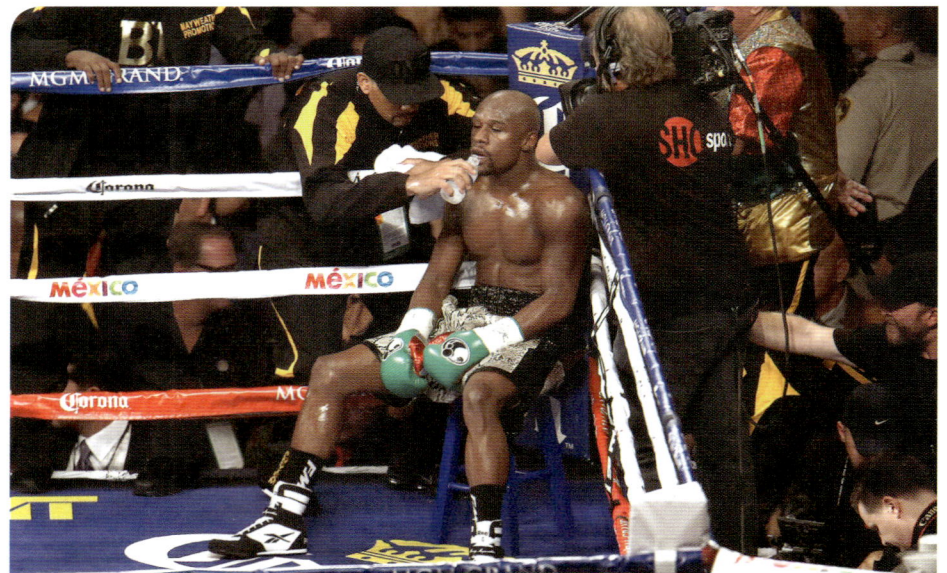

Boxers and jockeys often make themselves sweat to lose weight so that they can reach the required weight for competition, but this may make them vulnerable to dehydration

Fibre is found in the leaves, stems, roots, seeds and fruits of plants. The fibre content of some foods may be reduced when they are peeled and processed.

There are two types of fibre: **soluble** and **insoluble**. It is important to eat a variety of foods so you include both types in your diet.

- Oats, fruit and vegetables are sources of soluble fibre, which helps to reduce blood cholesterol levels.
- Wholegrain cereal and bread are sources of insoluble fibre, which is required as a bulking agent to prevent constipation.

Apply it

Look at a range of breakfast cereals. Read the nutritional information on the pack and write down the names of the vitamins and minerals contained in the cereal. Research why each of these is needed to maintain a healthy diet.

Factors affecting optimum weight

Sportspeople need to know their **optimum weight** – the most favourable weight to produce their best performance in their sport – so that they can make every effort to keep within this weight range.

There are two key ways to work out your optimum weight, you could use a height/weight chart or alternatively you could search online for a BMI calculator:

A number of factors affect your optimum body weight:

- **Height** – Generally speaking a taller person is likely to be heavier than a shorter person, although other factors may affect this.
- **Bone structure** – People with a heavier bone structure would normally be heavier in weight.
- **Muscle girth** – People with bigger muscles will weigh more.
- **Gender** – For women and men of the same height, the man is likely to have a higher optimum body weight, because of their heavier bone structure and bigger muscle girth.

Sportspeople and average weight

Bone structure and muscle girth play an important part in optimum weight. A person can be heavily built without being overweight – or, more accurately, **overfat**.

On many age and height-to-weight tables, some sportsmen and women may appear to be **overweight**. However, this is because their bone structure and muscle girth are greater than for the average person – no one would accuse them of being 'fat'.

Key terms

Soluble (fibre): can be digested by your body and can help to reduce the amount of cholesterol in your blood (see www.nhs.uk/conditions/Cholesterol).

Insoluble (fibre): cannot be digested by your body. As it passes through your gut it helps other foods move through your digestive system. It keeps your bowels healthy and helps prevent digestive disorders.

Overfat: having too much body composition as fat; men having more than 19 per cent of total body composition as fat and women over 26 per cent.

Overweight: having more weight than is considered healthy by medical professionals.

Link it up

For more information on height-to-weight tables and BMI see Component 1, Topic 3, Section 3.2.

Health and Performance

Apply it

With a partner, discuss the data given for the sportspeople in Table 2.2. Consider the information on optimum weight, and for the sportspeople the importance of their sport and their role in their sport, e.g. the position they play and their style of play.

Sources:
www.manutd.com, www.fifadata.com, www.bbc.co.uk, www.englandrugby.com.

Exam tip

Make sure you understand – and explain – the factors that influence optimum weight and why one athlete may be heavier than another, in the same sport or in a different sport.

Key term

Metabolic rate: the rate at which metabolic processes take place; the rate at which a body uses up energy.

Variation in optimum weight

As you have learned, sports vary widely in the demands they place on an athlete's body. For example, for some sportspeople such as weightlifters, strength is all-important; for others, such as long-distance runners, muscular endurance is the key factor.

These different demands mean that there are different optimum weights for different types of sport – and, indeed, for different roles within the same sport. For example, in rugby (probably more than any other sport) the players have very different roles according to the position they play. Forwards tend to be bigger, heavier, stronger players, while backs are usually smaller and slimmer as they need to be more agile.

Add in the broad differences in weight between men and women, and the range of optimum weights for sport is huge.

Sportsperson	Sport	Height	Weight
Wayne Rooney	Football	1.76 m	83 kg
Steph Houghton	Football	1.72 m	62 kg
Jessica Ennis-Hill	Athletics	1.65 m	57 kg
Mo Farah	Athletics	1.65 m	58 kg
Mako Vunipola	Rugby Union	1.80 m	121 kg
Anthony Watson	Rugby Union	1.85 m	93 kg

Table 2.2 Height and weight comparisons

Exam-style question

Mako Vunipola and Anthony Watson both represented England in the 2015 Rugby World Cup. They are roughly the same height as each other. Using the information in Table 2.2, explain the variation in their optimum weight according to their body build and their role in their sport.
(3 marks)

Energy balance for maintaining a healthy weight

Energy balance is the basis of weight control. It means taking in (eating) and using up (through work and exercise) an equal number of calories (or kilocalories); this is how body weight remains constant.

We all have our own rate of using up energy, which is known as our **metabolic rate**. This is why some people may eat less food but actually put on weight, while others appear to be able to eat anything without putting on any weight at all.

We measure energy in calories. Average calorie requirements differ between men and women. An average man will need about 2500 calories per day, while an average woman will need about 2000 calories per day.

'This is because men tend to be taller and heavier than women and therefore have more muscle.'

However, these are just averages. Actual needs will vary according to the person's age, their job and their exercise pattern, plus any additional factors. Teenagers, who are still growing, need more than these averages.

- Men aged 15–18 need about 2755 calories per day.
- Women between the age of 15–18 need about 2110 calories per day.

Hydration

As you read earlier in this topic, taking on enough water and fluid is important for any sportsperson, because **hydration** plays a role in every function of your body.

When you exercise, you can lose up to a litre of fluid every hour, mainly through sweating and breathing. If you don't replace these fluids, you may become dehydrated. This will affect both your general health and your performance.

How to maintain correct levels

Your hydration levels can change rapidly when you play sport or do exercise, without you even noticing it. However, there are some simple things you can do to keep your hydration up.

Before exercise

- Test the colour of your urine. The paler it is, the more hydrated you already are. If you urine is dark yellow to orange, you need to take on water or other fluids without delay.
- Drink at regular intervals throughout the day, try to drink around 500 ml of fluid at least four hours before you exercise.
- Just before you exercise – perhaps 10–15 minutes before – top your fluid levels up by drinking about 250 ml water.

During exercise

- If you feel thirsty, drink! Don't be tempted to carry on if you know you should stop for a water break.
- Think about the best way to have water on hand while you exercise, and make sure you have a supply with you, or nearby.

After exercise

- Start to drink as soon as you finish your exercise. The sooner you replace the fluid, the sooner you will recover.
- Don't drink alcohol straight after exercise. It is a **diuretic**, which means that it makes you produce more urine – and this removes water from your body.

> **Key terms**
>
> **Hydration:** being hydrated means the body has the correct amount of water in cells, tissues and organs to function correctly. The average recommended daily intake is 2.5 litres of water for men and 2 litres for women.
> **Diuretic:** making you produce more urine.

Health and Performance

Summary

Key points to remember:

Physical, emotional and social health

- Participating in sport can improve all types of health:
  - physical – better cardiovascular fitness, body composition, strength and muscular endurance
  - emotional – makes you feel good, relieves stress, increases confidence, fun and challenge
  - social – co-operation, friendship and good attitude
- Personal exercise programmes help individual promote their health
- Lifestyle choices have impact on fitness in terms of:
  - diet – balance of calories, energy and nutrients
  - level of activity – barriers exist, but can be overcome
  - work/rest/sleep balance – rest is important for recovery
  - recreational drugs – caffeine, alcohol and especially smoking all have an impact

Sedentary lifestyle

- Can lead to being obese – remember obese, overweight and overfat are different
- Brings risks to long-term health:
  - depression, coronary heart disease, high blood pressure, diabetes, osteoporosis, loss of muscle tone/posture
  - impacts on all components of fitness
- Health trends can be shown in graphs – make sure you can interpret them

Energy, diet, nutrition and hydration

- A balanced diet is very important in sport
- Macronutrients:
  - carbohydrates for energy (endurance)
  - fats for energy and to make muscles work
  - proteins to build and repair muscle
- Micronutrients – vitamins, minerals, fibre
- Optimum weight
  - affected by: sex, height, bone structure, muscle girth
  - varies according to activity or sport
  - needs correct energy balance for individual
- Hydration – need to maintain correct levels as you exercise

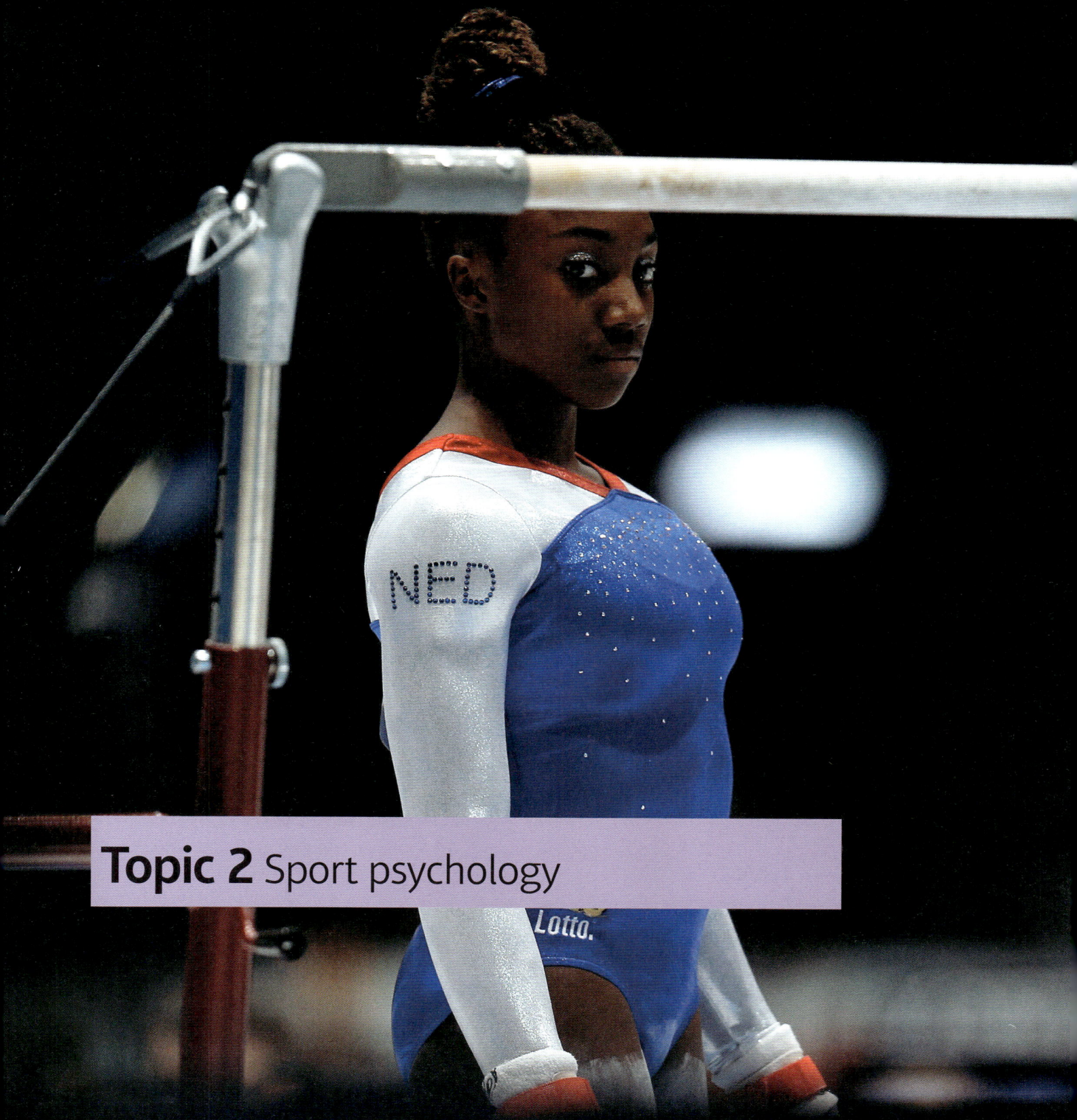

Topic 2 Sport psychology

2.1 Classification of skills (open/closed, basic/complex, low organisation/high organisation)

Work with a partner and name one of your practical activities that you are doing for GCSE PE, e.g. football.

Make a list of all the skills you need for your chosen sport (e.g. a penalty kick in football).

In this topic you will find out how to classify the skills you have listed.

Learning objectives

By the end of this section you will understand:

- how to classify sports skills as open/closed, basic (simple)/complex and low organisation/high organisation
- practice structures – massed, distributed, fixed and variable
- how to apply these to choose the best practice to develop a range of skills.

Classification of a range of sporting skills

Open and closed skills

Open skills are seen in sports such as netball and football, where the situation is always changing. The player has to continually adapt to the situation. For open skills, practices need to match the competitive situation – so for example, in football, players might start with three against one practice in a grid, then change to three against two practice as their skills improve.

Closed skills take place in a stable, predictable environment, and the player knows exactly what to do and when. These skills are not affected by the environment. Movements follow set patterns and have a clear beginning and end. The skills tend to be self-paced: for example, a free throw in basketball, a penalty in football and serving in squash or tennis.

Basic and complex skills

A **basic (simple) skill** is one that the player finds easy and needs little concentration to do. This could be a chest pass in netball, or a side-foot pass in football.

A **complex skill** needs the player's complete attention and concentration as it is technically difficult to perform: for example, a penalty kick in football, or a smash in tennis. These skills need to be practiced over and over again, so that they become easier when playing in a match or competition.

Taking a penalty kick is a complex skill. What are the complex skills in your favourite sport?

Low organisation and high organisation skills

A **low organisation skill** has clear, simple phases or parts: for example, a set shot in basketball. You can usually break the phases down and practice them separately, to improve your technique.

A **high organisation skill** has a lot of complicated phases or parts: for example, a somersault in trampolining. You cannot break these phases down and practice them separately, as they are closely linked together. To perform these skills you need attention to detail, good co-ordination and timing and quick thinking, especially in a competitive situation.

Practice structures

Practice sessions need to be planned according to the activity: for example, rugby, football and netball as team games; table tennis, badminton and tennis as individual or doubles activities; swimming, trampolining and athletics as individual activities. The practice will then also be based on the skill level, ability level, fitness and experience of the players taking part.

Massed and distributed practice

Practices can be:

- **massed**, where the skill is practised until it is learned, without taking a break – this type of practice is normally for athletes who are fit and experienced
- **distributed**, where the skill is practised over several sessions, or with rest breaks – this type of practice is normally for players of lower ability, experience or fitness level.

Fixed and variable practice

Fixed practice is where the skill is practised over and over again until it is perfected. For example, you might use fixed practice for a free shot in basketball or a somersault in gymnastics. Closed skills are normally practiced in this way so that the movement sequence can be perfected.

Variable practice involves practising the skill in a variety of different situations, so that it can be adapted to suit different competitive situations. Variable practice is essential for open skills: for example, in football where the game varies from match to match, in different weather conditions, according to the opposition, etc.

2.2 The use of goal setting and SMART goals to improve and/or optimise performance

Goal setting

Think about times when you have set yourself a particular goal in sport or physical activity, perhaps as part of your PEP. Your goal might be to improve your cardiovascular fitness levels, to increase your strength or to improve your hand-eye co-ordination.

Having a clear goal can help you by:

- helping you focus on what is important
- increasing your motivation to make progress
- helping you develop new strategies to meet that goal
- enabling you to monitor how well you are doing.

Some athletes feel that goal setting is boring and time-consuming, and this can deter them from doing it. However, research has shown that goal setting is incredibly effective and can have a dramatic and positive effect on performance.

You may end up setting one goal, or having a range of goals you want to achieve – but the most important thing is to choose the right goals for you. Often athletes pick goals like winning a certain race or getting a good place in a particular competition – but goals like this depend on how other people perform too. The best goals are those for your personal performance, independent of others.

SMART goals

Once you have identified your aims, you then have to work out a plan to achieve them. This is where SMART goals can help.

SMART stands for:

- **S**pecific
- **M**easurable
- **A**chievable
- **R**ealistic
- **T**ime-bound.

Specific

Having a specific goal means knowing exactly what the goal is. For example, an overall goal might be 'I want to be fitter', but this is not specific; neither is 'I want to be better at football'. A specific goal for someone doing fitness might be: 'I want to run 100 metres further in my Cooper test'. More specific goals can act as clear steps towards the overall goal. Before you decide what your specific goals should be, you should test your current fitness and performance levels.

Apply it

Prepare your own SMART goals for your sport.

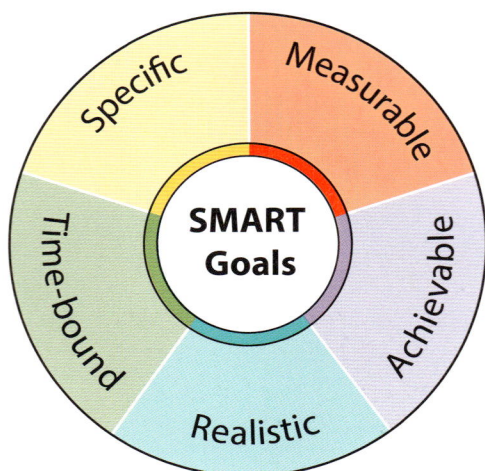

Figure 2.4 SMART goals

Measurable

A measurable goal is, as it sounds, one that you can measure. Having measurable goals means that you can know when you have achieved them. For example, the goal of running an extra 100 metres in the Cooper test is clearly measurable as you are recording results and comparing them with previous performance.

Achievable

Running an extra 100 metres in the Cooper test after six weeks' training may be achievable; running a full marathon after four weeks of running distances of six miles is probably not. It is important that your goals stretch you, but are possible to achieve. Setting unachievable goals can make you feel demotivated, and you are less likely to achieve your target.

Realistic

A goal may well be achievable in theory, but if it is to be achievable in practice you need to have the time and resources to complete it. For example: 'I want to get stronger biceps by being able to curl an additional 2kg after a six-week training programme' may be an achievable goal, but if the gym is not open at suitable times, or it's too far away or too expensive then it is not realistic.

Time-bound

Does the goal have a time limit? If not, it is easy to put off achieving it indefinitely! Setting a deadline for achieving each goal is important. For example, a PEP runs for 6–8 weeks so is time-bound, as the goals set have to be achieved within the set number of weeks.

Setting and reviewing targets

The tests you perform should help you to evaluate your current levels of fitness before setting your goals. For example, if you do the Cooper test, you will have your score for the test and can use this to set your goals for your PEP. If you have chosen to improve muscular endurance, you may have used tests for various muscle groups, such as the number of press-ups you can do in a set time, or the maximum you can do before you have to stop!

Setting the right targets will lead you to the right training methods: for example, to improve your cardiovascular fitness, or your muscular endurance.

Once you have set your goals or targets, you need to review your progress towards achieving them. You can run the same tests again, to see how well you are doing. If you do not seem to be making progress, or if you have already reached your target ahead of time, you can look at your goals again. They may need adjusting to ensure you get the greatest benefit and feel motivated.

> **Exam tip**
>
> You need to be able to explain what each letter in the term SMART means, and to give examples of how you might apply this. Make sure you have your ideas prepared before the exam.

> **Exam-style question**
>
> In the term SMART goals, explain what the A stands for and how this aspect would be used to plan a training programme. **(3 marks)**

2.3 Guidance and feedback on performance

Types of guidance

In physical education and sport, a coach will use different methods to guide learners to develop their skills and improve their performance. The way the coach gives guidance will influence how well the learner progresses.

Most coaches use a variety of different methods, taking into account:

* the individual learner's personality and learning style
* the learner's ability level in the activity
* the sport or skill being taught
* the facilities available.

The main methods a coach will use are:

* visual guidance
* verbal guidance
* manual guidance
* mechanical guidance.

Visual guidance

This type of guidance can be given in many different ways. For example, imagine a coach wants to teach you how to do a lay-up shot in basketball. The most common way to show you would be for the coach to give a demonstration themselves, or ask another learner to perform. They could also show you a video of a top basketball player making a lay-up shot, or use photographs or posters showing the different parts of the lay-up shot.

Visual guidance could also mean setting a target for the player to hit – for a lay-up shot, this would be the near top corner of the small square on the backboard.

Verbal guidance

Verbal guidance can be helpful – as long as it is clear. It can be difficult for beginners to understand verbal guidance, especially if it is to do with a difficult or complicated skill.

Verbal guidance is sometimes used before giving a demonstration, but is more often used at the same time as visual guidance, to back it up and support it. In the lay-up shot example, the coach would be verbally explaining and visually showing the learner how to hold the basketball, reach up towards the basket, then squeeze the ball against the backboard.

The words used in verbal explanation are important. In our basketball example, the performer will not know how hard to push the ball against the backboard, so the coach must explain that they need to squeeze the ball against the backboard, not throw it!

As performers improve, verbal guidance is crucial to give feedback on the performance.

Manual and mechanical guidance

Manual and mechanical guidance is when the coach is actually in contact with the learner as they perform the skill. Clearly, this is only possible in some sports. Using the example of trampolining again, the coach can work on the trampoline with the performer. If they are learning a seat drop the coach can make sure that their legs hit the bed at the same time as their bottom. This helps them to get the 'feel' of the movement, before they perform it on their own. For a more advanced move such as a somersault, the coach can make sure they get the full rotation, so again they can feel what they have to do to get the complete movement safely.

In trampolining the coach may also give verbal guidance on a back somersault, to explain the importance of timing when lifting the hips, tucking and then dropping the head back

Advantages and disadvantages of different types of guidance

Each type of guidance has advantages and disadvantages, depending mainly on the ability level of the learner. However, coaches for most sports use more than one method of guidance. The important thing is to choose the right type of guidance for the learner, the sport/skill and the situation and apply the best method – or combination – of methods.

Type of guidance	Advantages	Disadvantages
Visual	Visual guidance, through a demonstration or video, means that the learner knows what skill they have to perform and what it looks like.	If visual guidance is given in the form of a video, learners will not be able to ask questions to clarify their understanding.
Verbal	The coach can explain in further detail or emphasise specific points about the skill.	It can be difficult for beginners to understand verbal guidance, especially if it is to do with a difficult or complicated skill.
Manual and mechanical	The coach can help the performer to execute the skill safely and successfully and 'feel' how the movement should be done	This will not be possible for all sports.

Table 2.3 Advantages and disadvantages of different types of guidance

In a competitive situation, guidance and feedback is normally verbal, often given at the break or the end of a game. However, in many activities data can be collected in the form of **qualitative** and **quantitative** (notational) analysis and this can be used as guidance and feedback on the individual or team performance.

> ### Key terms
>
> **Qualitative**: information about qualities, which is difficult to measure.
>
> **Quantitative**: information about quantities, which can be measured.

Health and Performance

Feedback to optimise performance

There are different types of feedback that can be given to help you analyse and improve your performance.

Intrinsic

Intrinsic feedback comes from the performer themselves, as they think about how they feel they performed or what contribution they made to a team or game. This feedback may affect the motivation of the performer, so it is important that they feel that they have performed well and want to come back and continue with the activity. A novice performer may have little knowledge of the skill they are using, so they will not be able to assess their own performance as well as the coach or teacher – so for them extrinsic feedback is more important.

Extrinsic

Extrinsic feedback comes from an outside source: for example, from a teacher or coach. This sort of feedback is important for the performer as it will motivate them to improve and learn from their practice, as well as to return and continue with the activity. Extrinsic feedback could also come from teammates, family or friends.

Concurrent

Concurrent feedback is given at the time of the performance – for example, from the coach on the sideline during a match. This sort of feedback can be acted on immediately.

Terminal

Terminal feedback is given at the end of a game or performance. This sort of feedback has the benefit of being more reflective and giving an overview of the whole of the performance.

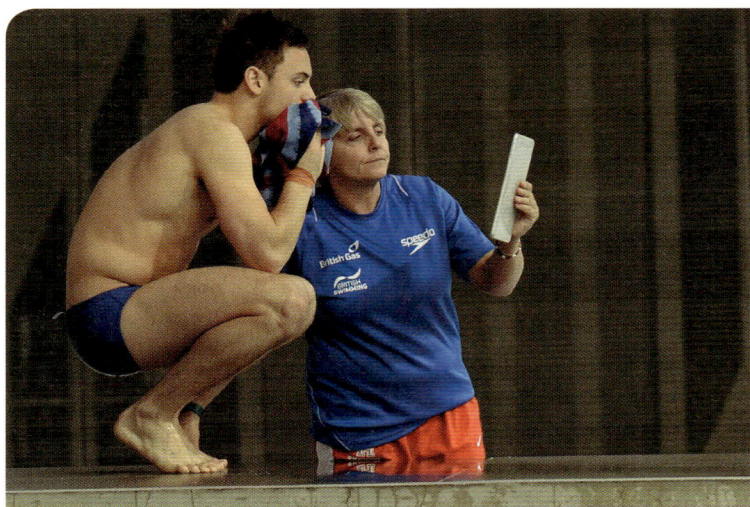

Which type, or types, of feedback do you find the most beneficial in your sport?

Interpretation and analysis of feedback data

Data can be gathered on a variety of sports. Coaches can analyse this data and feed this back to the performer, during the game, during a break or before the next game. Usually this is quantitative data, where you measure amounts, rather than qualitative data, where you look at how people feel about something, or what opinions people have.

Here are some examples of the quantitative data that can be collected in sport.

- Swimming – the time it takes for the swimmer to complete each length in a race.

- Racket games – the number of forced and unforced errors a player makes, and the number of winners they hit with a certain type of shot.
- Netball – the number of successful and unsuccessful shots the shooter makes and where each shot is taken from.
- Basketball – a shooting analysis for each player showing where the shot was taken from, what type of shot it was and whether it was successful.

Quantitative data can often be set out as a bar chart, graph or table – but it could be set up on a diagram of a playing field or court.

KEY

◯ = successful shot

Numbers indicate players' shirt numbers and positions on the court

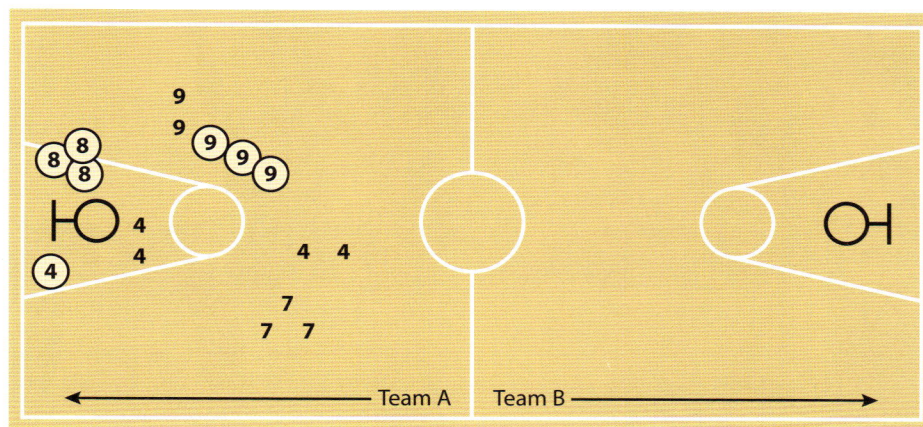

Figure 2.5 Diagram to show the shots taken by players on a court

Apply it

In a group, research sports data presented in graphic form; this could be in magazines or online. Choose an example that you think presents the information in the best way and explain your reasons to your group.

Look at Figure 2.5. In this example, the coach can see where all the shots have been taken from on the court, which of the players has been most successful and which of their opponents has been most successful. Seeing the data like this can make it easier to analyse, and use to influence tactics for the future.

Mental preparation for performance

How each athlete prepares mentally for competition will vary, not just with the athlete but also with the sport. Individual sports differ from partner or team sports, where you can encourage each other. In some individual sports, you can still get support and encouragement – for example, from a coach in swimming or athletics, or from your caddy in golf – but there comes a moment when it is down to you.

For most sportspeople, mental preparation starts long before the warm up for the game. Getting the right mindset is something you practise during training, and for which you may even get specialist support.

Health and Performance

England kicker Owen Farrell has a set ritual before taking a kick. How do you achieve the right mindset?

Practice

For one of your practical activities explain how you mentally prepare yourself before a competition or for a specific part of the game, e.g. taking a penalty.

Some sportspeople develop performance rituals: they follow the same routine every time they play or perform. One common example is when a rugby player taking a penalty or conversion visualises the perfect kick, looking up to the posts before they start their run up and visualising the ball going over and between the posts.

Other examples of mental rehearsal from athletics include:

- a sprinter at the start of the 100m, preparing and getting into their starting blocks and looking up the track
- a high jumper or pole vaulter practising their first step, then visualising their run up and jump, clearing the bar
- a discus thrower before their throw, seeing the discus flying through the air and landing for their best performance.

The pressure in these situations is great, and good mental preparation can help to ensure that athletes are able to focus on producing their best performance when it counts.

Summary

Key points to remember:

Types of skill

- Classification:
  - open (always changing) – closed (stable, predictable)
  - simple (easy, low concentration) – complex (hard, high concentration)
  - low organisation (clear, simple phases) – high organisation (complicated phases)
- Practice structures:
  - massed (learned without a break) – distributed (learned in sessions)
  - fixed (practised in single situation) – variable (practised in different situations)

SMART goals

- Having clear goals improves performance
- SMART goals are **S**pecific, **M**easurable, **A**chievable, **R**ealistic and **T**ime-bound
- SMART goals need to be set, monitored and revised to stay SMART

Guidance and feedback

- Different types of guidance with pros and cons:
  - visual – easy to understand, but harder to show difficult skills
  - verbal – can be hard to understand, but important for harder skills
  - manual/mechanical – gives 'feel' for movement, but not always practical
- Different types of feedback with pros and cons:
  - intrinsic – from yourself, so you need knowledge
  - extrinsic – from others, so you need their expertise
  - concurrent – at the time, so helps you straight away
  - terminal – after the event, so allows for reflection
- Graphs are useful for feeding back on performance – make sure you can interpret them

Mental preparation

- Varies according to athlete and sport
- Pre-warm up, during warm up, during event
- Mental rehearsal and rituals – helps some athletes to visualise what will happen

Topic 3 Socio-cultural influences

3.1 Engagement patterns of different social groups in physical activity and sport

Getting started

Think about the things that influence you to try or play different sports.

- What do you think influenced you when you were younger?
- How have things changed as you have got older?
- How is participation in sport promoted?

Make a list of things that might stop you taking part in physical activity, or sport and suggest ways in which these barriers could be removed.

Learning objectives

By the end of this section you will understand:

- the impact that gender, age, socio-economic group, ethnicity, disability, and the other people's influence have on participation in sport
- how to interpret data in graphs about participation rates
- how commercialisation and the media affect sport, and their impact on those involved
- trends in sport
- different types of sporting behaviour.

What affects who plays sport?

The number of people taking part in sport in the UK once a week is rising, but still over half the population – 58 per cent – play no sport. There are many reasons why some people take up sport and continue to be physically active, and why some people don't.

Gender

The idea that some physical activities are more 'male' and others more 'female' has mostly disappeared, but some activities still offer one sex more opportunities than the other. A boy who loves netball may struggle to find a team, while women's cricket, football and rugby are still less popular than the men's versions, but are growing. It is worth reminding yourself that, in most sports, competitions are still organised on gender lines: for example, with men's events and women's events in athletics.

Overall in the UK, a greater proportion of men than women play sport – 40.7 per cent of men as opposed to 31.2 per cent of women, according to Sport England's data for 2014/15.

The public perception of an activity can also be a problem: for example, how much coverage the different genders get in the media for the same sport.

Health and Performance

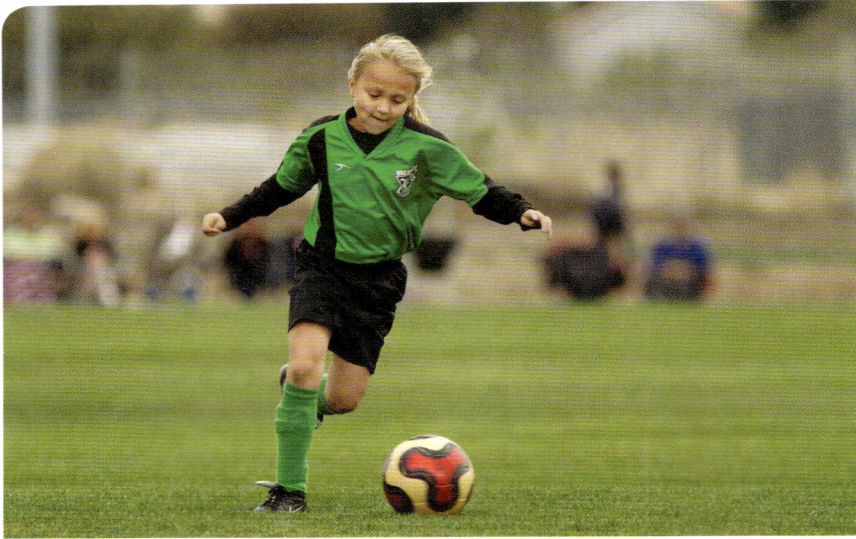

Starting to play football at a young age enables you to develop the personal skills necessary, such striking the ball correctly

Age

Age can affect performance and may also influence participation in physical activities. In most sports it is good to start young, although some competitive events may have age restrictions. For example, the minimum age for taking part in the London Marathon is 18, but under-11s can run in their local Parkrun if accompanied by an adult. Work and family responsibilities, as well as health problems, may prevent adults and older people from participating in physical activities.

Some sports lend themselves to being more suitable for younger people, such as gymnastics, which requires high levels of flexibility, strength and co-ordination, as well as the will to train intensively and acquire new skills quickly. Other sports tend to suit older competitors just as well, or even better, than younger competitors. Golf and bowls, for example, are seen as sports where older players can benefit from being mentally strong, good at tactics and patient.

Socio-economic group

Sometimes the media or a business talk about people in terms of 'ABC1s'. These are socio-economic groups or demographic groups, based largely on the occupation of the head of the household. If your parents are high-earning professionals or members of the aristocracy, you would be put in one group, but if they have low wages and do unskilled work, you would be put in a different group.

Groupings like this are generalisations, but they can say something about people's chances to access and take part in sport and the sort of attitude to sport or physical activity around them.

For example, most activities have some associated costs – hire of facilities, lessons, equipment, clothing, etc. Some sports, such as running, are quite inexpensive. Football may require boots and club membership, but these costs are minimal compared with, for example, golf, which requires a lot of expensive equipment and the payment of green fees or annual club fees. If people cannot afford to take part, their socio-economic status has influenced their involvement.

Your socio-economic group can also be seen to influence the type of sport you get involved in or experience. Polo, rowing and lacrosse are seen as traditionally 'wealthy', or 'upper class' activities, while netball, darts and boxing are often thought of as 'working class' sports.

These things can change. Football used to be thought of as a 'working man's sport', but now with mass coverage, millionaire players and billionaire club owners, the perception of the sport is very different!

Ethnicity

Ethnicity refers to a population whose members identify with each other and are united by common cultural, linguistic or religious traits. It can influence whether we play sport, what we choose to play and what sports we succeed in. It also influences other people's attitudes and our ability to progress performance-wise in sport.

There have been instances of racist abuse against non-white players, most notably in football, and it is still an issue that the sport works hard to combat. There are still far fewer black managers at the top level of football. In 2008, Paul Ince became the first black English manager in the Premiership.

Disability

People with disabilities take part in many sporting activities. Resources and opportunities for disabled people to take part in sport are increasing. However, more availability is still needed in schools, and at a local level, for people with disabilities who are not professional athletes or sportspeople.

The London 2012 Paralympic games were labelled 'the greatest Paralympic Games ever' by International Paralympic Committee (IPC) chairman Sir Philip Craven, attracting record crowds and many record-breaking performances from the athletes. There was also unprecedented media coverage, which has encouraged many people with disabilities to get involved in sport locally.

Influence of other people

Most people's choice of activity is influenced by others. People tend to choose the same activities as their friends, or members of their family, and are also influenced by sporting figures they admire.

- Children often take part in the same physical activities, follow the same sports and support the same teams as their parents. However, family responsibilities may prevent parents from participating in physical activities.
- The influence of your peer group – people of the same age, status and interests as you – is important. It is much easier to succeed with the encouragement and support of friends.
- Successful sportspeople may become role models, inspiring others to take up their sport. Being a role model brings with it responsibilities – for example, not taking drugs, displaying sportsmanship and conducting themselves well outside of their sport.

Interpreting and analysing data in graphs

In Section 1.2, you examined some of the graphs used to show data and trends in physical health issues. Graphs can also be a useful way to look at socio-cultural trends or issues.

Often, graphs used for this sort of subject matter are looking at people's opinions or ideas – qualitative data rather than quantitative data. With graphs of this sort, you need to pay even more attention to exactly what the graph is showing, reading all the surrounding text carefully.

Apply it

Research available sports for people with disabilities in your local area.

Apply it

With a partner, read the following text about tennis player Andy Murray. Which factors do you think influenced his involvement in tennis?

Andy Murray and his elder brother Jamie, were both born in Dunblane, Scotland. Andy and Jamie are able-bodied and played tennis from a young age. Their mother played and coached tennis and their maternal grandfather was a professional footballer. Andy started to play tennis from the age of three and would go to his local park to learn, play and train. His parents separated when he was ten. At 15, he was asked to train with Rangers Football Club, but opted to focus on tennis instead. He moved to Barcelona, Spain, to train and his parents had to find £40,000 to pay for his stay there. He is now one of the best tennis players in the world.

Health and Performance

Look at the graphs shown in Figure 2.6. Both are about people's opinion of the impact playing sport at school had on them – the **perceived** impact, rather than the actual impact.

The first graph shows data for men and women who don't currently take part in sport on a regular basis. Read the green bars, and you'll see that it shows that:

- 49 per cent of men and 48 per cent of women agree that if they had a better experience of sport at school they would play more sport now
- 37 per cent of men and 38 per cent of women disagree with this statement
- 15 per cent of men and 14 per cent of women don't know whether they would play more sport now.

Apply it

1 Look at the second graph carefully, and answer the following questions.
   - What statement are the people agreeing or disagreeing with?
   - What is the overall picture for men and women, using statistics from the top line?
   - How much do the responses of men and women vary?

2 Look at the two graphs together and compare the results. What does this show?

Currently less/not active

Men and women who **don't** currently participate regularly have very similar opinions on the impact of their experience of sport at secondary school age on their current participation levels.

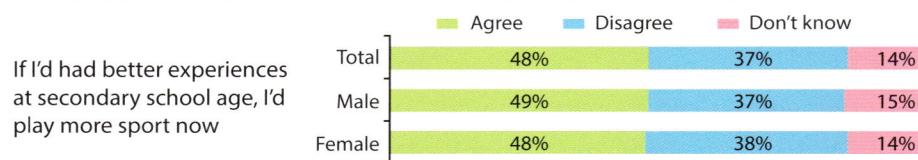

If I'd had better experiences at secondary school age, I'd play more sport now		Agree	Disagree	Don't know
	Total	48%	37%	14%
	Male	49%	37%	15%
	Female	48%	38%	14%

Currently regularly participate

Amongst regular participants, men value secondary school age experience more than women.

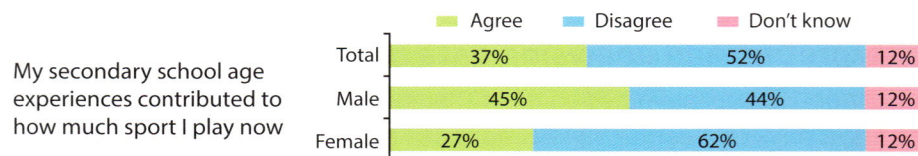

My secondary school age experiences contributed to how much sport I play now		Agree	Disagree	Don't know
	Total	37%	52%	12%
	Male	45%	44%	12%
	Female	27%	62%	12%

Figure 2.6 Perceived impact of school experience of sport on later participation

Material reproduced with permission from Sport England, www.sportengland.org

168

3.2 Commercialisation of physical activity and sport

Commercialisation means making something available on the market, or using something to make a profit. For sport, this involves lots of things that many of us take for granted, such as advertising boards at the side of pitches, sponsors' names on shirts or competitions and venues that are named after companies.

It is worth remembering that sport has not always been heavily commercialised – and that some sports still aren't. If you look back at footage from the 1966 Football World Cup Final, there are no adverts, no sponsors' branding and no players holding up boots for the cameras to see.

Commercialisation has developed as sport has become more professional – where people who play sport are paid, and people who want to see them will pay to do so. As professionalism grew, so did advertising and sponsorship, because larger audiences were available for marketers to target.

When TV coverage of sport began, it meant that advertisers and sponsors could reach millions of people at a time for some sports. World events such as the Olympics and the Football World Cup are now globally available to watch, either through television or other **media** formats. This has had a huge impact on individual players, groups, organisations and spectators.

Commercialisation, the media and sport

Increased media coverage has meant that sport has become more and more commercialised. If there were no TV, radio, newspapers and internet, sport would be very different! Because the media are there, it is inevitable that companies will try to exploit this opportunity to promote and to sell their goods and to increase their profit.

All major sports associations now see the media as a great shop window to publicise their sport, gain sponsorship, sell products and encourage more people to take up their sport – or at least follow it. Companies that invest and promote sports expect to promote their products and increase their revenue, so the sports that gain the most are those that can create large, loyal groups of viewers, readers, listeners and interactive consumers.

Today people talk about 'media sports' – those that dominate the media and are the most commercialised. We can also talk about the 'golden triangle': sport, media and business – three elements that are now inextricably linked in modern sport. Because the media and businesses invest so much money into sport, they can influence what happens. For example, Sky TV pays the Premier League over £5 million for each team per live match it shows, so they can dictate the timings of the games, in order to reach the audiences they want.

Links with sponsors also help to get more people involved in sport, which is especially important for games and activities that need to break down stereotypes, such as women's football or basketball. The extra money also provides equipment and funding for teams and players which may mean

> **Key terms**
>
> **Commercialisation**: making something available on the market; using something to make a profit.
>
> **Media**: the main means of mass communication (television, radio, newspapers and internet).

Health and Performance

Research what percentage of media coverage is dedicated to women's sport. Do you think this is enough?

being able to play nationally or internationally. At the higher levels, expert commentators in the media can give viewers a better insight and more knowledge of the game.

At all levels, but especially at grass roots level, the sponsor's product has to be considered suitable for endorsement. For example, if the sponsor is a cigarette company, there are issues associated with the negative health implications of smoking and the question 'would a sporting endorsement encourage young people to smoke?' If a suitable sponsor can be found then there are many advantages. Clubs and teams can grow, more people can be involved and they can invest in new kit, equipment and facilities.

Exam-style question

Assess the positive and negative impacts on a school netball team accepting sponsorship from a national bakery company producing cakes and biscuits. **(6 marks)**

Fashion

Many activities require the 'right' equipment – for example, you need boots to play football. Some brands of sports equipment can be fashionable – and expensive – partly as a result of media coverage of famous sportspeople. Sports stars can make a lot of money by endorsing a company's equipment, such as Rory McIlroy in golf. Sales of sports equipment and clothing are influenced by the time of year. For instance, sales of tennis equipment increase around Wimbledon fortnight in June/July, and more fitness clothing and equipment are sold around New Year.

Advantages and disadvantages of commercialisation

Table 2.4 shows some advantages and disadvantages of commercialisation in sport.

Advantages	Disadvantages
• Provides many sources of funds for individuals, groups and competitions • Can support athletes who might otherwise not be able to take part • Individual sports people and sports clubs can become rich and famous • Can support sport at a national and international level • Promotion of elite sport may be tied in with support for grass roots level sport, spreading the benefits • Brings sport to a wider audience, so raises awareness • May make people aware of sports or activities they didn't know about • May encourage more people to get involved for the first time • Promotes an active lifestyle, which is good for health • Can raise standards among athletes, who are seen as role models by the public	• Product promotion by successful sportspeople can make people want high-priced products they can't afford • Sponsors may demand things are done a certain way, which could clash with the ideals of an individual or group • Beauty parade effect – the most attractive athletes may get most support, while other good sportspeople miss out • Seat prices for events may be too expensive for many people • Audiences may find their enjoyment of sport interrupted or spoiled – for example, through advertising breaks • Sponsors can determine where and when events are put on, which may exclude some people • Marketing links may be seen as inappropriate because they push products that are not part of a healthy lifestyle – for example, chocolate

Table 2.4 Advantages and disadvantages of commercialisation in sport.

Exam-style question

Some sports have higher participation rates than others. Explain two ways in which the media can **discourage** participation in some sports. **(4 marks)**

Exam tip

Make sure you read the question carefully, and note any words in bold. Here, you need ways in which the media discourage participation, not encourage it.

Health and Performance

Interpretation and analysis of graphical representation

The commercialisation of physical activity and sport is increasing year on year. This can be seen in the media and in the volume of branded merchandise that is now sold.

The English football Premier League is now officially known as the Barclays Premier League due to a sponsorship deal with Barclays, and all the clubs in the Premier League have sponsorship agreements with companies who display their brands and products on team shirts and around stadiums. The Arsenal FC stadium, for example, is now known as the Emirates Stadium as the club are sponsored by the airline Emirates in a long-term deal worth a reported £150 million.

Professional sport has become 'big business' and many companies, both in the United Kingdom and globally, invest millions of pounds in sports to increase awareness of their brands and commercial products.

Trends in revenue for some of these clubs can be seen during the football season with merchandise sales increasing in the period August to May. Other factors can also influence how much money a club makes from sales of merchandise, such as its position in the Premier League.

The higher a club finishes, the more attractive it becomes to potential fans/customers. The limited number of seats in a stadium also means clubs can charge a premium for tickets in response to increased demand.

Also, the higher a club finishes, the more valuable players it will look to attract to compete in elite domestic and European competition. Season ticket income is an important contribution towards the costs of signing and paying players.

Graphs or charts are a useful way of seeing at a glance different trends in sport. Understanding how to interpret the information you see in a table, graph or chart is an important skill.

Exam-style question

The graph below shows the final position of 17 Premier League clubs for the 2014/15 season and the corresponding adult season ticket price for those clubs in 2016.

1   What overall pattern can you see in the prices of season tickets for 2016?

2   What was the 2014/15 position of the team that has the most expensive season ticket price in 2016?

3   Find out (look on the internet) which clubs were the top four at the end of the 2014/15 season. Why do you think Club no. 3 charges so much more for their season tickets than Club no. 4? What other factors might be involved?

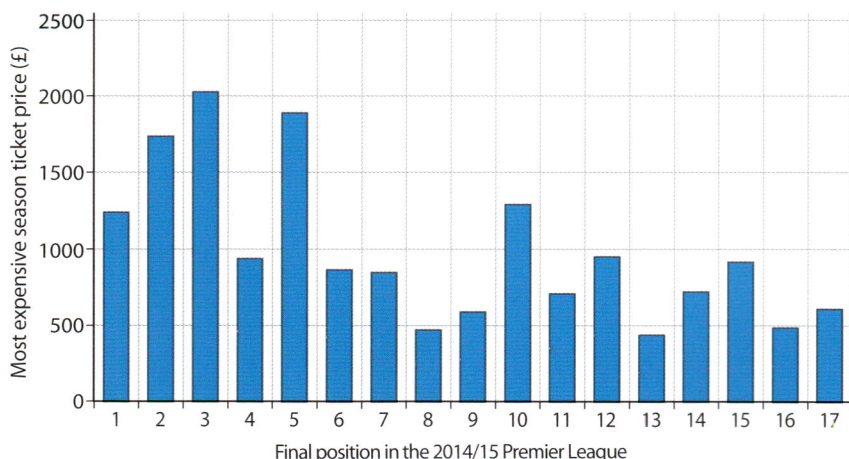

Figure 2.7: Graph to show the final position of 17 Premier League clubs for the 2014/2015 season and the corresponding adult season ticket price for those clubs in 2015-16.

3.3 Ethical and socio-cultural issues in physical activity and sport

Deviance in sport has been happening for many years and in various formats. One example would be within the game situation when someone tries to gain an advantage by breaking the rules without getting caught by the officials: for example, diving in the penalty area to try to get a penalty. Outside the game situation, it could be by taking performance-enhancing drugs. This is called **negative deviance.** All sports have rules and negative deviance occurs when the rules are broken and the referee, umpire or judge has to administer the rules. **Positive deviance** is when someone still acts outside the norm but with no intention to harm or break the rules, for example, when someone continues playing when they are injured, or when someone accidentally injures another player.

Sportsmanship and gamesmanship

Sportsmanship

Sportsmanship is when the player or competitor plays to the rules and does not cheat. For example, in football, if you know that you were the last to touch the ball, you do not claim it as your throw-in or goal kick; or in golf, if you accidently touch the ball with your club, you concede a stroke and you do not pretend that it did not happen.

Sportsmanship is playing the game and winning or losing honestly. This is the basis of sport, and is emphasised in things like the Olympic oath, which is taken by a chosen athlete from the host nation on behalf of all the competitors.

At the end of a match or competition, it is traditional to shake hands and congratulate your opponent, whether you have won or lost, each showing respect to the other having played the game.

At the top level of sport, sportsmanship plays an important and positive role for the sport. The players are role models, watched by millions of people, including many children who will copy their heroes.

Gamesmanship

The opposite of sportsmanship is known as **gamesmanship**. Gamesmanship is when you aim to win by whatever means possible, within or outside of the rules.

For example, you may break the rules by taking illegal performance-enhancing drugs, as many top sports stars have done. In a typical game situation, gamesmanship could mean claiming a catch in cricket when you know the ball

Sportsmanship has an impact on the sport itself, as it can promote the sport and encourage children to play 'in the right spirit'

Key terms

Deviance: behaviour that falls outside the norms or what is thought to be acceptable; goes against the moral values or laws of the sport.

Negative deviance: deviance that has a detrimental effect.

Positive deviance: deviance where there is no intention to cause harm or break the rules.

Sportsmanship: qualities of fairness, following the rules, being gracious in defeat or victory.

Gamesmanship: Bending the rules/laws of a sport without actually breaking them.

Apply it

Research the Olympic oath online and consider how it fits with the principles of sportsmanship.

Health and Performance

Give an example of gamesmanship you have experienced in your sport

did not touch the bat, or in tennis by claiming that your opponent's shot was out when you know it was in.

Some special terms have been developed to describe particular sorts of gamesmanship. In many field games, we talk about 'professional fouls', when an attacker is deliberately fouled to stop him or her scoring when they are in a good shooting position. In cricket, the phrase 'sledging' is used when the fielding team make unsuitable comments to the batsman to break their concentration when the bowler is running up to bowl to them.

Remember: if you cheat, you lose the inner satisfaction of victory, as well as the respect of your opponents.

Interpreting graphs

Graphs are used less often for data on ethical and socio-cultural issues in sport, but they can still be a useful way to display information or encourage discussion.

Figure 2.8 shows the number of red cards awarded in Premiership football matches over eight seasons, from the 2007/8 season to the 2014/15 season. The bottom line shows the number of 'straight' red cards issued (meaning the player is sent off immediately); the top line shows the number of red cards shown after two cautions (yellow cards) were issued to the same player during a single match.

A graph like the one below provides useful statistics which can help you to understand about trends in sport. For example, you could compare the number of cards issued between one season and another; or by adding

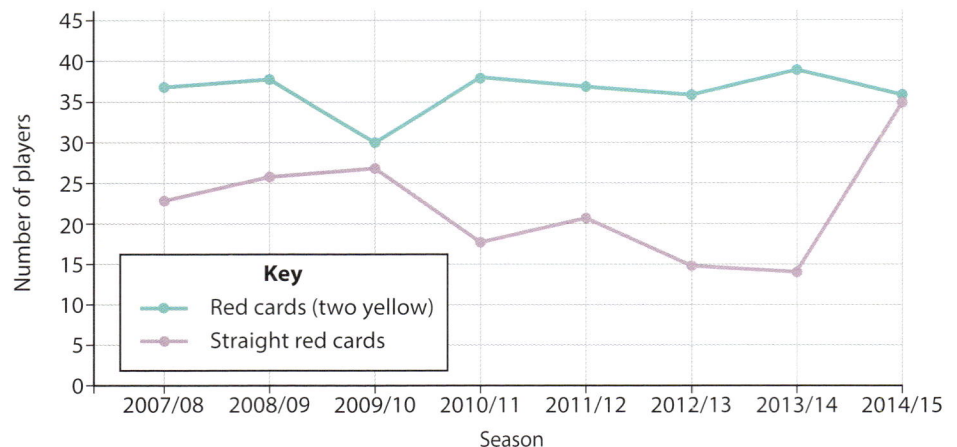

Figure 2.8 Graph to show the number of red cards given out over a number of football seasons

up the numbers of both types of card awarded in a particular season, you can work out the total number of cards issued each season. You could also calculate values such as the mean, median or mode across the eight seasons, which you could use to support any analysis or conclusions you reach about patterns and trends.

Season	Red cards (two yellow)	Straight red cards	Total number of red cards issued
2007-2008	23	37	
2008-2009	26		64
	27	30	57
2010-2011		38	56
	21	37	58
2012-2013		36	51
	14	39	
2014-2015	35		71

Table 2.5: Total number of red cards given in Premiership matches from 2007/08 to 2014/15

Apply it

- Look at Table 2.5, which has been partially completed. Use the information from the graph to help you fill in the blank spaces in the table.
- With a partner, discuss what this information reveals about the general trends in fouls and misconduct in football. Are the numbers of red cards on the increase or are they declining? Is this the same for 'straight' red cards and for red cards given after two yellow cards? What factors might account for this?

Summary

Key points to remember:

Engaging in sport

- Participating rates vary according to:
  - gender – some sports still seen as 'male' or 'female'
  - age – some sports suit younger people (e.g. gymnastics) or older people (e.g. golf, bowls)
  - socio-economic group – can affect choice of sport, but things change; cost can be a factor
  - ethnicity – some sports more common in certain groups; racism in sport
  - disability – resources and opportunities may be fewer
  - people – peer group, family, role models
- Graphs can help show socio-cultural trends – make sure you can interpret them

Commercialisation of sport

- Commercialisation – making something available on the market, or using something to make a profit
- Commercialisation, the media and sport are connected:
  - media coverage
  - sponsorship
  - fashions
- Commercialisation has:
  - advantages – e.g. more funding, wider audience, active lifestyle, awareness
  - disadvantages – e.g. higher prices, sponsors lead sport, 'beauty parade'

Ethical and socio-cultural issues

- Different types of sporting behaviour
  - sportsmanship – competitor plays to the rules and does not try to cheat
  - gamesmanship – competitor aims to win by any means, within or outside of the rules
  - deviance – behaviour that falls outside the norms of what is thought to be acceptable
- Graphs can be used to display data on these issues

Preparing for your exam: Component 2 Health and Performance

The Edexcel GCSE (9-1) Physical Education consists of two externally examined papers. This section of the book has been designed to help you prepare for the exam paper covering Component 2.

Overview of the exam paper

Component 2 covers all the topics related to Health and Performance. The written exam will be 1 hour and 15 minutes and will be out of 70 marks. This component will be worth 24 per cent of your final marks.

The examination will also include multiple-choice questions but, unlike Component 1, there will be fewer. These will be followed by short-answer questions which will be worth either two, three or four marks. There will again be two nine-mark extended writing essay questions. You must answer all questions. You should make sure you allow enough time to complete these – try to spend at least 15 minutes on each of these questions to plan and write your answer as well as checking over all your answers at the end.

Exam strategy

The way the questions are worded in the exam will give you a strong clue as to the objectives you are being assessed against and the level of detail required in your answer. See page 118 for the objectives you'll be assessed on in the written exam.

The important words in an exam question are called '**command words**'. Familiarise yourself with these and get to know what is needed for each type of word. Figure 2.9 shows examples of some of the most common ones.

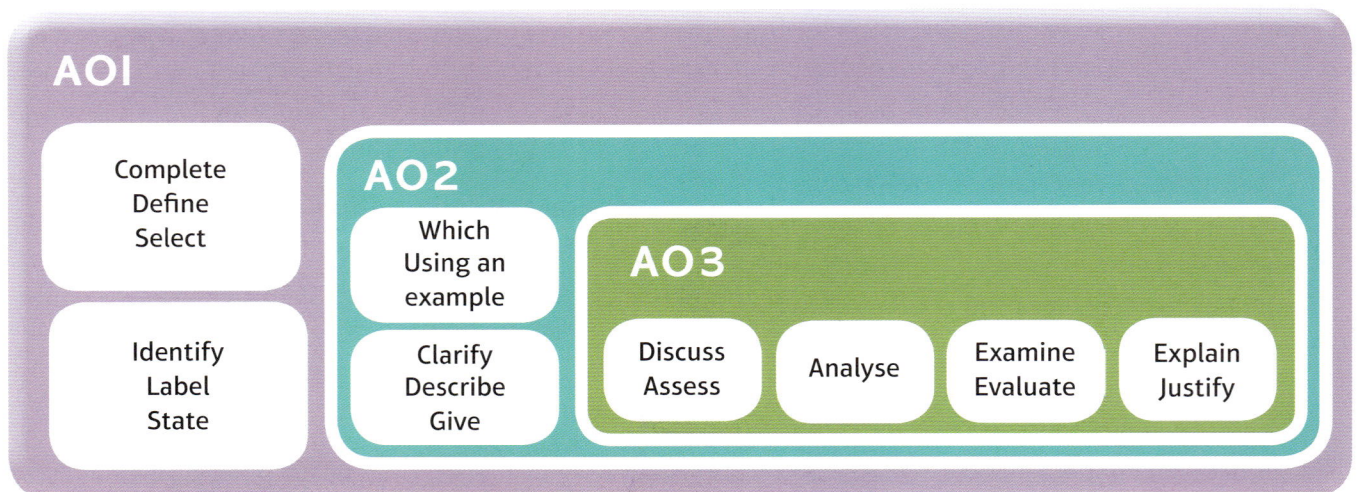

Figure 2.9 Examples of common command words used in assessment objectives

Preparing for your exam

Any question which begins with 'label' or 'identify' is usually assessing A01 objectives.

Table 2.6 gives some definitions of command words, which will help you understand how much detail you need to include in the answers you provide in your exam.

Command word	Definition
Assess	Requires a reasoned argument of factors in order to reach a judgement
Analyse	Break something down into its component parts
Calculate	Requires computation (use of mathematical skills) in relation to data
Classify	Group items or place them on a scale based on their characteristics
Complete	Add information to something (e.g. a graph, table, chart or sentence)
Define	Give the meaning of a word or term
Describe	Give an account of something without reasons. Statements in your response need to be linked to each other
Discuss	Explore the situation/problem, giving different or contrasting viewpoints, e.g. advantages or disadvantages
Examine	Justify or exemplify a point using analysis or evaluation
Explain	Justify or exemplify a point. Must contain some linked reasoning
Evaluate	Review/analyse information, bringing it together to form a conclusion/judgement based on strengths/weaknesses. Come to a supported judgement of a subject's qualities in relation to its context
Give	Involves the recall of a fact or an example
Identify	Requires a selection from a given resource, such as an option from a multiple-choice question, or analysis of data from source material, such as a graph
Justify	Give reasons for your answers
Label	Requires you to add named structures or features to a diagram
Select	Make a choice based on an evaluation of information you are given
State	Involves the recall of a fact but can also require you to analyse information
Using an example	Provide an example to support the point you're making
Which	Mainly used in multiple-choice questions where you'll need to select an answer from a set of options

Table 2.6 Command words

Now let's look at examples of some questions and responses of the kind you may find in your exam paper.

Component 2, Question 5

Describe how and why a sportsperson would include carbohydrate loading in their diet. **(3 marks)**

Exam tip

Read the question! The question asks **how** and **why** a sportsperson uses carbohydrate loading so make sure you cover both areas. It uses the command word 'describe', so make sure you link your statements, e.g. don't just say what carbohydrate loading is, but say how and why it could be used by a sportsperson.

Average answer

❶ Carbo-loading is used by endurance athletes. It is where a runner consumes increased amounts of carbohydrates in the days leading up to a competition so they have more energy.

❶ Identifies increased consumption of carbohydrates before an event but lacks detail. No mention of why – more energy is vague.

Verdict

This question targets assessment objectives A01 and A02. It is an average answer because although the student has identified the type of sportsperson who might increase their consumption of carbohydrates there is no detail about how or why the athlete would use carbohydrate loading.

A01. The student **knows and understands** the basics of carbohydrate loading.

A02. The student **has not applied** the knowledge. There is no link about why an athlete would use carbohydrate loading.

Strong answer

❶ An endurance athlete may reduce the amount of training 4-5 days before an important competition (this is called tapering) and reduce their carbohydrate intake. Then in the 24-48 hour period before the race they would increase their carbohydrate intake to increase their glycogen stores. ❷ This means that they will be able to utilise these stores for longer in the race and delay fatigue. Consequently, they should perform better late in the race.

Verdict

❶ Detailed analysis of how carbohydrate loading is used by endurance athlete.

❷ Reasons provided for use of carbohydrate loading.

This is a strong answer. The student has given a detailed description of how carbohydrate loading is achieved in the context of a specific sport and also linked this to the benefits the athlete hopes to achieve from the process.

A01. The student clearly **knows and understands** the concept of carbohydrate loading and describes it in detail.

A02. The student **has also applied** the knowledge. There is a clear link between both how and why a sportsperson uses carbohydrate loading and an explanation of which type of athlete would benefit from this.

Component 2, Question 14

Evaluate the advantages and disadvantages of the increasing commercialisation of sport and the media for the player/performer and sponsor. *(9 marks)*

Exam tip

The command word is 'evaluate'. Advantages and disadvantages of commercialisation is asked for so make sure you cover both areas. The focus is narrowed to the performer and sponsor so make sure you concentrate on these two aspects. You should also remember to come to a supported judgement of the relative merits of each viewpoint.

Average answer

Commercialisation of sport is about the increasing use of business in ❶ sport. Most football teams now have sponsors' names on their shirts and even competitions like the Barclays Premier League have sponsors.

A lot of stadiums are sponsored now, like the Amex stadium at Brighton. This means that the sponsor's name can be seen on television. One of the main advantages of commercialisation in sport is that there is more money in sport and players get paid extremely high salaries. Television companies, particularly SKY, now pay huge amounts ❷ of money to broadcast sport. This is good as it means there is more sport to watch on television.

The disadvantage of commercialisation is that players now cheat more in order to win.

Footballers dive to get penalties and in athletics lots of athletes take drugs. They also earn too much money in my opinion. Lots of football clubs also now have very rich owners. Managers often get sacked when results are not good – sometimes after just a few games.

❸ Sport has also been 'jazzed up' to make it more attractive. All in all, I think the commercialisation of sport has been a good thing because players now earn more money and there is more sport on television.

❶ Defines commercialisation but reference to sponsors doesn't really address the question – a hint of an advantage, i.e. exposure on TV.

❷ Identifies an advantage and disadvantage of commercialisation to player but no analysis, i.e. why do they cheat more?

Offers their own opinion about players' salaries but doesn't back this up with any reason.

❸ Reference to owners and sport being made more attractive to the spectator is not relevant to question.

Verdict

This is a lower level response.

A01. The student has demonstrated that they **know and understand** some of the advantages and disadvantages of commercialisation of sport in relation to the player/performer and sponsor – albeit at a fairly superficial and shallow level.

A02. The student has not **applied or linked** the information. For example, why do players cheat? Because of the rewards. These are not only financial but also include fame, etc. What are the disadvantages of this fame? The answer could include points such as media intrusion into private lives, need to maintain a suitable image, etc.

A03. The student has not **analysed** or **evaluated** the question. What has been the impact of increased money in sport? Why are sponsors so keen to pay millions of pounds to clubs/players? What happens if a player's behaviour on or off the field causes embarrassment to the sponsor?

Preparing for your exam

Strong answer

Sport has seen huge changes over the last 20 years since businesses, the media and commercialisation have become commonplace.

Being a professional sportsperson is now an extremely lucrative profession. This means they can concentrate on training without financial worries. ❶ Salaries are very high due to the influx of money from the media, sponsors and wealthy owners of clubs. Some would argue that the salaries paid to professional footballers are obscenely high and that they have lost touch with the core fans. Being a professional sportsperson also provides fame and adulation from the public. Many endorse products and earn as much from endorsements and adverts as they do from the sport itself – for example Jessica Ennis-Hill endorses Adidas and Olay as well as being the face of Santander bank. Roger Federer is one of the highest paid sportsmen in the world who makes more from his endorsements than he does from tennis.

With this fame and fortune comes some downsides. First of all, there is now more intrusion into players' personal lives and often stories are front page news instead of confined to the sports pages. Any indiscretions are seized upon and are in the public eye. There is an expectation that sportspersons ❷ are squeaky clean as they are role models to younger people. There is also an increased temptation to cheat – whether this is taking drugs in order to win competitions or diving to win penalties in football. This is because of the increased pressure to succeed and win due to both the financial rewards and fame.

The pressure may also come from coaches and the public. This puts the performer in a difficult position particularly if they feel that others are cheating and they need to do so themselves to keep up.

Sponsors are now commonplace in sport – businesses pay huge amounts of money to have their name placed on a team's shirt or associated with a competition or even a stadium. This is because they get more publicity having their name projected into every living room in the country through television coverage. Their product gets associated with excellence in the sporting field and will encourage more sales of the product.

The disadvantage for sponsors is when a team or a player is either performing badly or gets discredited. For example, sponsorship has been withdrawn when athletes have come under criminal investigation. None of the businesses want to have their name tarnished.

❶ Good analysis of the advantages and disadvantages of commercialisation to the player/performer backed up with relevant examples.

❷ Further analysis about advantages and disadvantages of commercialisation, media and sponsors, which is backed up with more relevant and topical examples which demonstrates understanding of the issue being addressed.

❸ I believe that the influx of money and sponsorship has largely been good for sport. Sport is more entertaining, there is more sport to watch on TV for the public, players earn huge salaries and standards of performance continue to grow. However, sport needs to be careful that it does not lose its soul and be overwhelmed by business. There is already a case that it has too much influence – for example, dictating kick-off times and the scheduling of games/tournaments.

❸ Nice conclusion which also exhibits some analysis of the topic, i.e. sport losing its soul.

Verdict

This is a high level response.

A01. The student **knows and understands** the advantages and disadvantages of commercialisation and media to the player. Makes clear reference to some of the issues.

A02. The student **applies** their knowledge to the question with good examples which support the various points being made. The examples are relevant and topical.

A03. The student has **analysed and evaluated** the question. The dilemma for sponsors and behaviour of athletes is addressed and there is analysis of the pressure on athletes to perform well.

Individual and team activities

Getting started

You will no doubt have taken part in a variety of sporting activities already and you may represent your school and/or play for a team outside of school in your sports. This is your chance to use your skills and enthusiasm for your sport for your GCSE examination, but look at the criteria first, take your teacher's advice and choose wisely so that you achieve as many marks as possible towards your final grade.

Learning objectives

By the end of this topic you will understand:

- what you need to do for the practical component of your course
- what activities you can do
- how you will be assessed and marked on your practical performances
- how to prepare effectively for your performances.

What do I need to do for my practical performance?

The practical part of the course is designed to test your skill in a range of practical performances. It will provide 30 per cent of your final grade; 10 per cent from each of three practical activities.

You need to choose **three** activities in total and you will need to perform three different physical activities, in the role of player/performer. You can choose either:

- **two** team activities and **one** individual activity, or
- **two** individual activities and **one** team activity.

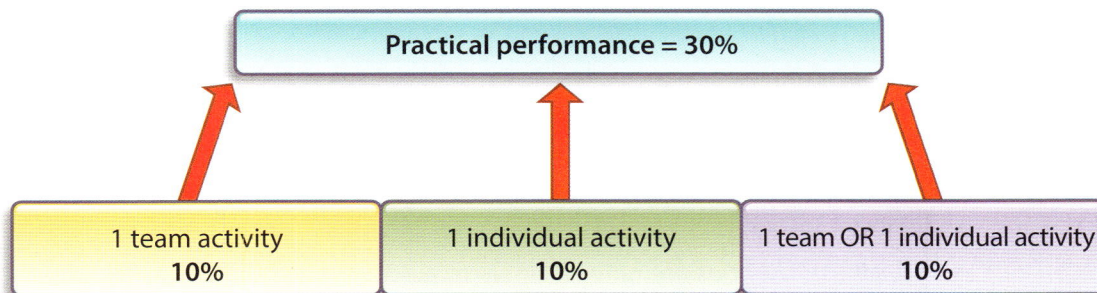

Practical performance = 30%		
1 team activity 10%	1 individual activity 10%	1 team OR 1 individual activity 10%

Figure 3.1 How the grading for your practical performance works

Practical Performance

What activities can I choose?

There is a set list of team and individual activities that you can choose from.

Specialist activities*	Individual activities
Association football	Amateur boxing
Badminton (doubles)	Athletics
Basketball	Badminton
Camogie	Canoeing
Cricket	Cycling
Dance (group or pair)	Dance
Gaelic football	Diving
Handball	Golf
Hockey	Gymnastics
Hurling	Equestrian
Lacrosse	Kayaking
Netball	Rock climbing
Rowing	Rowing
Rugby league	Sculling
Rugby union	Skiing
Squash (doubles)	Snowboarding
Table tennis (doubles)	Squash
Tennis (doubles)	Swimming
Volleyball	Table tennis
	Tennis
	Trampolining
Specialist activities*	
Blind cricket	Boccia
Goalball	Polybat
Powerchair football	
Table cricket	
Wheelchair basketball	
Wheelchair football	
Wheelchair rugby	

Table 3.1 GCSE PE approved activities

*Specialist activities are only available to students with a physical disability

Your teacher will help you to choose carefully. There are some combinations of activities that are not allowed and specific rules apply to some of the activities – it is vital to check with your teacher before making your final choices. For example, if you want to choose diving, this must be platform diving and if you want to do gymnastics, you can only do floor routines and apparatus.

Your teacher will also help you ensure you get the right combination of activities. For example, if you choose to do tennis as an individual activity, you are not allowed to choose doubles tennis as a team activity.

Your school will probably be able to offer a selection of these activities. It may also allow you to include one or more out-of-school sports, such as equestrian activities, kayaking or golf. You should discuss this with your teacher, as special arrangements will be necessary, both during the course and when doing your assessment.

If you have a physical disability there are specialist activities that you can choose from, in addition to the other sports. These will be assessed based on the relevant activity's National Governing Body classification criteria.

At the start of your course, neither you nor your teacher may be sure which activities will be the best for your assessment. To begin with you may do more than three practical activities. By the time you have completed four or five activities, you should have a good idea of your standard in each. Then you can decide which your three best activities are, and you can be assessed on these.

Specialist activities are available to those with a disability

Practical case study

Emma is taking GCSE Physical Education. She is good at several sports, but she has not yet decided which three she will offer as her practical activities for the exam.

She is an excellent athlete, representing both the school and her athletics club, so she decides to choose this as an individual activity.

Emma has to choose two other activities, one of which must be a team activity. She likes badminton (singles – she doesn't play much doubles), netball and volleyball. However, she is not sure which two will give her the best scores. Emma takes some time to look at the criteria for each of the activities with her teacher, and they discuss her level of performance in each. They assess which are currently her two best activities and how much she can improve over the next two years before the examination/**moderation**.

Emma is lucky; whichever two activities she selects, she will have the right combination: either two team activities (volleyball and netball) and one individual activity (athletics), or two individual activities (athletics and badminton singles) and one team sport (volleyball or netball).

After looking at the sports criteria with her teacher, Emma decides that her next best sport is badminton singles – she won't have to rely on a partner to practise doubles with. She also decides on netball. She is at about the same level as she is at volleyball, but she is in the school team for netball and so gets regular practice and matches.

So Emma's chosen activities are:

- athletics (individual activity)
- badminton singles (individual activity)
- netball (team sport).

Key term

Moderation: the assessment of work to ensure it is in accordance with agreed criteria and procedures.

Practical Performance

How you will be assessed

The assessment of your three practical activities can take place at any time during your course. Usually this will be at the end of a block of work on the activity, but it may be towards the end of your two-year course.

For each of your three activities, teaching and assessment will be carried out over a number of sessions, totalling around 12 hours. These sessions will usually be a series of practices in the skills of the activity, including small-sided games and the full game for team sports and individual sports, although this will vary according to the activity. During the assessment you will be set tasks by your teacher, who will be aiming to allow you to perform to the best of your ability.

Recording your teacher assessment

This assessment will be filmed to produce evidence to justify the marks you have been awarded. A camera will be set up in a position that will give the best possible recording of your performance. You will have to give your name and student number, and say what activity you are doing. Then the recording will begin and your performance will be recorded. The unedited video then acts as evidence, to justify the mark you have been awarded by your teacher.

Moderating your performance

At the end of your course, normally between March and May of your second year (Year 11) your assessment will be 'moderated'. An assessor (**moderator**) will visit your school and check that you are being assessed and marked accurately using the set criteria; they also ensure marking is consistent between other students and schools.

When the moderator comes in – moderation day – you will be assessed (again) and marked by the moderator. The moderator may be present for all of your practical activities or just for some of them. This depends on the number of people from your school taking the course, or the activities themselves (for example, for skiing, video evidence would be required). Your teacher will mark you in each activity before moderation day using the set criteria, and the moderator will mark you on the moderation day, against the same criteria.

Your teacher will work with you to make sure that filming goes as smoothly as possible and meets the requirements, ensuring that, for example:

- you can be identified in a team game, by wearing a numbered bib
- the camera angles and types of shot capture the performance well
- the equipment is working properly.

Depending on how many are taking the course at your school, and on factors such as being overseas, you may have to be moderated completely by video. In this case, your video will be sent to the moderator to confirm your marks.

The marking criteria

When your teacher looks at your performance during your course, and when the moderator looks at it on moderation day, they will assess it against set criteria. There are criteria for each sport and activity, and there will be particular things the moderators are looking for in each of the activities you do.

For each sport or activity, there are levels of performance; within each level, there are criteria for which marks will be awarded.

Levels

For each sport or activity, the criteria are set out in levels, from level 1 to level 5. Level 1 is the lowest level and level 5 is the highest.

When you are assessed, the moderator will first decide which level your performance should be placed in. They use a 'best-fit' approach, to see which of the levels in the guide best describes the quality of your performance.

Marks

Moderators then assess the mark you should get within that level. Here they look in more detail at your performance against the criteria, to work out your mark.

For example, if you are being assessed in table tennis, the assessors may decide that you are at level 3. This means they can give you between 11 and 15 marks. To decide your final mark for this activity, they would look at your skills in certain strokes, like topspin drives, forehand and backhand and forehand and backhand loops, as well as how consistent you are and how well you use tactics. If you do these well, you could get 15 marks; if not, you might get 11 marks.

How your marks are decided

For each of your activities, you will be assessed against two main criteria:

- your performance of skills and techniques in isolation or unopposed situations
- your application of skills and techniques and decision making under pressure – during conditioned practices or competitive situations.

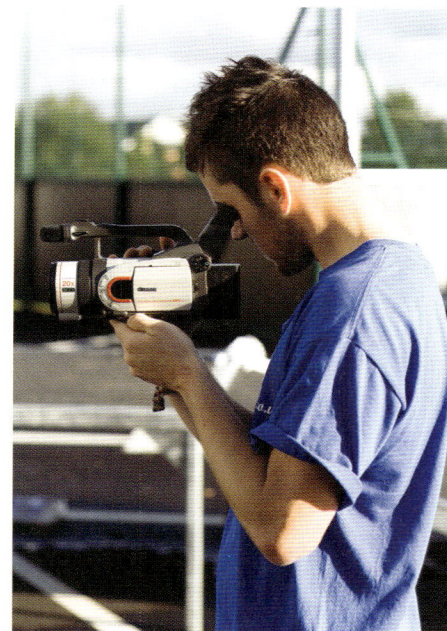

Your performance will be recorded for moderation

Practical Performance

There are more marks available in competitive situations

The marks you can get for each of these are very different. For each of your activities, you can get:

- a maximum of 10 marks for isolated skills
- a maximum of 25 marks for conditioned practices and competitive situations.

The second mark, for performance in conditioned practices and competitive situations, scores a lot more than the skills in isolation, because sport is mainly about performance in the competitive situation.

Isolated skills

Some activities will be similar, and will have comparable types of assessment. For example, in a team game such as football, netball, rugby or basketball, you will practice skills such as passing and shooting to show that you can perform the skill well, you can shoot a set shot correctly with good technique and score from various positions in a practice session.

In an individual activity this could be:

- in swimming, performing a tumble turn in front crawl after swimming 10 metres
- in trampolining, performing a front somersault but not in a 10-bounce routine.

This performance is marked out of 10 marks using the criteria set out in the *Practical Performance Assessment Guide*.

Your isolated skills can earn you up to 10 marks

Conditioned practices and competitive situations

You will perform in a variety of conditioned practices, where there are certain limits and instructions concerning what you have to do.

For example:

- in table tennis, you may have to only play forehand shots, so if your opponent plays the ball onto your backhand, you have to move around the table to play a forehand
- in basketball, it may be that you can only score with a jump shot from outside the three-second area
- in netball, it could be that you have to have at least six passes to teammates before you can shoot
- in football, it could be a 3v1 practice in a 10 m² grid, where you will be expected to find space, call for the ball and make good, accurate, short passes when you have the ball
- in trampolining, it could be a short sequence including a front somersault (such as a half turn, tuck jump, front somersault, pike jump, out bounce)
- in a racket game, it could be a short sequence (such as, in badminton: a high service, high clear (return), smash (return), drop shot (return).

The final part of the assessment is the competitive situation. For example, you could be assessed on:

- a full game, for team games such as football, netball, hockey, rugby or basketball
- a game, for racket sports such as badminton, table tennis or tennis
- individual activities such as:
  - in trampolining, performing a 10-bounce routine
  - a floor routine in gymnastics – 60–90 seconds
  - in swimming, performing a 100m front crawl
  - in athletics, performing a 1500m race or high jump or shot put.

In this part of the assessment, your teacher will mark you out of 25, again using the criteria set out in the *Practical Performance Assessment Guide*. In this situation you must perform as if it was in a competition, e.g. as fast as you can in the swimming and athletics or best quality of performance in trampoline and gymnastics.

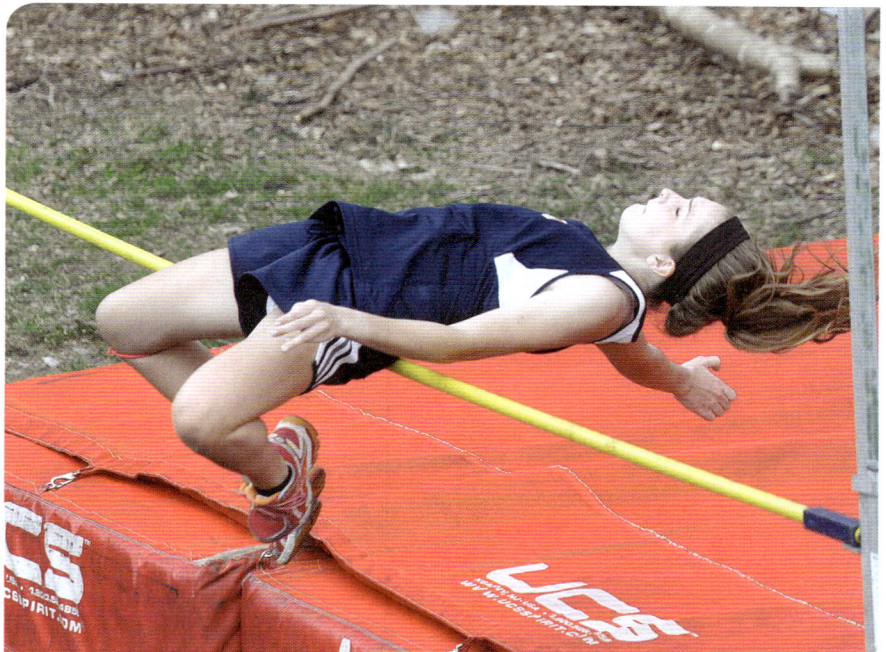

Your conditioned practices and competitive situations will earn you up to 25 marks

Practical Performance

Practical case study

On moderation day, Jack has to perform his three practical performances:

- football (team game)
- basketball (team game)
- trampoline (individual activity).

He has made sure that his combinations fit the requirements, with two team activities plus one individual activity.

Jack knows that preparation starts before moderation day: he has to get things ready for the day to give himself the best chance to perform well. He has a timetable for the day, he knows his partners and group for each practice and each activity, and he is clear about the positions he is in for each team game. He knows his bib colour and his bib number for each activity and what practices he has to do in each sport. He also makes a list of everything he has to take to school on the day, including the correct kit, water and the snacks he may need.

Jack is keen to score at the higher end of the levels in each sport he is doing. He has made sure that he knows what mark he is currently at and what he wants to improve to on the day. He has also discussed with his teacher what he needs to do to achieve his SMART goals on the day.

In both of the team games Jack has scored well in the individual practices and the conditioned games, but he needs to make sure that, in the game situation, he:

- does not make any unforced errors, such as bad passes or misjudgements
- influences the game
- shows good communication skills.

In trampolining – his individual activity – Jack again does well in the individual skills, but he knows he must make sure that he:

- shows good technique at all times
- completes the 10-bounce routine with good height and no travel or gain
- finishes with a good somersault and out bounce.

Before each activity, he goes through a routine to calm his nerves and prepare himself emotionally. He knows he will need to apply his knowledge and skills to achieve his best performance. Jack knows that this is not just an ordinary performance but his own 'Cup Final', so he needs to prepare well and do his absolute best on the day.

Total marks

For each activity, you can get a total of:

10 marks for individual skills + 25 marks for competitive situation = 35 marks

You do three activities for your practical performance, so overall a total of:

35 marks × 3 activities = 105 marks

How to get a better mark

Your marks for individual skills are important, but the marks for conditioned practices and competitive situations are crucial to getting a good mark overall.

- When playing in the game situation, remember that performing the skills effectively and with good technique is very important. This could mean making sure you point your toes in trampolining, or pointing to the ring when you complete a free throw or jump shot in basketball.

- Be aware throughout your preparation and your performance that choosing good strategies and demonstrating good decision-making skills are important, and will gain you marks. For example, passing to a teammate instead of shooting yourself when they have a better chance of scoring than you.

- It will help you to know what your teacher and the moderator are looking for, so you need to know the criteria before you start each practical activity. You can find these criteria in the *Practical Performance Assessment Guide*.

Understanding the criteria will also help you to assess your performance as it is now, before you start your practical activity course.

Preparing for your practical performance

Linking theory and performance

During your course you will be learning theory in some lessons and improving your practical activities in others. These two elements complement each other. Understanding the theory behind what you physically do will help you improve your performance, and performing will allow you to apply the theory you have learned.

Having a strong understanding of the relevant theory from Components 1 and 2 of the course will benefit your performance in a number of ways.

- **Using SMART goals** – in Component 2, Topic 2 you learned how to set SMART goals for yourself. If you do this during your preparation for your practical activities, you have a better chance of achieving your goals – and ultimately getting the best mark of which you are capable.

- **Understanding your psychology** – in Component 2, Topic 2 you also studied the importance of the emotional/psychological aspect of sport – how you think and how you cope when training or taking part in physical activities. Having a good understanding of what drives you can help you demonstrate psychological control in a game situation – perhaps enabling you to manage your anxiety or channel your aggression in a positive way. Knowing the theory can also make you more alert to the motives and actions of other players. It can also help you to keep trying your best after you have made a mistake or missed an opportunity.

- **Being aware of socio-cultural influences** – in Component 2, Topic 3 you looked at how people are influenced by their backgrounds and situations.

Practice

Choose one of your practical activities. Be honest with yourself and think about which level you are currently performing at in your chosen sport (against the criteria in the *Practical Performance Assessment Guide*). Ask others for feedback and ask your teacher what he or she thinks. Think about what you need to do to reach the next level. When you understand why you are not at a higher level, you can work on improving your weaker points.

Practical Performance

Practice

Think ahead to your practical performance and make some notes on how you might apply theory from Components 1 and 2 to your particular activities. Make sure you review your notes regularly, to ensure that you are applying the theory.

Sportsmanship is about playing fairly, respecting your own team and opponents and accepting victory or defeat graciously

If you apply this theory during your practical performance, it can help you communicate more effectively with other players and demonstrate your individual role in achieving the collective outcome.

- **Applying sportsmanship** – remember to be a good 'sportsman' and play to the rules.

Emotional/psychological and physical preparation

Getting ready for your assessment starts from the moment you begin your course. Your assessment is your personal 'Cup Final': you will have prepared for two years for it, so you will want to do the best that you can.

To do your best, you will need to make sure that you:

- do the work, in the classroom and at home
- understand how the course and assessment work, so that you know what you are aiming for
- keep yourself in the best shape you can, physically and emotionally, so that you are always prepared.

As the assessment gets closer, during the lead-up and even on the day itself, there are some simple but important things you can do to make sure that you can perform at your best.

Emotional/psychological preparation

Having a good attitude and an understanding of what is required of you can make all the difference to how you perform on assessment day. Here are some tips to help you arrive emotionally and psychologically prepared for the task ahead.

- Try using visualisation techniques to help you get tricky or complicated skills right. Think of your best performance in each of your activities and how it made you feel. For example, if you often serve into the net in tennis, visualise doing it perfectly before you serve.

- Increase your self-confidence by doing everything you possibly can to prepare for the day. If you get nervous before assessment, take a moment to sit quietly to reassure yourself that you are ready to give the best performance of your life.

- Be aware of your weaknesses as well as your strengths. This will help you to make fewer mistakes on the day. For example, if in a basketball game you often lose the person you are marking, keep this in mind during the game situation in the assessment; be prepared to act on it and correct your error.

How do you and your team support each other?

- Think about what you will do if you do make a mistake. Be ready to keep your head up, keep performing and be even more determined to do well.

- Get to know and be supportive to the other students in your team activities. Developing a 'team spirit' will help your whole group perform better.

- Remember: good sportsmanship – not gamesmanship.

- Make sure you know the details of what you are about to do. This will help you shape and target your performance. You should be clear on:
  - your target mark for each of your three activities and what the assessment asks for to get that grade
  - the order of the activities you will be assessed in
  - what you will do in your warm up and cool down for each activity
  - what practices you are going to do in each activity, and who you will work with
  - what skills you will be demonstrating in each activity
  - how you will rest and recover between each activity
  - the assessment criteria, should the moderator talk to you.

- Make sure you understand the rules and etiquette of your activities and the health and safety aspects of your sports – and that you follow them on the day of assessment.

Practice

For your team activity, think about your weakest skill. Make sure you know what the skill should look like at its best then visualise yourself doing this perfectly.

Link it up

Review Component 2, Topic 2 on sport psychology. As you read, think about how you could apply the theory to your own practical performance.

Practical Performance

Physical preparation

By the time you reach your assessments you should be thoroughly prepared in health and fitness. Throughout the course, you should make sure that you:

- have a healthy, balanced diet – see Component 2, Topic 1
- get enough sleep and rest – see Component 2, Topic 1
- train effectively for continual improvement – see Component 1, Topic 3
- develop the skills you need for your chosen activities – see Component 2, Topic 2.

However, there is no point in being at the peak of fitness and highly skilled if you are not organised.

- Know what activities you are doing for assessment and get all the equipment for each activity ready at least the day before.
- Check your kit and equipment to make sure it is clean and functioning properly – and, if appropriate, that you have spares to take with you.
- Know your timetable for the day and make sure you arrive in good time. Remember to leave plenty of time to do your warm up.
- Write out your warm up routines, especially where you need a different warm up for each of your activities.
- Make sure you have your diet and meals planned for the day, and take any snacks, drinks and water bottles you may need.
- The night before have a healthy, balanced meal – and get a good night's sleep.

Practice

Choose one of your practical activities. Devise your warm up for that activity including the three phases: for example, cardiovascular/increasing heart rate (jogging), stretches (lunges for legs and arm rotations for upper body) and skill (jump shots in basketball). Write out your warm up in detail so that you know it and can follow it.

What is your warm up routine?

Practical case study

One of Asher's team sports is basketball. He is a guard and one of the skills he uses in the game is a jump shot. Unfortunately, this is always the skill that lets him down when he is assessed at school. When he is in a game situation he loses his nerve when shooting just outside the edge of the zone – and then he loses his technique.

Asher wants to improve this skill for the moderation, so he first gets his teacher to correct his technique, so that he will know the points to concentrate on. He discovers that the key for him is pointing to the ring when he finishes his shot. So when he practices, he goes through the technique, making sure he is looking at the ring and concentrating on finishing his shot pointing to the ring.

As he practices, he tries to calm his nerves by telling himself he can do it – so that he believes he can do it. He looks at the ring and visualises the ball arching and dropping through the ring and then when he does do it he tells himself – yes, you can do it!

Asher sets out three spots around the key that he normally shoots from in a competitive situation and practices at each spot until he has scored three times in a row. Then he moves on to the next spot, aiming to get nine in a row in total. If he does get 9/9, he takes one more, just to see if he can get the magical 10/10! As he improves, Asher gets a defender in, first of all for passive defence then he introduces a gradually more active defence. He records his practice scores to see if he is improving. He then focuses on his training experience when playing in practice and in matches.

Summary

Do

- make sure you have your timetable for the day
- know your three practical activities
- know your number and bib for moderation day
- know your team or partner for each activity and each practice
- know what you need to bring to school for the assessment
  - special things for each activity (such as your routine schedule with tariff for trampoline)
  - any equipment you need for your group
- know the practices you will be using for:
  - your team activities
  - your individual activities
  - your skill practices
- know all the practices and the order you will be doing them in
- know what mark you have set as your target and what the criteria are for you to get that mark
- know your weaknesses and try to make sure you overcome them on the day
- know your SMART goals.

Do not

- expect to turn up on the day and for everything to be done for you
- expect to get a good mark if you do not organise yourself and give your best performance
- expect to get the same mark your teacher gave you if you do not perform up to that mark on moderation day
- expect your teammates to make all the effort in the team games
- expect the other students to cover for you if you are not trying your hardest
- expect the others to do all the work, such as setting up the practices and carrying out and collecting the equipment
- forget any of the special equipment you need
- forget your snacks and water.

Aim and planning analysis

Getting started

The aim of your Personal Exercise Programme, often referred to as your PEP, is to improve your physical fitness by putting into practice much of the theory which you will have learned during the course. This will have two advantages. It will give you the opportunity to, firstly, use and apply your newly acquired theoretical knowledge and, secondly, it will improve your level of fitness. This in turn should help you to improve your practical performances in your chosen sports.

Learning objectives

By the end of this topic you will understand:

- what a PEP involves
- how your PEP will be assessed
- how to plan an appropriate PEP
- how to carry out and monitor your PEP
- how to analyse and evaluate your PEP.

Throughout your course you have learned about the theory of physical education. You have studied modules on human anatomy and physiology, on fitness and on the principles and methods of training.

For the final part of your course you will need to use this knowledge and understanding to plan, perform, analyse and evaluate a programme designed to improve a chosen aspect of your personal health and fitness. By focusing on a specific area you will gradually improve your fitness and enhance your performance in the activity you have chosen.

What is a Personal Exercise Programme (PEP)?

A PEP is a training programme that is specific to you and to your chosen physical activity or sport. It shows exactly how you plan to train in order to improve or **optimise** your performance, and records how you actually trained and improved your fitness over 6–8 weeks of monitored training.

Your PEP can be based on any physical activity from the activities list shown in the specification – it could be one of the three activities you have chosen for your practical performance, or another activity from the list. If you are unsure which activity or sport you should choose, ask your teacher for advice.

Link it up

Review Component 1, Topic 1 for information on anatomy and physiology and Component 1, Topic 3 on fitness and physical training. These will help you to plan and analyse your PEP.

Key term

Optimise: make most of.

Link it up

For more information on the activities you can use for your PEP please review Component 3.

Personal Exercise Programme (PEP)

Platform diving is one of the 23 individual activities from which you can choose. Which will you choose?

Link it up

Refer to Component 3 to see the activities that you can choose from.

Link it up

Review Component 1, Topic 3, Section 3.5 for information about PAR-Q.

How will I be assessed?

You will be assessed on your ability to analyse your plan and evaluate your PEP at the end of monitored training. You will **not** be assessed on how much you improve your performance, or on how well you actually carry out the plan.

You can submit your PEP in two ways:

- a written PEP, with a maximum of 1500 words (not including PAR-Q, graphs, charts, tables or training record forms)
- a verbal PEP; this will be recorded and should be a maximum of 15 minutes long.

Aim and planning analysis

When writing your PEP, you should start with an overall aim for your programme. You need to be able to say what you are trying to achieve – where you want to get to by the end of the planned programme. You will be expected to identify which components of fitness you want to improve and justify why these choices are suitable and how they will improve your performance.

In the introduction to your PEP, you should give the following information:

- your name and age
- the sport you have chosen for this programme (for example, hockey, rugby, athletics or swimming)
- how much experience you have in the sport you have chosen
- your current standard of performance (for example, you play for the school team)
- your strengths and weaknesses in this sport or activity.

You will need to think and plan carefully. A solid and clear plan at the beginning will help you to monitor and evaluate as you work through your PEP.

Are you ready?

Before you start any training programme you need to assess your readiness for training – and this is true for your PEP. You will need to use a suitable PAR-Q and complete it to make sure that you are healthy enough to start an exercise programme. Once you have completed a satisfactory PAR-Q, you can go ahead and examine which aspects of fitness you want to improve in your PEP.

Exam tip

Make sure you include the results of the PAR-Q in your final PEP report.

What do you want to improve?

You need to identify the component, or components, of fitness you want to improve. You should also make sure that the components you choose can be linked to SMART goals:

- cardiovascular fitness (aerobic endurance)
- muscular strength
- muscular endurance
- flexibility
- body composition

- agility
- balance
- co-ordination
- power
- reaction time
- speed.

You will see that these include basic components of fitness, such as cardiovascular fitness, but you can include components of skill-related fitness.

To make a good and informed choice, you will need to use at least two principles of training:

- individual needs – this is going to be your programme – not anyone else's – it needs to work for what you want to achieve
- **specificity** – your programme needs to fit with the particular requirements of your chosen sport or activity, so your training must be the right type and duration to enable you to meet these requirements.

When you have decided which aspects to focus on, you should state each one and say why you want to improve them. This could be improving cardiovascular fitness and muscular endurance in order to keep running at pace for the duration of a football match.

Analysing your fitness levels

You will need to analyse your own personal fitness levels and carry out tests to determine your current level of fitness. This will help you analyse and decide what you need to do in order to improve in the areas you want to develop. By testing yourself throughout your PEP, you can monitor your progress accurately. Make sure you record the results of each test you take.

Make sure that the tests you choose match the areas of fitness that you are working to improve. Use recognised fitness tests, such as:

- Cooper 12-minute run test
- Harvard step test
- grip dynamometer
- one-minute sit-up test
- one-minute press-up test
- 30m sprint test
- vertical jump/Sargent jump test
- wall sit, sit and reach test.

Link it up

Review Component 1, Topic 3, Section 3.3 for the principles of training, including individual needs and specificity.

Key term

Specificity: the particular requirements of an activity.

Link it up

Review Component 1, Topic 3, Section 3.2 for information on the components of fitness.

Which tests will you choose? Why?

Personal Exercise Programme (PEP)

Link it up

Review Component 1, Topic 3 , Section 3.2 for information on the types of tests available and what you can use them for.

Perform each of the tests you are using and work out your score. Record your score or current level now and decide what you would like to score in the test/s when you have completed your PEP. Use SMART objectives to help you plan.

Use of data

You will need to present and interpret mathematical data in your PEP. Graphs or bar charts are good ways of presenting results. For example, if you do the Cooper 12-minute run test you could take your resting heart rate before you start your warm up. Take your working heart rate as soon as you complete the run, and again every minute until it returns to your resting heart rate (or for five minutes, whichever is shorter) after you have completed the test. This is your recovery heart rate. Plot your recovery rate at one-minute intervals to make your graph.

You may devise your own appropriate tests. For example, if you choose to do circuit training, you could work out your exercises, devise your circuit and then test yourself on each exercise, including data such as:

- number of sit-ups you can do in one minute (or 30 seconds)
- number of press-ups you can do in one minute
- maximum time you can hold the plank position.

Re-test yourself after you have completed your 6–8 week programme and record the results.

Practice

1. Decide which test or tests you will use to assess your current level of fitness in the relevant components of fitness. For example, if you want to improve your cardiovascular fitness you may decide to use the Cooper 12-minute run test.

2. Explain the test and how you will perform and record it.

3. You may add in a secondary goal – for example, improving your muscular endurance or flexibility, so you could do the sit and reach test.

4. Add some daily exercises to your programme designed to improve this component of fitness.

Setting goals

When you have decided which aspects of fitness you are going to work on and you have assessed your current levels of fitness, you can progress to setting goals that will help you to achieve your overall aim. For example, your overall aim might be:

- I want to improve my general fitness level and be able to play a bigger part in the last 15 minutes of our football matches as I sometimes get substituted towards the end of the game.

However, the specific goal for your PEP would be:

- I want to improve my cardiovascular fitness and muscular endurance.

Use what you have learned about the methods of training, FITT and goal setting to help you. The FITT principle helps you determine how often you should train, how hard and for how long, and also what type of training you should choose.

Setting goals and applying SMART goals will help ensure that your plan can be achieved and that you stay motivated.

Remember your goals must be realistic and achievable. It would be unrealistic, for example, to say 'I want to run a marathon at the end of eight weeks.'

Link it up

In Component 2, Topic 2, Section 2.2 you learned about SMART goals. Review this when you are setting your goals for your PEP. To review FITT see Component 1, Topic 3, Section 3.3.

Planning your programme

After you have set your goals you need to plan your programme. You should apply your knowledge of the principles of training and the methods of training to develop a suitable programme that will enable you to reach those goals. Things to include are:

- how many training sessions you will need
- which sessions you will perform on which days of the week (for example, I will train on Monday, Wednesday and Saturday and I will do this particular session on Monday)
- which methods of training will you use, e.g.
  - to improve your cardiovascular fitness in order to keep running for the whole of the football match you could do long runs four times a week (continuous training)
  - and to improve your flexibility and muscular endurance, or your general fitness, you could add in some circuit training.

You also need to outline what you will do in your sessions: your warm up and cool down, and your main activities in each method. For example, you may decide to include a daily 15-minute set of exercises or you may add in a circuit training session once a week. If you do this you could produce circuit training cards to show what you will do at each station, with photographs of yourself doing the activity and an explanation of what is involved.

You should try to use progressive overload to ensure that the programme gradually becomes harder as you get fitter. Plan enough rest and recovery time so that your body adapts to the training.

Remember you will be expected to justify your plan. State why and how improving the fitness components you have chosen will have an impact on your performance, and why the methods of training will help you to achieve that improvement.

Planning is vital to ensure you get the best out of your PEP

Carrying out and monitoring the PEP

Now that you have created your training programme, you need to carry it out and monitor its progress.

Everything that you achieve in a training session should be recorded and reviewed against your goals. For example, in swimming, the planned goal could be to improve your time over 100 metres. On the way to achieving this target, you would measure other results, such as:

- your best time over 25 and 50 metres
- your resting heart rate and recovery rate (as a guide to fitness levels).

If your first activity is running, you could monitor your training by:

- explaining the run routes in your programme
- recording when you did your run, how far it was and what your time was (you could download an app to help you do this)
- adding a note about how it went (for example, I didn't run this session so well this week which may be because I played football yesterday).

Do the same for your second activity. For example, record how your flexibility or circuit training went. Think about whether the session was better because you had a longer warm up, for example.

You should also record any other relevant data from your training sessions: you will need to refer to it when evaluating the impact of your programme on your chosen aspect of fitness. Here are some examples of the type of data you could collect.

- During cardiovascular exercise, monitor your heart rate before you start, when working and during recovery (at one-minute intervals over five minutes).
- When exercising to improve muscular endurance, you could record, for example, the number of press-ups in one minute or the number of press-ups without stopping for a rest.

Re-testing

You could decide to do a re-test part-way through your programme – for example, after three or four weeks – or wait until you have finished the programme. You must be careful to carry out the tests in exactly the same way that you did them at the start of your programme.

If you leave the re-testing to the end of your programme, you must also carry out the tests in exactly the same way that you did before you started.

Remember every time you test your fitness levels, make sure you record the results and include them in your PEP.

Adapting your programme

As you progress through your programme, you will need to reflect on whether you are on track to achieve the goals you set. If not, you could consider adapting it: for example, changing the intensity or duration of your training.

You should record any changes and explain them in your PEP. You will also need to evaluate how any change has impacted on your performance and the effectiveness of your programme.

Other things you can do

A number of other factors could help you to reach your goals.

- If you are exercising more, consider what and when you eat. For example, you might choose to change your diet and include food groups that are relevant to your goal. If you are working on building muscle, you could decide to include more protein, or if you are doing a lot of long-distance running your intake of carbohydrates might increase, especially before a performance.
- Fit exercise around your work or study commitments and make sure you always allow time for recovery.
- You can also work on your tactics or strategies. You might change tactics for the next race, saving some energy for the last part of the race or distributing your pace more evenly over the whole course.

Evaluating your PEP

When you have completed your six- or eight-week programme, you need to analyse and evaluate the data (results) and write it up.

Evaluating your programme means considering a number of questions.

- Was it successful? Did it improve or optimise your performance?
- If so, why? If not, why not?
- How do you know whether it was successful or not? What evidence do you have?
- In what way did your performance in your chosen activity improve?
- What could you do to develop your level of fitness further?

If your fitness or performance has not improved, there may be obvious reasons (for example, you got an injury after week three). If something happened, you would explain what occurred and the implications for your training (you had to wait three weeks before starting again). However, you should also show how you adapted your programme (you could not run, but you could do flexibility exercises).

Presenting your results

You will be expected to present your data graphically, using graphs, charts, tables or diagrams. For example, you will need to show the objective results from your tests. With each graph or diagram, you should explain the main points below it. When explaining the raw data, you need to make sure that you include a suitable comparison of your pre- and post-PEP fitness test results.

Personal Exercise Programme (PEP)

You will also have subjective results, which you should write up. For example, you might want to explain that you feel fitter and no longer lack pace at the end of a game of football, and are no longer substituted towards the end of the game.

Moving on

Planning and following a PEP should give you the skills and knowledge to help you plan your fitness for the rest of your life – a valuable skill.

When you have finished your six- or eight-week programme, you should think about what you would like to do for your next PEP. Using the principle of progressive overload, start planning your follow-up programme to take you to the next level.

From the principles of training and methods of training listed below, explain which ones you have used in your programme and how you will use them to move on.

Apply it

Principles of training

- ☐ Individual needs
- ☐ Specificity
- ☐ Progressive overload
- ☐ FITT (Frequency Intensity Time Type)
- ☐ Rest and recovery
- ☐ Reversibility

Methods of training

- ☐ Continuous
- ☐ Fartlek
- ☐ Circuit
- ☐ Interval
- ☐ Plyometrics
- ☐ Weight/resistance

Summary

Key points to remember:

Your PEP

- Specific to you and your chosen sport
- About improving or optimising performance
- Choose carefully – ask your teacher for advice
- Assessment is of your planning and evaluation, not your performance

Planning

- Work out your overall aim
- Assess your current fitness
- Set your goals

- Plan your programme:
  - number of sessions
  - methods of training
  - warm up; main activity; cool down

Carrying out and monitoring

- Record your results
- Re-test part-way through
- Adapt your programme

Analysing and evaluating

- Evaluate impact on your performance
- Think about how best to present your results

Glossary

Abduction: a movement that pulls away from the midline of the body (the opposite of adduction, see below).

Acute injury: a sudden injury that is usually associated with a traumatic event, such as crashing into another player during sport, causing your bone to crack, muscles to tear or ligaments to snap.

Adaptation: your body's response to training and how your body changes to cope with new activity.

Adduction: a movement that pulls towards the midline of the body (the opposite of abduction).

Adrenaline: a hormone that increases rates of blood circulation and breathing.

Aerobic respiration: the process of releasing energy from glucose, using oxygen.

Aerobic target zone: the range within which you want your heart rate to be as you exercise.

Aesthetic appreciation: enjoying something because it is pleasing to look at: for example, as an observer rather than a participant.

Agility: the ability to control the movement of the whole body and change position quickly.

Alveoli: tiny sacs at the end of the bronchioles, where gas exchange takes place.

Alveoli: tiny sacs within our lungs that allow oxygen and carbon dioxide to move between the lungs and bloodstream.

Anabolic steroids: drugs that mimic the male sex hormone testosterone and promote bone and muscle growth.

Anaemia: a condition where there is a lack of red cells or haemoglobin in the blood.

Anaerobic exercise: working at a high intensity level without oxygen for energy production.

Anaerobic respiration: the process of releasing energy from glucose, without using oxygen.

Analgesic: a painkilling, or pain relieving drug.

Anatomy: the bodily structure of humans and animals.

Antagonistic pair: muscles that work together to create movement.

Antibody: chemical that destroys a pathogen.

Artery: a muscular tube that carries blood away from the heart.

Articulate: act as a joint.

Articulation: the state of having a joint; being a joint.

Axes: lines around which the body/body part can turn.

Axis: an imaginary straight line round which a body or object rotates.

Balance: being able to keep the body stable, while at rest or in motion.

Basic (simple) skill: is one that the player finds easy and needs little concentration to do.

Beta blockers: drugs that are used to control the heart rate and have a calming and relaxing effect.

Blood doping: an illegal attempt to improve performance in sporting events. This happens by artificially increasing the number of red blood cells in the bloodstream, boosting the blood's ability to bring oxygen to the muscles.

Blood pressure: pressure of the blood against the walls of the blood vessels, especially the arteries.

Body composition: the percentage of body weight that is muscle, fat or bone.

BPM: beats per minute.

Bronchioles: smaller branches coming off the bronchi.

Bronchitis: inflammation of the lining of the bronchial tubes.

Bronchus (pl. bronchi): tube along which air passes from the trachea into the lungs.

Carbohydrates: the body's main source of energy.

Cardio-respiratory system: the interaction of the heart and lungs to supply oxygen to muscles during exercise.

Cardiovascular fitness: your ability to exercise your whole body for long periods of time, sometimes called stamina or aerobic endurance.

Cardiovascular: to do with the heart, blood and blood vessels together.

Cartilage: a firm, connective tissue.

Glossary

Central nervous system: nerve tissues that control the activities of the body.

Circumduction: moving a part of the body in a circular or conical shape, as with a ball-and-socket joint like the hip.

Closed skill: takes place in a stable, predictable environment, the player knows exactly what to do and when.

Commercialisation: making something available on the market; using something to make a profit.

Complex skill: a complex skill that needs the player's complete attention and concentration as it is technically difficult to perform: for example, a penalty kick in football, or a smash in tennis.

Co-ordination: the ability to use two or more body parts together.

Coronary heart disease: when your coronary arteries are narrowed by a slow build-up of fatty material within their walls.

Cramp: painful, involuntary contraction of a muscle, usually caused by fatigue.

Cusp: a triangular fold or flap of a heart valve.

Dehydration: the loss of water and salts essential for normal body function.

Depressant: a substance that lowers the level of physiological or nervous activity in the body.

Depression: a persistent feeling of sadness and loss of interest in life.

Deviance: behaviour that falls outside the norms or what is thought to be acceptable.

Diaphragm: the primary muscle used in the process of inspiration, or inhalation. It is a dome-shaped sheet of muscle that separates the chest from the rest of the body cavity.

Diastole: the phase of the heartbeat when the heart muscle relaxes and lets the chambers fill with blood.

Distributed: where the skill is practised over several sessions, or with rest breaks – this type of practice is normally for players of lower ability, experience or fitness level.

Diuretic: making you produce more urine.

Diuretics: drugs that elevate the rate of urine production.

Dorsi-flexion: bending or flexing the toes upwards, bringing them closer to the shin.

E-cigarette: electronic cigarette; battery-powered vaporiser that simulates the feeling of smoking.

Effort: the force that is applied by the user of the lever system.

Endorphins: chemicals in the brain that, like serotonin, are another of your body's natural 'feel-good' chemicals.

Erythrocyte: red blood cell.

Exercise: physical activity that maintains or improves health and fitness.

Expiration: breathing out.

Explosiveness: the rate of force development is at the maximum for any type of muscle action using explosive power.

Extension: a straightening movement that increases the angle between body parts (the opposite of flexion).

Fartlek: a method of training for runners where the terrain and speed are constantly changing.

Fats: a rich source of energy, but many modern diets provide more than our bodies need.

Feedback: information received before, during or after a performance about the performance.

Fitness: the ability to meet the demands of the environment.

FITT: training principle based on frequency, intensity, time and type.

Fixed practice: where the skill is practised over and over again until it is perfected.

Flexibility: the range of motion of your joints or the ability of your joints to move freely.

Flexion: a bending movement that decreases the angle between body parts (the opposite of extension).

Free sugars: extra sugar added to food and drink.

Frontal axis: an imaginary line passing horizontally through the body from left to right, allows flexion and extension.

Frontal plane: an imaginary line dividing the body vertically from front to back.

Fulcrum: the point around which the lever rotates.

Gamesmanship: Bending the rules/laws of a sport without actually breaking them.

Gaseous exchange: the delivery of oxygen from the lungs to the bloodstream and the removal of carbon dioxide from the tissues.

Glucose: a major source of energy for most cells in the body.

Glycogen: the stored form of carbohydrate primarily located in the muscles and liver and readily available as an energy fuel.

Growth hormone (GH): is used by some athletes to increase their muscle development. Athletes are tested at regular intervals to check for the use of steroids, but GH is used to gain the same advantage.

Guidance: information to aid the learning of a skill; can be given visually, verbally, manually or mechanically.

Haemoglobin: a red protein in the blood that transports oxygen.

Health: a state of complete emotional/psychological, physical and social well-being and not merely the absence of disease and infirmity.

Heart rate: the number of times the heart beats per minute.

High organisation skill: has a lot of complicated phases or parts: for example, a somersault in trampolining.

High-density lipoprotein cholesterol (HDL): highdensity lipoprotein cholesterol, sometimes known as 'good' cholesterol, which removes 'bad' cholesterol in the body.

Hydrate: take on water.

Hydration: being hydrated means the body has the correct amount of water in cells, tissues and organs to function correctly.

Hypokinetic disease: a disease caused by a lack of physical activity or sedentary lifestyle.

Immune system: the structures and processes in your body that stop disease.

Insoluble (fibre): cannot be digested by your body. As it passes through your gut it helps other foods move through your digestive system. It keeps your bowels healthy and helps prevent digestive disorders.

Inspiration: breathing in.

Interval training: physical training involving alternating stages of high- and low-intensity activity.

Karvonen formula: a test to find out an individual's optimum heart rate.

Lactate accumulation: when lactic acid gathers in the muscles/blood due to increased work intensity, e.g. moving from aerobic to anaerobic exercise.

Lactic acid: a colourless acid produced in muscle tissues during strenuous exercise.

Leukocyte: white blood cell.

Lever: a rigid rod (bone) that turns round a pivot (joint).

Lifestyle choice: the choices we make about how we live and behave that impact on our health.

Ligament: strong, flexible connective tissue that connects bones to other bones.

Load: the force that is applied by the lever system.

Longevity: how long a person lives.

Low organisation skill: clear, simple phases or parts: for example, a set shot in basketball.

Macronutrients: are the types of food that you need in large amounts in your diet: carbohydrates, fats and proteins.

Massed: where the skill is practised until it is learned, without taking a break – this type of practice is normally for athletes who are fit and experienced.

Media: the main means of mass communication (television, radio, newspapers and internet).

Mechanical advantage: a large load can be lifted with a relatively small amount of effort (applies to first and second class levers).

Mechanical disadvantage: third class levers cannot lift as heavy a load with the same amount of effort, due to the position of the effort and load from the fulcrum.

Metabolic rate: the rate at which metabolic processes take place; the rate at which a body uses up energy.

Glossary

Metabolism: the chemical processes within a living organism that keep it alive.

Micronutrients: are the parts of your food that you need for normal growth, but only in small amounts – what we usually call vitamins and minerals.

Moderation: the assessment of work to ensure it is in accordance with agreed criteria and procedures.

Moderator: someone who carries out the moderation of parts of a subject examination, such as coursework, projects and special studies, which are marked initially by teachers.

Muscle fatigue: when muscles get tired.

Muscle fibres: make up voluntary (skeletal) muscle; divided into type I, type IIa and type IIx.

Muscular endurance: the ability to use voluntary muscles many times without getting tired.

Muscular strength: the amount of force a muscle can exert against a resistance.

Narcotics: drugs that affect mood or behaviour, inducing drowsiness and relieving pain.

Negative deviance: deviance that has a detrimental effect.

Norm: a pattern or standard.

Open skill: seen in sports such as netball and football, where the situation is always changing.

Optimum weight: the most favourable weight to produce their best performance in their sport – so that they can make every effort to keep within this weight range.

Ossification: the process of development from cartilage to bone.

Osteoporosis: a condition causing the bones to become brittle and fragile from loss of tissue, resulting from hormone changes, or a deficiency in calcium or vitamin D.

Overfat: having too much body composition as fat; men having more than 19 per cent of total body composition as fat and women over 26 per cent.

Overtraining: training beyond your body's ability to recover.

Overuse injury: sustained from repeated action, such as shin splints caused by running.

Overweight: having more weight than is considered healthy by medical professionals.

Oxygen debt: The amount of oxygen needed at the end of a physical activity to break down any lactic acid.

PAR-Q (Physical Activity Readiness Questionnaire): a self-screening tool that can be used by anyone who is planning to start an exercise or training routine.

Passive smoking: breathing in the smoke from other people's cigarettes.

Pathogen: an agent that causes disease, such as a virus.

Peptide hormones: these are often used to produce the same effects as anabolic steroids, namely, to increase muscle growth, and to assist in recovery from injury and heavy training sessions.

Perceived: what someone thinks or feels to be the case.

Performance: how well a task is completed.

Physiology: how the whole body or a body part functions.

Plane: an imaginary flat surface that divides the body into sections.

Plantar-flexion: extending or pointing the toes down, away from the shin.

Plasma: the fluid part of blood.

Plyometrics: exercises where muscles use maximum force in short intervals of time.

Positive deviance: deviance where there is no intention to cause harm or break the rules.

Power: the ability to undertake strength performances quickly.

Progressive overload: gradually increasing the amount of overload to improve fitness but without injury.

Protocol: official procedure; set way to do something.

Pulmonary: to do with the lungs.

Qualitative: information about qualities, which is difficult to measure.

Quantitative: information about quantities, which can be measured.

Reaction time: the time between the presentation of a stimulus and the onset of movement.

Recovery: the time required for the repair of damage to the body caused by training or competition. Alternatively, the period between sets of a given exercise or between intervals in an interval training session/workout.

Respiration: the movement of air from outside the body into the cells within tissues.

Rest: the period of time allotted to recovery.

Reversibility: gradually losing fitness instead of progressing or remaining at the current level.

Rotation: movement around a single axis or pivot point.

Sagittal axis: an imaginary line passing horizontally through the body from front to back.

Sagittal plane: an imaginary line dividing the body vertically into left and right sides.

Sedative: a drug that has a calming or sleep-inducing effect.

Sedentary lifestyle: where there is little, irregular or no physical activity.

Serotonin: a neurotransmitter believed to regulate your mood.

Social health: ability to interact with others, adapt to social situations and form relationships.

Socially acceptable drugs: legal drugs found in everyday products, such as caffeine, nicotine or alcohol.

Soluble (fibre): can be digested by your body and can help to reduce the amount of cholesterol in your blood (see www.nhs.uk/ conditions/Cholesterol).

Somatotype: body shape or type.

Specificity: the particular requirements of an activity.

Speed: the rate at which an individual can perform a movement or cover a distance.

Sportsmanship: qualities of fairness, following the rules, being gracious in defeat or victory.

Steroid: a drug, which can have harmful side effects, that is sometimes used illegally by athletes to help them become stronger and more muscular.

Stimulant: a substance that raises the level of physiological or nervous activity in the body.

Stimulants: drugs that have an effect on the central nervous system, such as increased mental and/or physical alertness.

Stroke volume: the amount of blood pumped by the heart during each beat.

Structure: how something complex is put together (called anatomy in animals and plants).

Systole: the phase of the heartbeat when the heart muscle contracts and pumps blood from the chambers into the arteries.

Target zone: The range within which an individual needs to work for aerobic training to take place (60-80 per cent of maximum heart rate).

Tendons: fibrous tissues that join bone to muscle.

Thrombokinase: a substance involved in blood clotting.

Trachea: the tube that takes air into the chest, also known as the windpipe.

Training threshold: a safe and effective level to train at.

Transverse plane: an imaginary line dividing the body horizontally from top to bottom.

Variable practice: involves practising the skill in a variety of different situations, so that it can be adapted to suit different competitive situations.

Vascular: relating to blood vessels.

Vascular shunting: process that increases blood flow to active areas during exercise by diverting blood away from inactive areas; achieved by vasodilation and vasoconstriction.

Vein: tube that carries blood back to the heart.

Vena cava: large vein bringing deoxygenated blood into the heart.

Venous: to do with the veins.

Vertical axis: imaginary line passing vertically through the body, allows rotation of the body in an upright position.

VO_2 max: the volume of oxygen an athlete can consume while exercising at maximum capacity.

Well-being: the state of being comfortable, healthy or happy.

Index

Note: Page numbers in **bold** indicate where definitions of key terms can be found.

abduction **10**, 11, 12
abrasions 107
active lifestyle, benefits of 64–5
activity level 133
acute injury **103**
adaptation **85**, 99
adduction **10**, 11, 12
adrenaline 23**, 136**
aerobic exercise **36**, 97
aerobic respiration **36**
aerobic target zone 86, 90
aesthetic appreciation 129
age and sport 166
agility **71**
alcohol, effects on health 137
alveoli **32**
   exercise increasing 101
   gas exchange in 33
anabolic steroids **109**
anaemia **29**, 111, 147
anaerobic exercise **34**
anaerobic respiration **36**, 37
   and muscle fatigue 40
analgesics **110–11**
anatomy **2**
antagonistic pair **19**
antibodies **29**, 30
aorta 24, 25
arteries **25**, 26, 27, 28
articulate/articulation **21**
averages
   calorie requirements 150–1
   fat percentage 68
   heart rate 41, 100, 126
   stroke volume 46
   weight for sportspeople 149
axes of rotation **56**, 57–8

balance **71**
balanced diet 133, 144
ball and socket joints 9, 10
bar charts 141–2
basic (simple) skills 154
beta blockers **110**

biceps curl 17, 54
biceps muscle 15, 16, 17
   antagonistic with triceps 19
blood clotting 23, 30
blood distribution 28
blood doping **108**, 112
blood plasma 30
blood platelets 30
blood pressure **26**
   beta blockers lowering 110
   and BMI 141–2
   exercise reducing 101
   nicotine increasing 136
   and sedentary lifestyle 140
blood vessels 26–8
body composition 66, **68**, 127
body mass index (BMI) 69
body pump 97
body temperature regulation 23
bone density 99, 127
bone growth 4
bone marrow 3
bone structure and optimum weight 149
bones 4–8
   anatomical names 6–8
   classification 4–5
   fractures 105–6
   growth and development 4
   skeletal 7
   storage of calcium and phosphorus 3
   vertebrae 8
BPM (beats per minute) **41**, 87, 100, 126
breathing 31
   effect of smoking on 135
   effects of exercise on 35, 43
bronchi **32**
bronchioles **32**
bronchitis **136**

caffeine 112, 134
calcium 3, 147
calorie requirements 133, 150–1
capillaries 27–8, 101
carbohydrate loading 146

carbohydrates **38–9**, 144–5
cardiac (heart) muscle 14
cardiac output 43
   graphs 47–8
   maximum 100
cardio-respiratory system **22**
   cardiovascular system 22–30
   effects and benefits of exercise 100–1
   respiratory system 31–5
cardiovascular fitness **66–7**, 126
cardiovascular system **22–30**
   effect of smoking on 136
   efficiency of 66–7
   working with respiratory system 33–5
cardiovascular warmup 114
cartilage **4**, 5
   damage to 107
cartwheels 59–60
central nervous system (CNS) **112**
cigarettes 135–6
circuit training 92
circulatory system 22–30, 41–3
circumduction: **12**
closed skills 154
clothing, protective 104
co-operation 130
co-ordination **72**
commercialisation of sport **169–71**
   football clubs 172
competition
   attitude to 131
   eating prior to 39
   social aspects to 131
competitive situation
   assessment 189
   marks for 188, 190–1
complex carbohydrates 39, 145
complex skills 154
concurrent feedback 160
concussion 105
condyloid joints 9, 10
connective words, exam skills 119, 121, 122, 123
continuous training 90–1
cool down 113
   phases and activities 116
   purpose/importance of 104, 113–14
Cooper 12-minute run test 77
coronary heart disease **100**, 136, 139

cramp **37**, 41
cusp **25**

data gathering 76
dehydration **148**
deltoid muscles 15, 16, 17
deoxygenated blood 24, 25, 26, 27
depressants **135**
depression **139**
deviance **173**
diabetes 140
diaphragm **32**
diastole **26**
diet, balanced 133, 144
disability 167
dislocations 106
distributed practice 155
diuretic **110, 151**
doping 112
dorsi-flexion **10**, 11, 12
drug-taking 108–12
dynamic balance 71
dynamic stretching 115

e-cigarettes **136**
effort **51**
emotional health 127–9
endorphins 128
endurance *see* muscular endurance
endurance athletes, carb loading 146
energy balance for healthy weight 150–1
energy production 36–7
energy sources 38–9, 144–6
engagement in sports, factors affecting 165–71
enjoyment of exercise/sport 128–9
equipment
   checking 104
   and fashion 170
   protective 104
erythrocytes **29**
erythropoietin (EPO) 111
ethical issues 173–5
ethnicity 167
exam preparation
   fitness and body systems 118–23
   health and performance 176–81
exercise **63–4**
   effect on breathing 35, 43

Index

effect on health and fitness 63–5
effect on heart 41–3
effect on muscles 40–1
long-term effects 98–101
expiration **31**
explosiveness **94**
extension **10**, 11, 12
external obliques muscle 15, 16, 17
extrinsic feedback 160

Fartlek training **91–2**
fashion and sport 170
fast twitch (type II) muscle fibres 20
fat percentage 68
fatigue, muscle 40
fats **38**, 145
feedback on performance 160–1
fibre, dietary 148–9
first class levers 52
fitness **63**, 64
    classes 96–7
    five components of 66–70
    and health 65
    skill-related 71–4
fitness level
    analysing own 199–200
    establishing current 89–90
    measurement of 47
fitness tests 75–7
    health-related 77–8
    skill-related 79–80
FITT principle **84–5**
fixed practice 155
flat bones 4, 5
flexibility 66, 68
flexion **10**, 11, 12
forward roll 58
fractures 105–6
frame size 70
free sugars **39**
frequency, FITT principle 84
friendships 130–1
frontal axis **57**, 58
frontal plane **56**, 57, 59
fulcrum (pivot) **21, 51**, 52, 53, 54

gamesmanship 173–4
gaseous exchange **32–3**

gastrocnemius 15, 16, 18, 19
gender
    and optimum weight 149
    and sport engagement 165
glucose **36**, 37
    and carbohydrates 38–9
    and diabetes 140
gluteal muscles 15, 16, 18
glycogen **6, 36**, 145, 146
goal setting 156–7, 200–1
golfer's elbow 107
graphs, interpreting and analysing 44–8, 167–8, 172, 174–5
growth hormones 111
guidance on performance 158–9

haemoglobin **29**, 32
hamstrings 15, 16, 18
    antagonistic with quadriceps 19
hand grip strength test 78
Harvard step test 77
health, defined **63**
health, fitness and well-being 124–52
Health Related Exercise (HRE) 23, 126
heart 24–6
    effect of smoking on 135–6
    effects of exercise on 41–3, 100
heart disease 135–6
heart rate **41**
    graphs 44–5
    maximum 42
    measuring 90
    variation in 41
    see also resting heart rate (RHR)
heart rate reserve (HRR) 87
height
    and BMI calculation 69
    height/weight chart 70
    and optimum weight 149, 150
high altitude training 112
high-density lipoprotein cholesterol (HDL) **135, 139**
hinge joints 10
hip flexors 15, 16
hormones
    adrenaline 23, 136
    growth 111
    insulin 140
    peptide 111

serotonin 30
testosterone 109
hydration **148**, **151**
hypertrophy, muscle 98
hypokinetic disease **63**

immune system **30**
individual needs 82, 199
influence of others 167
injuries 105–8
prevention of 103–5
treatment of minor 107–8
insoluble fibre **149**
inspiration **31**
insulin and diabetes 140
intensity, FITT principle 84
interval training **88**, 93
intrinsic feedback 160
involuntary muscles 14
iron 29, 147
irregular bones 5
isolated skills 188

joints 9–12
ball and socket 10
candyloid 10
classification 9–10
hinge 10
and movement 11–12
pivot 9–10

Karvonen formula **86–7**

lactate accumulation **40**
lactic acid **37–8**, 40
latissimus dorsi muscle 15, 16, 17
lean body mass 69
leukocytes **29**
lever **3**
lever systems 51–5
lifestyle choices 133–5
positive and negative impacts 135–7
ligaments **9**, 13, 99
injuries 106, 107
line graphs 142–3
load **51**
long bones 4–5
longevity **132**

lung disease 136
lungs 31, 32
effects of smoking 135, 136
exercise increasing efficiency 35, 99, 101

macronutrients **144–6**
manual guidance 159
marathon runners 43, 70, 82
programme for 88–9
marking of practical performance 187–91
massed practice 155
maximum cardiac output 100
maximum heart rate (MHR) 42, 86, 87
mechanical advantage and disadvantage, levers **54**–5
mechanical guidance 159
media coverage of sport **169–70**
mental challenge of sport 129
mental preparation 161–2
practical performance 192–3
metabolic rate/metabolism **150**
micronutrients **147–8**
minerals 3, 147–8
moderation of practical performance **185, 186–7**
moderator **186**
movement analysis 50–61
lever systems 51–5
planes and axes 56–61
muscle fatigue **40**
muscle hypertrophy (size) 99
muscle tone, loss of 140–1
muscle types 13–14
muscles, voluntary
antagonistic pairs 19
effect of exercise on 40–1
fast and slow twitch fibres 20
location and role of 15–18
muscular endurance **2**, 66
health benefits 127
marathon runners 70, 88
tests for 77, 78
weight/resistance training 94–6
muscular strength **2**, 66, 67
health benefits 127
tests for 78
weight/resistance training 94–6
musculo-skeletal system 2–21
bones 4–8
effects and benefits of exercise 99

Index

functions of skeleton 3–4
  joints 9–11
  ligaments and tendons 13
  movement 11–12
  muscles 13–20
myofibrils, muscle fibres 20

narcotics **110–11**
negative deviance **173**
nicotine 134–5, 136
norms **75**
nutrition 144–9

obesity 69, 70
one-minute press-up test 78
one-minute sit-up test 78
open skills 154
optimise **197**
optimum weight **149–50**
ossification **4**
osteoporosis **127**, 140
overfat 139, **149**
overload training 83, 84
overtraining **85**, 103
overuse injuries **103**, 105–6
overweight 139, **149**
oxygen debt 33, **34**, 43
oxygenated blood 24, 25, 26, 27, 28

PAR-Q (Physical Activity Readiness Questionnaire) **102–3**
passive smoking **136**
pathogens **29**
pectoralis major muscle 15, 16, 17
PEDS (performance-enhancing drugs) 108–12
peer group influence 167
PEP (personal exercise programme) 196–204
  promoting personal health 132
peptide hormones 111
perceived impact of school sport **168**
performance **63**, 64
  feedback on 160–1
  guidance on 158–9
  mental preparation for 161–2
performance-enhancing drugs (PEDS) 108–12
personal exercise programme (PEP) 132, 196–204
phosphorus 3
Physical Activity Readiness Questionnaire (PAR-Q) **102–3**
physical training 62–117

drugs 108–12
fitness components 66–80
health-fitness link 63–5
injuries 105–7
injury prevention 103–5
injury treatment 107–8
long-term effects of exercise 98–101
principles of training 81–97
warm up and cool down 113–16
physiology **2**
pilates 97
pivot joints 9–10
planes of motion **56–7**
planning 201
plantar-flexion **10**, 11, 12
plasma **30**
plyometrics **94**
positive deviance **173**
posture, poor 140–1
potassium 148
power **73**
power athletes, timing of protein intake 146
practical performance 182–95
  assessment 186–7
  choosing activities 183–5
  mark allocation 187–91
  preparing for 191–5
practice structures 155
Premier League football 172
principles of training 81–5
progressive overload **83**
protective equipment and clothing 104
protein intake, timing of 146
proteins 145
protocol, defined **77**
psychology of sport 153–63
pulmonary arteries 24, 25, 26, 27
pulmonary, defined **25**
pulmonary veins 24, 25, 27
pulse (heart rate) 41

quadriceps 15, 16, 18
  antagonistic with hamstring 19
qualitative analysis **76, 159**
quantitative data analysis **76, 159, 160–1**

reaction time **73**
readiness for training 198

recovery and rest **85, 99**
recovery rate, heart 41, 45, 48, 100, 200
recreational drugs 134
red blood cells 29
    blood doping 112
    exercise increasing 101
    iron creating 147
    production in bone marrow 3
relaxation exercises 116
resistance training 94–6
respiration, defined **32**
respiratory system 31
    inhaled and exhaled air 31
    main components of 32
    structure of alveoli 32–3
    vital capacity and tidal volume 31
    working with cardiovascular 33–5
rest **85**, 99
    breathing rate 35
    following minor injuries 107–8
    stroke volume 46, 47
resting heart rate (RHR)
    effect of exercise on 100
    indication of fitness 41, 42, 44, 100, 126
    Karvonen formula 86–7
    return to during cool-down 116
reversibility (loss of fitness) **85**
RICE (Rest, Ice, Compression, Elevation) 107–8
rituals 114, 162
rotation **9**, 12
roughage (fibre) 148–9
rules, playing to 104–5

sagittal axis **57**
sagittal plane **56**
Sargent jump test 79
second class levers 52–3
sedatives **135**
sedentary lifestyle **63, 138–41**
selenium 148
self-esteem 128
serotonin **30, 128**
short bones 4, 5
side effects of drugs 108, 109, 110, 112
simple (basic) skills 154
simple carbohydrates 39, 145
simple fractures 105
sit and reach test 79

skeletal muscle 14, 21
skeleton
    functions of 3
    structure of 6–7
    vertebral column 8
skill-related fitness, components of 71–4
    agility 71
    balance 71
    co-ordination 72
    power 73
    reaction time 73
    speed 73
skills classification
    basic and complex skills 154
    low and high organisation skills 155
    open and closed skills 154
slow twitch (type I) muscle fibres 20
SMART goals 156–7
smooth muscle 14
social health **130–1**
socially acceptable drugs **134**
socio-cultural influences 164–75
socio-economic group 166
sodium 148
soft tissue injury 107
soluble fibre **149**
somatotype **4**
somersaults 58–9
specificity **82–3**, 103, 199
speed **73**
spinning 97
sport engagement patterns 165–71
sport psychology 153–63
sportsmanship 173
sprains 106
sprint test 79
static balance 71
static stretching 115
steroids, anabolic **67**, 109
stimulants **112, 134**
strains 107
strength *see* muscular strength
stress fractures 105–6
stress relief 64, 128
stretching
    cool down 116
    warm up 115
stroke volume **42**

output 43

exercise 100

s 45–7

structure, defined **2**

sugars 39

   simple carbohydrates 145

systole **26**

target heart rate 87

target setting and reviewing 157

target zones **83**, 86

tendons **3**, 13, 99, 107

tennis elbow 107

tennis players, programme for 89

terminal feedback 160

third class levers 53–4

thresholds of training 86–8

thrombokinase **30**

tibialis anterior muscle 15, 16, 18, 19

tidal volume 31

time, FITT principle 84

tobacco 135–6

torn cartilage 107

trachea **32**

training methods

   choosing 88–90

   circuit 92

   continuous 90–1

   fartlek 91

   interval 93

   plyometrics 94

   weight/resistance 94–6

training optimisation 102–3

training principles 81

   FITT 84–5

   individual needs 82

   and injury prevention 103

   progressive overload 83

   specificity 82–3

training threshold **86**

training thresholds 87–8

trampolining 57, 159

   case study of practical work 190

   twist jumps 60–1

transverse plane **56**

trends in physical health issues 141–3

trends in sport 172

triceps dip 52

triceps muscle 15, 16, 17

   antagonistic with biceps 19

tucked front somersault 58–9

twist jumps, trampolining 60–1

type, FITT principle 84–5

variable practice 155

vascular **14**

vascular shunting 28

vasoconstriction **23**

vasodilation **23**

veins **25**, 27, 28

vena cava **24**

venous **24**

verbal guidance 158

vertical axis **57**, 60

vertical jump test 79

visual guidance 158

vital capacity 31, 101

vitamins 147

VO_2 max **35**

   test to measure 77

voluntary muscles 14

   location and role of 15–18

warm up 113

   phases and activities 114–16

   purpose/importance of 104, 113

water 148

weight/height chart 70

weight issues

   body mass index 69

   lean body mass 69

   and metabolic rate 150–1

   optimum, factors affecting 149

   sportspeople and average weight 149

   terminology 139

   variation in optimum weight 150

weight/resistance training 94–6

well-being **131–2**

white blood cells 29–30

work/rest/sleep balance 134

yoga 97

zinc 148